EVERYTHING WAS SET TO GO

Weapons had been cleaned and oiled, combat gear had been neatly packed, ammunition had been issued, intelligence reports had been brought up to date, letters home had been written.

After the sun set behind the western horizon and the quarter moon appeared, the only job left for the 2nd Marine Division's 20,000 men, particularly the nearly 3,000 Marines of the three initial assault battalions, was to attain some final spiritual communion.

The officers who would lead the assault units could do no more than offer their good wishes and a few high-flown sentiments. Their words were not going to save lives, but there was reason to believe that the spirit they might instill would result in a few more yards on the morning's bloody beaches. . . .

Also by Eric Hammel
from Jove

ACE! A MARINE NIGHT-FIGHTER PILOT IN WORLD WAR II
(with R. Bruce Porter)

76 HOURS
The Invasion of Tarawa
ERIC HAMMEL AND JOHN E. LANE

JOVE BOOKS, NEW YORK

This Jove book contains the complete
text of the original hardcover edition.
It has been completely reset in a typeface
designed for easy reading and was printed
from new film.

76 HOURS
THE INVASION OF TARAWA

A Jove Book / published by arrangement with
the authors

PRINTING HISTORY
Pacifica Press edition published 1985
Jove edition / March 1988

ISBN: 0-515-09485-4

Jove Books are published by The Berkley Publishing Group,
200 Madison Avenue, New York, New York 10016.
The name "JOVE" and the "J" logo
are trademarks belonging to Jove Publications, Inc.

PRINTED IN THE UNITED STATES OF AMERICA

10   9   8   7   6   5   4   3   2   1

For the Fallen

CONTENTS

GUIDE TO ABBREVIATIONS

1stLt	First Lieutenant
1stSgt	First Sergeant
2ndLt	Second Lieutenant
Amtrac	Amphibian Tractor; LVT
Arty	Artillery
Asst	Assistant
BAR	Browning Automatic Rifle
BGen	Brigadier General
Capt	Captain
Cdr	Commander
cm	Centimeter
CO	Commanding Officer
Col	Colonel
Comdr	Commodore
CP	Command Post
Cpl	Corporal
D-Day	Day of invasion
D+1	Day after invasion
D+2	Two days after invasion
D+3	Three days after invasion
Ens	Ensign
Exec	Executive Officer
F6F	U.S. Navy Hellcat Fighter Plane
FM1	Field Music 1st Class
GySgt	Gunnery Sergeant
HQ	Headquarters
IMAC	I Marine Amphibious Corps
KIA	Killed in Action

Konkyochitai	Special Base Force
LCdr	Lieutenant Commander
LCM	Landing Craft, Medium
LCVP	Landing Craft, Vehicle, Personnel
LVT	Landing Vehicle, Tracked; amphibian tractor; amtrac
Lt	Lieutenant
Lt(jg)	Lieutenant (Junior Grade)
LtCol	Lieutenant Colonel
M1	U.S. .30-caliber Garand rifle
M2	U.S. .30-caliber carbine
M3	U.S. Stuart light tank
M4	U.S. Sherman medium tank
Maj	Major
MGen	Major General
mm	Millimeter
Mustang	Officer formerly an enlisted Marine
NCO	Non-Commissioned Officer
Noncom	Non-Commissioned Officer
Pfc	Private First Class
PhM3	Pharmacist's Mate 3rd Class
PlSgt	Platoon Sergeant
Pvt	Private
RAdm	Rear Admiral
Recon	Reconnaissance
Sgt	Sergeant
SSgt	Staff Sergeant
TBS	Field Radio
TBX	Field Radio
TNT	Dynamite
TSgt	Technical Sergeant
VAdm	Vice Admiral
VMAC	V Marine Amphibious Corps
WIA	Wounded in Action
WO	Warrant Officer

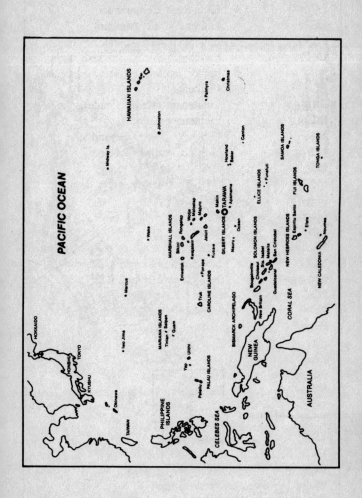

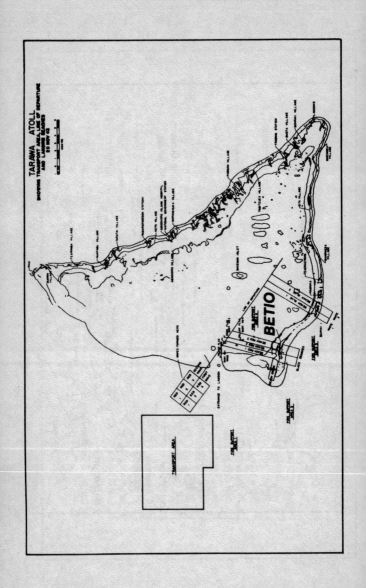

LEGEND

- ■ Above-ground building
- ◧ Covered bunker
- ▨ Anti-tank ditch
- ⅂ Seawall
- ⊃ Aircraft/truck revetment, log
- ⬭ Open excavation
- ▧ Open supply dump
- △ Searchlight
- ⬭ Observation tower
- ◌ Wooded area
- ■ Reinforced concrete above-ground structure
- T Over-water latrine
- ○ Large shellhole or bomb crater
- ⅄ Edge of reef
- ⚓ Sunken ship
- ⊢ Barbed wire
- ▴▴▴ Concrete tetrahedrons

- ◼ 8" Naval mount
- ◆ 14 cm Gun
- ⊂= 12.7 cm Gun, twin-mount
- ⊙ 80mm Gun
- ● 75mm Mountain Gun
- ◆ 70mm Howitzer
- ○ 70 mm Gun
- ● 37 mm Rapid-fire Gun
- ⊂ 13 mm Machine Gun, twin-mount
- ○ 13 mm Machine Gun, single-mount
- ▩ Large covered bunker
- ▨ Covered pillbox
- ⊏┅┅ Covered trench
- ▭▬ Defensive barrier, above ground
- ⋀⋀ Fire & Communication trench
- ◆ Radar

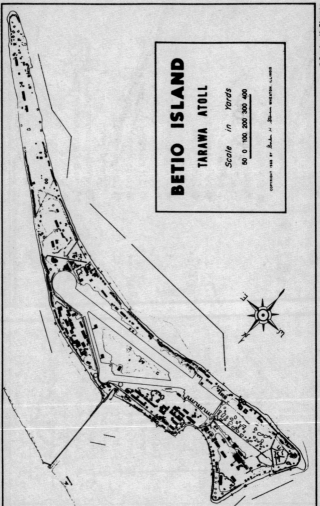

BETIO ISLAND

TARAWA ATOLL

Scale in Yards

50 0 100 200 300 400

COPYRIGHT 1988 BY Gordon H. Stevens WHEATON, ILLINOIS

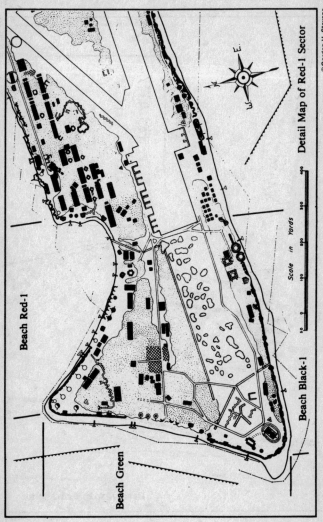

Beach Red-1

Beach Green

Beach Black-1

Detail Map of Red-1 Sector

Scale in Yards

0   100   200   300   400

©Gordon H. Stevens

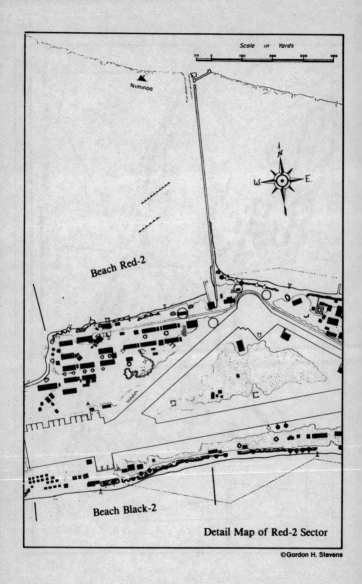

Scale in Yards

Niminoa

Beach Red-2

Beach Black-2

Detail Map of Red-2 Sector

©Gordon H. Stevens

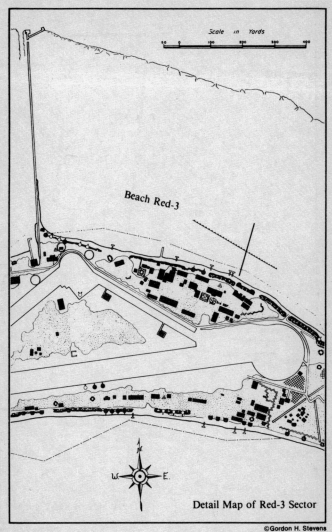

Scale in Yards

Beach Red-3

Detail Map of Red-3 Sector

©Gordon H. Stevens

Prologue

The inshore tide had gently carried him from the lagoon. He looked strangely fat and shiny in his bursting blouse and trousers; the buttons and seams were straining. His corpulent hands swished gently back and forth in the inch or two of water that kept surging in around him. His torso gently rolled back and forth as he hung balanced on his right hip.

His canvas-covered steel helmet was firmly buckled beneath his chin, the strap now straining against the oozing folds of shiny, distended flesh. One slightly more powerful surge of the tide wrenched him a bit farther up on the sandy shelf, feet first. The sudden movement proved too much for the cloth encasing his outsized right leg. There was a fine tearing noise and a long bubble of slick white flesh oozed from beneath the rotting fabric.

His left hand scraped once against a small jagged piece of coral, and a small blue rift appeared in the ruined flesh. Clear, thin fluid spurted from the broken hand, and the skin folded back to reveal a length of meat and bone.

Another surge of the incoming tide flipped him on his back, revealing an ugly blue-green patch beneath a charred area of his faded green shirt. Seawater flowed over sharp, spiny, broken rib ends through the depression in his chest.

His dead eye sockets seemed to scan the sky as the water gently lolled his head from side to side. The puffy, bloated lids did not quite close over the remnants of jellied slime left by the feeding lagoon fish.

A rusted watch on his distended, boneless wrist showed the time to be nine o'clock, but the watch had stopped five days since. The band was covered by blistering folds of mottled blue-white skin.

Two of the living happened upon him. Shouldering their rifles, they prepared to remove him from the sea, which had regurgitated his vile bulk from its depths and committed him once again to land.

The more haggard of the living, the elder, roughly grabbed him by his leather-shod feet, just as the younger leaned over to collect his arms. A vile rumbling erupted from within him, and from between rotting yellow-green teeth and purple lips he gurgled the stench of his decay into the face of the young man, who dropped his dead arms, irreverently cursed, and turned his head an instant too late to keep his breakfast from covering the face of the dead warrior.

Breathing heavily, the two tired men lifted the crumbling remains and half dragged them down the beach to where other men were scraping holes and committing hundreds of dead young men.

The air, washed though it was by the tepid sea breeze, had a strange, dark quality about it.

The only sounds were the high-pitched grunts of order and oath, and the soft crunching of hundreds of tired feet upon the ageless golden sand.

Part I
BEFORE

1

Four days before the surprise Japanese attack on Pearl Harbor, a company of Imperial Japanese Navy bluejackets—known in the West as "Imperial Marines" and in Japan as *rigosentai*—was designated the Gilbert Invasion Special Naval Landing Force and placed under the control of the naval air arm. The 250 infantrymen and officers, plus a contingent of Korean labor troops, were mustered on Jaluit, in the Japanese Marshall Islands, and sent eastward on December 8, 1941. Their objective was Makin Atoll, in the neighboring British Gilbert Islands.

On December 10, 1941, the Japanese force landed at Butaritari Island. Following the bloodless landing, labor units began to work on a seaplane base while the *rigosentai* explored and plundered the remaining fifteen Gilbert atolls.

At 0300, December 24, a roving Japanese contingent landed at Betio, in Tarawa Atoll, and looted a store run by the Burns-Philp Company, a leading cultivator and shipper of copra from British-mandated islands throughout Melanesia and Micronesia. The Japanese found fewer than a dozen Europeans living on Betio. One, Edward Harness, master of the interisland government steamer *Niminoa*, asked permission to board his vessel to fetch his personal belongings. There, Harness took advantage of a lapse in his captors' attentiveness and ran the steamer aground on the coral reef. The Japanese blew *Niminoa's* oil tanks to prevent the Europeans from escaping; then they left the atoll.

A second Japanese force landed at Betio on December 27, made a peaceable survey of the small coral sand islet, and left.

Sensing a sinister purpose in the attention to their nondescript island, the Europeans decided to sail to safety aboard a twenty-foot cutter they had hidden with an engine on one of the nearby islets. The small party picked up six American sailors

5

whose ship had been sunk off Nonouti and several civil administrators who were living around the Gilberts group. The overladen boat arrived safely in the Fijis after a thoroughly miserable but uneventful journey.

Except for making occasional spot-checks to the South, the Japanese remained within Makin Atoll. They were developing it with limited resources as the easternmost base screening the Marshalls. The League of Nations had ceded the Marshall Islands to Japan following World War I, and they had been subsequently developed into a major naval and supply center.

Things remained quiet until the predawn hours of August 17, 1942, when the 93-man garrison at Butaritari was destroyed by a two-company force of U.S. Marine Raiders under the command of LtCol Evans Carlson. In a daring, picturesque stroke, Carlson's Raiders landed from two large transport submarines and launched a bloody attack against the isolated, unsupportable Makin garrison.

The Makin raid had been mounted in the hope of drawing major Japanese fleet units from the vicinity of the Solomon Islands, which had been invaded at Guadalcanal on August 7. However, the Japanese response could hardly have been less dramatic.

On August 19, two days after Butaritari stopped transmitting routine messages, four large Japanese reconnaissance aircraft from Kwajalein, in the Marshalls, discovered no sign of life there. On the following day, an advance detachment of *rigosentai* flown in from Jaluit found the scene of a bloody fight, but no signs of any Americans. A full company of *rigosentai* landed several days later and, while combing the rubble of the thickly wooded island, discovered nine Marine Raiders who had been left behind in the hurried departure of the main force. These men were executed some months later.

The Japanese began expanding in earnest throughout the Gilberts, diverting modest resources to the effort. Nauru and Ocean Islands were seized on August 25 and 26, respectively. On August 28, a second company of *rigosentai* landed on Butaritari, and Abemama Atoll was occupied between August 31 and September 4. Except for restoring the base at Butaritari, the Japanese were mainly concerned with lightly screening the Gilberts; they anticipated no major effort by the Allies, who were committing all their meager resources in the Solomons.

Using Butaritari, in Makin, as a northern anchor, the

Japanese landed the main body of the 1,500-man Yokosuka 5th Special Naval Landing Force at Betio, in the South, on September 15, 1942. After establishing a base camp, the Betio force did little more than scour surrounding islands and atolls in searches for (nonexistent) radios in the hands of European missionaries or islanders still loyal to the British Crown.

On December 11, 1942, a battalion-sized construction unit arrived on Betio to build an all-weather bomber strip and formal beach defenses. The war was a year old, and the tide had turned against Japan in the Solomons; the eastern edge of the Empire could become the scene of a battle at any time.

2

From the time in the early 1920s when American military planners had begun suspecting that there might be a war between the United States and the Empire of Japan, it had been consistently determined that the soundest means for achieving victory would be to follow a path directly across the Central Pacific to Tokyo.

There was never any fear among American military analysts that the Japanese might be capable of knocking the plan askew or of putting up much resistance.

Following World War I, Japan, an American ally, had been given the task of overseeing the former German colonies in the Marshall and Caroline Island groups in the eastern Central Pacific and the Palau Islands in the western Central Pacific. By the middle of the succeeding decade, the Japanese had constructed defenses around the Marshalls' abundant and excellent fleet anchorages, which would serve as major bases for the Imperial Navy's tactical arm, the Combined Fleet. The Mariana Islands, which included the American protectorate at Guam, were similarly prepared to support the Combined Fleet.

As the Japanese dug in, American naval planners fabricated and endlessly updated their plans for war in the vast region. Although the plans themselves changed with new developments in deployment and weapons, the basic strategy remained the same: move from east to west across the region and seize Tokyo.

The plan was a shambles by Christmas, 1941. Guam, the small naval base from which the seizure of the Marianas was to be mounted, was by then lost to the Japanese. By April, the main American bases in the Philippines had surrendered. By July, Australia and New Zealand were in danger of being cut off from North America by a Japanese thrust through New Guinea and the Solomons in the direction of the New Hebrides and Samoa. Far from being able to mount a decisive thrust through the Central Pacific, the Allies, and chiefly the United States, were hard pressed to defend Australasia. Lacking bases in the Philippines and Guam, the U.S. Navy dropped its reactive plans for the Central Pacific and rushed every available resource to the South Pacific in the hope of blunting the Japanese drive there.

The Allies bogged down in the Solomons; they were lucky they did not suffer a catastrophic defeat there. Guadalcanal took six months to decide, although the Japanese nearly ended it in two.

If the Japanese tide were to be contained, more time would be needed to produce weapons, launch ships, build warplanes, collect supplies, support Britain in North Africa and Europe, bolster defenses at a score of out-of-the-way strategic strong-holds, and develop the aggressive traits of the millions of newcomers swelling the ranks of the conservative peacetime military.

Still, for all the necessary combat elsewhere, the eyes of the professional planners remained on the Central Pacific. The plans had been written by 1930, and the doctrines by which they would be achieved had been perfected by 1940. It was to be a Navy show, with the Marine Corps as the striking arm.

The Marshall Islands were to have been the first target because Kwajalein, the largest natural fleet anchorage in the world, was there and because the Marshalls had been the easternmost of the Japanese Central Pacific holdings; an attack from east to west would reach them first. Before December, 1941, no thought had ever been given to seizing the Gilberts; they were British until then, and friendly.

In February, 1943, the Japanese redesignated the Betio garrison 3rd Special Base Force (*konkyochitai*). In mid May it was bolstered by the arrival of the Sasebo 7th Special Naval Landing Force, which had been involved in combat in the Solomons.

American intentions in the Central Pacific were no mystery to the Japanese, and American successes in the Solomons increasingly indicated that the United States had the capability to mount its longstanding plan to sweep through the region. Efforts to construct formidable defensive and air installations on the Empire's eastern boundary were redoubled following the defeat at Guadalcanal. As long as the Allies were unable to effectively monitor Japanese activity in the Gilberts, they were unable to seriously threaten the building program.

By July, 1943, Makin boasted a modern seaplane base accommodating a group of amphibious fighters and reconnaissance bombers. The airfield at Betio, under construction since October, 1942, had been the scene of a trial landing by a medium bomber in January, 1943, and the main runway, a secondary runway, and support facilities were nearing completion by midsummer.

Although they might have anticipated it, the Japanese could not be certain that they would ever have to put their Gilberts defenses to the test. The Americans, who had taken charge of the Pacific War, were waging a slogging, yard-by-yard campaign in the Solomons, and they seemed hard pressed to maintain their momentum. But the fact was that the Japanese had yielded the initiative following Guadalcanal, and the ability to choose battlegrounds was in the hands of the Americans.

The United States had not developed its freewheeling bypass strategy by mid 1943, but the seeds of this highly mobile method for waging the island war had been planted. It was within the scope of American abilities to conserve limited resources by mounting expeditions against lightly held or uncontested areas, almost at will. The limitations were almost purely technical, the result of burgeoning airpower and its effect upon warmaking in the vast Pacific.

Well before the close of combat on Guadalcanal, in early February, 1943, the United States had reaffirmed the guidelines by which it had always intended to mount its Central Pacific sweep. Two criteria had to be met: combat had to take place within the range of land-based aircraft launched from secure, permanent bases; lines of supply to the point of conflict had to be secured by land-based aircraft.

Thus, determining the course of the Pacific War became a matter of knowing the combat ranges of land-based aircraft. Action could take place only within the radius of a round-trip bomber flight or at the extremity of a fighter's operational range from a friendly base.

The Marshall and Caroline groups were too far from the nearest Allied airbases to be seriously considered. If the

Central Pacific sweep was to be mounted at all, it would have to begin at the Gilberts.

The options were thus narrowed to two: seize an undefended island and build a protective fighter strip, or seize a defended island with an airbase. The ramifications were simple: time could be a factor in the first case; lives could be a factor in the second.

Given the still-limited resources of the American carrier air arm and its vulnerability to submarine attack, the U.S. Navy strongly opted for a brief fight to seize an existing airfield. For its part, the U.S. Marine Corps was itching to test itself against a defended beach, a task for which it had been preparing since 1775, the year the Corps was founded.

The solution was simple: Betio would be assaulted.

3

The work began in March, 1943, when the U.S. 2nd Marine Division was assembled in its entirety for the first time since being activated in San Diego on February 1, 1941. The three infantry regiments, three artillery battalions, and elements of most of the divisional support battalions had been at Guadalcanal for as long as five months or as little as five weeks. By the day's inexact standard, the division was a veteran combat unit.

The 2nd Marine Regiment (2nd Marines) was the most seasoned of the division's infantry regiments. In August, 1942, it had replaced a detached regiment of 1st Marine Division and landed and fought at the outset of the bitter campaign. B Company, 2nd Marines, had been the first American unit to land on Japanese-held soil in the Pacific War.

The 8th Marines had been on garrison duty in American Samoa until November, 1942, when it had been sent to Guadalcanal. It had been in a few big fights.

The 6th Marines had been sent to Guadalcanal in January, 1943, almost as an afterthought. Its combat had been tedious and bloody, but of just over a month's duration.

Some artillerymen, headquarters troops, engineers, communicators, and medical personnel had also shaken down in the Solomons, although portions of such units never left New Zealand.

Some units had returned to New Zealand in February. These had been in tropical combat the longest and had suffered for the experience, losing many veterans to fatigue, malaria, dengue, beriberi, and a few diseases with unpronounceable names and improbable symptoms. Those units that had been sent to Guadalcanal later and had arrived in New Zealand later were in better shape, having mainly had the opportunity to weed out dead weight.

In the end, every squad of every rifle platoon of every rifle company of the nine rifle battalions had its share of seasoned combat veterans, men who had seen and mastered death. These men would be invaluable in the long months of training that lay ahead, for they would instruct the green replacements arriving from the States. All the veterans brought back lessons and grudges, and all could in some way impart their knowledge and feelings to their new comrades.

Of one thing they could all be certain: as one of only six combat-experienced American divisions in the Pacific, 2nd Marine Division would soon be facing combat again.

In the months following the Guadalcanal experience, and largely as a result of it, extensive staff, command, and organizational changes were undertaken. Some officers had been unable to cope with their jobs and had to be sent home. Others had ideas too good to pass up or talents too important to jeopardize and had been sent to Stateside training commands or to the many new fighting units then forming. Still others had fallen ill under the inhuman duress of jungle warfare and had to be relieved and sent home for cures and eventual reassignment.

Whenever possible, staff and command assignments moved veterans into key positions. However, officers were sent directly from the States who had to be given choice assignments because of seniority. Most were professionals smart enough to listen to subordinates newly wise to the ways of war in the Pacific. Others were hard cases, incapable of bending to the new rules the new war imposed.

As post-combat shuffles continued—endlessly, it seemed to some—many infantry platoons were stripped of their greatest assets, platoon leaders and staff NCOs who had proven their worth in combat. Many of the lieutenants were given command of companies or moved to staffs at all levels, and many of the sergeants were offered the chance to win commissions. While some men were receiving rewards they had well earned, the rifle companies were losing good men to jobs not nearly as important as leading troops in what would be a rifleman's war.

Many of the spirited platoon leaders and seasoned enlisted Marines were replaced by green troops from the States who had been Marines for only a few months. These men were accepted by the veterans, but coolly, for even veterans of a few hours of fighting are disdainful of men who have never seen combat.

. . .

The story of K Company, 3rd Battalion, 2nd Marines, is a good example of the problems faced by all the rifle companies of 2nd Marine Division.

K Company, 2nd, had been at war from the moment it landed as a support unit on Gavutu, a small island near Guadalcanal, on August 8, 1942, the second day of the American South Pacific offensive. The company had taken its casualties, nursed its wounds, and sat around on garrison duty for several months until called to fight on Guadalcanal. Early in November, 1942, after participating in several minor actions, the 3rd Platoon was sent on an independent mission to a large neighboring island to destroy a Japanese observation station. The mission was successful, and the platoon leader, 1stLt Jim Crain, was decorated and marked for higher responsibilities.

Shortly after the 2nd Marines was shipped to New Zealand, Jim Crain was promoted to captain and given K Company. As a result of combat casualties and illness, he was the surviving officer. For a short time, he had no officers, and few noncommissioned officers who had had much responsibility on The Canal. The company's ranks had been radically thinned by illness. At one point, K Company, 2nd, was down to half its authorized strength of 180, and many of the troops were green replacements.

Over the next few months, Jim Crain was forced to build almost from the ground up. His executive officer, 1stLt Clint Dunahoe, was green. The 1st Platoon went to 1stLt Ott Schulte, who had been commissioned at Quantico that winter. Second Lieutenant Mike Hofmann got 2nd Platoon as his first command. Third Platoon went to 2ndLt Jim Fawcett, who had enlisted in the Corps in 1939, had gone to tanks, and had been commissioned due to the shortage of officers. Fawcett had missed Guadalcanal, but he was the only K Company officer who had ever exercised authority over enlisted Marines, having been a tank commander. The last company officer, 2ndLt Tom Becker, got Weapons Platoon; he was also green.

Most of 2nd Marine Division's senior Regular officers—staffers and troop leaders—were lieutenant colonels who had been in some form of combat in Central America. Many of the numerous senior Reserve officers in the division had seen combat in France, but few had been on active duty between the wars. Very few 2nd Marine Division senior officers had served at Guadalcanal.

On May 1, 1943, MGen Julian Smith took command of 2nd Marine Division. He was 58 years old, a 1909 graduate of the Marine Corps Basic School. Although he had seen no action in the new war, he was a blooded, decorated combat veteran with decades of rigorous staff and command experience.

LtCol Dave Shoup, the division's operations officer, would be the chief orchestrator of any combat by the division. His staff department was responsible for training and coordinating the movement and actions of the regiments and battalions in an active campaign. Well under 40 years of age, Shoup was a blooded combat veteran who had commanded troops in Central America and China. He would write the Tarawa plan.

The Division Chief of Staff was Col Merritt Edson, a thin-lipped whisper-voiced redhead, one of the toughest officers in the Corps. Red Mike Edson wore a Medal of Honor earned at Guadalcanal, where he had first commanded a battalion of Raiders, then a full regiment of 1st Marine Division. He was an unusual choice for the largely noncombatant post he held, but he outranked all the other colonels in the division, and he was being groomed for a general's billet. He was 46 years old.

None of the infantry regiment commanders had seen action in the Pacific. The commander of 10th Marines, the division's artillery regiment, had been briefly involved at Guadalcanal, but his job was largely that of a trainer and a coordinator for battalions that would be parcelled out to the infantry regiments.

LtCol Ray Murray, commander of the 2nd Battalion, 6th, was a fine example of the rapid rise of junior peacetime officers in the wartime expansion of the Marine Corps. A 1934 graduate of Texas A&M, Murray was commissioned in June, 1935, at age 22. By late 1941, the 6'5" Texan was a captain serving with the 6th Marines in Iceland. As a 29-year-old major, he had commanded the 2nd Battalion, 6th, in first combat at the close of the Guadalcanal campaign. Murray (who was to serve as the model for "Highpockets" in Leon Uris's *Battle Cry!*) was promoted to lieutenant colonel in mid 1943 at age 30. Most of the other rifle battalion commanders were Ray Murray's contemporaries or even younger.

A typical rifle company commander was Capt Warren Morris. A native of Arkansas, Morris graduated from Oklahoma University in 1941 and immediately enlisted in the Marine Corps as a private at age 23. He was commissioned in November, 1941, and saw first combat near Guadalcanal in August, 1942, as a platoon leader with the 2nd Battalion, 2nd Marines. After gaining a reputation as a highly motivated troop leader, Lefty Morris was given command of F Company, 2nd, in mid 1943, at age 25.

Seasoned or green, hero or laggard, leader or led, 20,000 U.S. Marines would be on hand on November 20, 1943, to undertake the Pacific War's first large-scale amphibious assault against a defended beach. Ready or not.

4

Until mid 1943, the American Pacific War strategy had been largely determined by Japanese deployments in the critical South Pacific area. All available resources and manpower had been committed there to stem the Japanese threat. Guadalcanal was the Pacific War's turning point. Once the Japanese relinquished the initiative, the Allies became the attackers and the Japanese struggled in vain to regain the lost initiative. Limited U.S. resources continued to be diverted almost exclusively to the South Pacific, but reserves were also slowly built up for use elsewhere. After a year of steady combat in the South Pacific, there was enough material and manpower for the American strategists to begin work on mounting the long-planned Central Pacific sweep.

The Pacific War was a naval and naval-air war in which ground forces were relegated to the role of seizing naval bases and land for protective airfields. As a result of the dominant naval influence, Navy officers and units they commanded had prime responsibility for the conduct of the war. Thus, the U.S. Fifth Fleet was created to oversee the conduct of the war in the Central Pacific.

Of the three Marine divisions deployed in the Pacific in mid 1943, the 2nd was best suited for undertaking the opening of the Central Pacific sweep at Tarawa. First Marine Division had been engaged the longest in the bitter Guadalcanal fighting, and it was not yet available. The new 3rd Marine Division was just deploying in the theater and would require months of training before it could be used offensively.

Second Marine Division was placed under the administrative control of the new V Marine Amphibious Corps (VMAC), commanded by MGen Holland MacTyre Smith, known later as "Howlin' Mad." Although unblooded in the new war, Smith was a stubborn and argumentative professional who could be

17

counted on to tenaciously defend the interests of his Marines within the Navy-dominated councils responsible for conducting war in the Central Pacific.

The newly created V Amphibious Force went to VAdm Richmond Kelly Turner, whose appointment signaled the singular importance of the new command and its role in the war. Kelly Turner had been pulled from Third Fleet's III Amphibious Force in the South Pacific, a command he had created almost entirely alone in the long months it took to arrive at a decision at Guadalcanal.

In addition to the seizure of an Allied foothold in the Central Pacific, the Tarawa invasion plan arose from the Navy's and Marine Corps' need to adequately test doctrines and equipment developed over the preceding decade. Chances for success were good, the Navy tacticians thought, because new techniques in naval bombardment would practically annihilate any defending force. The Marines were skeptical about that, but unruffled; their own tactics and equipment, they averred, would take care of any serious opposition.

It was thought that Tarawa would be more of a demonstration than a fight.

When 2nd Marine Division left Wellington on November 1, 1943, it was generally believed that another in a long series of landing exercises was to be conducted at Hawkes Bay, New Zealand, a rocky inlet that had been used for such purposes during the preceding months. The troops were not enthusiastic about going to Hawkes Bay, for terrible accidents in the surf there had consistently taken lives.

There were two very good reasons for covering the departure for Tarawa with the Hawkes Bay story: to keep the true story out of Japanese hands and to account for the possibility that some fainthearted souls might decide to stay on the beach if they knew that a battle was in the offing. Only four men of 20,000 stayed behind—and the Japanese were not fooled.

On November 7, with 2nd Marine Division still a day away, RAdm H. E. Kingman, commander of the Tarawa fleet support units, completed the task of assembling his warships at Noumea, in New Caledonia, the major headquarters base for the South Pacific's Third Fleet. Kingman's force consisted of battleships, light and heavy cruisers, and destroyers, all of which would take part in pummelling Betio to its basic component, coral dust. Kingman and his subordinates were confident that the Marines would have to make nothing more than an administrative landing.

On the same day, November 7, one of the Marine Corps' hedges against naval overconfidence arrived at Noumea. The first Marine medium tanks to be deployed in the Pacific arrived with C Company, I Marine Amphibious Corps (IMAC) Tank Battalion. The 16 Sherman M4 tanks, each mounting a 75mm gun, would be the best means for cracking the many pillboxes known to be on Betio.

Second Marine Division made landfall on November 8 at Mele Bay, Efate, where the assault and support battalions immediately undertook a final series of practice landings.

While the troops were moving back and forth between their ships and the beaches, the division staff and the staff of the 2nd Amphibious Tractor Battalion were sweating out the arrival of 50 new LVT-2 amphibian tractors (amtracs). The division had departed from Wellington with 75 old-style LVT-1 amtracs, a hybrid vehicle that had been adapted rather than specially designed for combat. This was an important distinction, given the welcome some Marines were expecting on the beaches.

The adaptation of the amphibian tractor to a combat role was probably the most significant state-of-the-art amphibious warfare innovation from the Guadalcanal campaign. Designed in the 1930s by Donald Roebling as a rescue vehicle to be used by rangers in the Everglades, amphibian tractors had come to the attention of the Marine Corps in 1940 and had been adapted for carrying cargo; it was intended to be no more than a tracked amphibious truck capable of delivering supplies across water too shallow for standard landing craft. Protected by a pair of interior-mounted light machine guns, two tractors had been thrown into a combat situation in the early fighting at Guadalcanal, and alert innovators had seen a new potential for the basic vehicle. The older LVT-1 tractors were upgunned and armored with boilerplate in New Zealand while designers in the U.S. worked on an improved model. By the autumn of 1943, the first 100 LVT-2 production models were sitting on the docks at San Diego, ready for shipment to 2nd Marine Division. The Navy had room for shipping only 50 of the new tractors, and the schedule was so tight that they would have to arrive at Mele Bay while the practice landings were being undertaken or they would not be used at Tarawa. A provisional company was formed and crews were sent to Samoa to intercept them, thus affording drivers and maintenance teams a little time to familiarize themselves with the new innovations on the trip to Efate. There was no chance to test the new vehicles in the water.

All hands were assembled on November 10 and given the traditional Marine Corps Birthday message and a special meal. The fleet sailed on November 13. D-Day at Betio was a week away.

On November 14, RAdm Harry Hill, the Tarawa task force commander, transmitted the following message to all ships: "Give all hands the general picture of the projected operation and further details to all who should have this in execution of duties. This is the first American assault of a strongly defended atoll and . . . the largest Pacific operation to date."

The troops were assembled. Rumors were rife. The consensus ran to the recapture of Wake Island; betting ran the same way.

The Marines were first told that a reinforced regiment of the U.S. Army's green 27th Infantry Division was to mount an amphibious assault against Butaritari, in Makin Atoll. Second Marine Division, designated Southern Attack Force, drew Betio, in Tarawa Atoll. The codename for the operation, for what it was worth to the troops, was GALVANIC.

Tarawa Atoll is a wedge-shaped string of islands lined up along the edge of a large natural lagoon. The point of the wedge is to the east, and the open base is to the west. The target, Betio, is the westernmost island of the southern arm. There is one entrance into Tarawa Lagoon through the rugged coral reef that surrounds the entire atoll. Betio is wedge-shaped, point to the east, base to the west.

Four initial assault battalions were designated: the three battalions of the 2nd Marines reinforced by the 2nd Battalion, 8th Marines. Command of the initial assault would be in the hands of Dave Shoup, who had succeeded to command of the 2nd Marines from his position as Division Operations Officer when the previous regimental commander fell ill on the journey to Efate; Shoup had been spot-promoted to full colonel.

The initial assault battalions would land on Betio's north shore, from the lagoon side. The order from west to east would be 3rd Battalion, 2nd; 2nd Battalion, 2nd; 2nd Battalion, 8th. The 1st Battalion, 2nd, would be regimental reserve under Colonel Shoup's direct control.

Three primary beaches were marked out along the western half of Betio's northern shore. The 3rd Battalion, 2nd, would assault the westernmost, Red-1; the 2nd Battalion, 2nd, drew Red-2, in the center; the 2nd Battalion, 8th, drew Red-3, to the east.

The boundary between Red-2 and Red-3 was a 500-yard-long pier running from the beach to the north side of the reef that ringed Betio; it separated the 2nd Battalion, 2nd, from the 2nd Battalion, 8th, and would serve as a regimental boundary in the event additional battalions of the 8th Marines were committed.

The boundary between the 2nd and 3rd Battalions, 2nd, was at the eastern edge of a cove-like indentation in the north shore; 3rd Battalion would land into the indentation, and 2nd Battalion would land on the straight stretch of beach between the indentation, on the right, and the pier, on the left.

The 1st Battalion, 2nd, would land behind the assault battalion that made the most exploitable initial gains.

The 1st and 3rd Battalions, 8th Marines, were the Division Reserve, under the direct control of MGen Julian Smith, commanding general of the 2nd Marine Division. Smith could do as he wished with the division reserve without having to seek authority from higher headquarters. If all went well, the 3rd Battalion, 8th, would be landed on Bairiki, the island adjacent to Betio, to provide patrols and work details throughout Tarawa Atoll. The 1st Battalion, 8th, was to be aboard boats in the lagoon during the initial landings; it would be sent into Betio or back aboard its ship, depending on how things went.

The reinforced 6th Marines was designated Force Reserve and placed under the direct control of the VMAC commander, MGen Holland Smith, who was also in direct command of the Butaritari landings. (In fact, he would be aboard ship nearer Makin than Tarawa.) He could make use of all or part of 6th Marines at Makin or turn over all or part of it to Julian Smith for use at Tarawa.

It was a flexible enough plan, given the limited manpower—

a very standard plan. Given the Navy's boasts about the likely results of the prelanding bombardments, it appeared doubtful that the 6th Marines would ever be committed. Even the commanders of the 1st and 3rd Battalions, 8th, had doubts that their units would see combat.

A controversy attended the attachment of the 50 new LVT-2 tractors to 2nd Marine Division. The problem arose from the existence of a wide, rugged coral reef around all of Betio, and from unique tidal conditions that might render large numbers of standard landing craft useless in the assault.

In all parts of the world there are two kinds of tides, and they change with the lunar cycle. These are called "spring" tides and "neap" tides. Both are composed of the familiar high and low daily tides, but neap tides average less depth than spring tides. The cycle is weekly, with the neap tides occurring during the first and third quarters of the moon; thus, a high tide during the first quarter of the moon—during the "neap" phase—has a lower average depth than a high tide during the adjacent "spring" phase. Compounding the weekly and monthly phases is the semiannual cycle; all tides grow to greater depths during one half of the year, then diminish on the average during the second half of the year.

Betio was to be assaulted during the neap phase of the lower semiannual cycle, during a period when the daily tidal cycle would be lowest. However, it was expected that there would be sufficient water over the reef to float shallow-draft landing craft, which drew about 40 inches of water.

Up to this point, there seemed to be nothing to make the tides at Tarawa different from the tides anywhere else in the world. Modern armies do not wait six months for better tidal conditions—they use their material strengths to overcome nature.

However, at certain latitudes—Tarawa's among them—there is a rare tidal condition called a "dodging" tide. Whereas the spring and neap tides occur with clocklike regularity, dodging tides, as the name implies, may occur irregularly as many as several times in any given day. A low dodging tide is lower than a low neap tide. Tarawa was to be attacked during a period when dodging tides *might* occur.

It was assumed in planning that standard tides at Betio would be uniformly lower in mid November than they would be a month later. The planners had accounted for the low neap cycle, had tested equipment in expectation of it, and had come away with some assurance that the plan could be made to fit the conditions of nature. The margin for error was slim and would not accommodate a dodging-tide condition during the landing. The planners rated the chance of running into a dodging tide at Betio on the morning of D-Day as less than one in four—acceptable odds.

The hedge against the entire tidal question was the amphibian tractor; the more the division had, the better able it would be to cope with adverse tides.

Betio's reef is from 500 to 800 yards from the beach and averages 50 yards wide. There was only one boat passage in that reef, a narrow cut opposite the center of the northern beach, about 500 yards from shore. A narrow pier, 500 yards in length, connected the passage with the island. If the tide was too low to float boats over the reef, and if there were not enough amtracs, almost the entire assault force would be channelized into the pier, or the troops would have to wade at least 500 yards through gunfire to get to the northern beaches from the reef.

Because of the barrier reef and *expected* low tidal conditions, the three initial assault waves—six augmented companies, about 1,500 men—would be transported to the beaches aboard nearly all of the 75 old and 50 new amtracs. Troop leaders could elect to ride their individual tractors far inland.

If the water was high enough at the reef, subsequent troops and supplies would be ferried in aboard light and medium landing boats. If the water was too low for all or some of the boats, the tractors would be used to shuttle additional troops.

Aside from possible tidal difficulties, the initial waves would be tractor-borne, simply because armored tractors offer better protection against small arms fire than the plywood sides of the landing craft.

It was a neat plan, and the planners were proud of it.

But there was one dissenting voice, authoritative and persistent.

Among the old-time Tarawa residents included in the planning to lend their expertise was the former Resident Commissioner of the Gilbert Islands, Maj Frank Holland. While other former residents said there *might* be a dodging tide problem, Holland emphatically and repeatedly said that there *would* be a problem.

If anyone should have known for certain, it was Frank Holland, who had resided on Bairiki Island, right next to Betio, for 15 years. With little else at hand for relieving the boredom of his duties, Holland had spent a great deal of time mastering the tidal cycles. He was not simply skeptical about the chance of having sufficient water over the reef for the lightest landing craft, he *knew* there would not be enough.

Holland approached LCdr Louis Fabian, the amphibious squadron beachmaster, at Mele Bay and begged him to tell the brass that the Marines would be facing sure death if they intended to land on November 20. There would be no chance of occurrence of dodging tides only five weeks later, at the end of December.

Holland was extremely distraught throughout the Mele Bay exercises. Many senior Marine officers were subjected to his highly emotional pleadings, and all were put off by them. They insisted that a long-range multiservice amphibious operation the size of GALVANIC was too complex to alter. Plans and schedules had been worked out months in advance, there would be cargoes waiting in a dozen ports for the ships charged with delivering troops and material to Betio, and other operations involving the same ships had been tightly scheduled. There was no way to alter the plan, short of cancelling the operation.

Major Holland was also rattling the troops. For this transgression, he was quietly moved from the ship bearing the command element of the 2nd Marines to another ship bearing a back-up battalion.

Nothing could be done to stop the assault.

Young Marines, eager for battle, were told that tiny Betio, less than two square miles of coral sand, was to be pummelled into oblivion by the Navy's largest ships. They were assured that the whole affair would consist of walking ashore and picking up the pieces. They were obliged to laugh when discussing the Japanese commander's boast that a million men would not take Tarawa in a thousand years of battle.

5

The intelligence summaries at the heart of the American plan to seize Betio were paradigms of calm, careful assessment of often oblique clues.

For example, the Betio garrison was accurately counted to within a half-dozen defenders. Since Betio is a coral and sand island whose highest point was a manmade sand-covered bunker ten feet above sea level, the Japanese could not build the usual sort of latrine trenches on the island itself. Instead, they were forced to build wooden latrines on tiny piers over the water, relying on tidal currents to sweep their droppings out to sea.

The Japanese are a fastidious race, and the elimination of bodily wastes falls within certain cultural norms that were known to American intelligence. Once the initial intellectual breakthrough was made, counting defenders at Betio became a matter of counting the latrines, multiplying by probable numbers using a single latrine, and arriving at a result. The estimate was 4,840 defenders. The actual number was 4,836.

Of the 4,836, only 2,619 were combat troops, *rigosentai* of Sasebo 7th Special Naval Landing Force and fighting troops attached directly to the headquarters unit, 3rd Special Konky-ochitai. Several hundred additional naval ratings and officers could put up a fight, but the bulk of the remainder were Korean, Okinawan and Japanese laborers, all noncombatants.

Although the Japanese commander, RAdm Keichi Shiba-saki, was grossly outnumbered, he had several undeniable advantages. It was his ground; there were only so many ways for invaders to get ashore; he had internal lines of communication; and he could defend from one of the most extensive defense complexes in that part of the world.

His armaments consisted of four 8-inch Vickers naval rifles captured from the British in Southeast Asia; four 14cm guns;

six 80mm antiboat guns; four 12.7cm twin-mount dual-purpose guns; eight 75mm dual-purpose guns; ten 75mm mountain guns; six 70mm battalion guns; nine 37mm antitank guns; 27 13mm single-mount and four twin-mount infantry machine guns; 31 13mm single-mount and twin-mount dual-purpose antiaircraft machine guns; several dozen 7.7mm Nambu-Hotchkiss medium infantry machine guns; a much larger number of old-style Nambu and new-style Rahambu 7.7mm light infantry machine guns (bipod-mounted, like an American Browning Automatic Rifle); hundreds of standard .25-caliber Arisaka bolt-action infantry rifles; and assorted small arms of various types. Mobile defenses consisted of 14 light tanks, each carrying a coaxial 7.7mm machine gun and a turret-mounted 37mm antitank gun.

The defense of Betio was to be based on fixed positions employing interlocking bands of fire and secondary fallback positions. Unengaged units would form a mobile reserve and reaction force.

Most of the crew-served weapons were emplaced in coral-and-log bunkers and pillboxes, all connected by an extensive, protected trench system. A number of concrete-and-steel positions had been constructed, and more were planned. These varied in size and shape, but most shared these characteristics: a concrete-slab floor set from three to five feet below the surface with four or five steel-rod-reinforced concrete walls at least twelve inches thick and five to eight feet high. Several such pillboxes sported steel gun cupolas similar to tank turrets. Roofs of most emplacements were flat and covered with alternating layers of coral, sand, coconut logs and sandbags. The final layers were tapered to conform with the topography, a hedge against casting shadows that would show up on intelligence photos. Many emplacements were so cleverly camouflaged that they could not be seen head-on. All pillboxes had two to four firing apertures and at least two entrances, and all could be reached through protected, often covered, trenches.

Betio is too small to support any sort of tactical movement by a defending force, so the defenses were set at or near the periphery, at the water's edge. Many emplacements, in fact, were set directly into the four-foot-high log or coral-block seawall that bordered most of the island. And a number of strong emplacements were built beneath the 500-yard-long pier connecting the north shore with the reef entrance. One-man emplacements, usually hardly more than a dug-in steel gasoline drum, were spotted all over the island. These could be used both as fighting holes and bomb shelters; most had camouflaged covers. A network of tank traps radiated from the southwest tip of the island to protect a huge concrete structure mounting the Vickers naval rifles.

Inland, large half-buried concrete command and barracks structures had been placed between 50 and 100 yards apart across the central portion of the island. These rectangular bombproofs consisted of two or four rooms on either side of a central corridor giving off to entrances at either end. Walls were up to 55 inches thick. Dozens of coconut-log buildings—sleeping quarters and messhalls for the troops, offices, machine shops, and storage buildings—were spotted all across the island. Many dozens of tents all over the island provided shelter for several thousand construction laborers.

The very first Allied attacks against targets in the Gilberts opened on September 18, 1943, when American carrier aircraft and land-based American B-24 heavy bombers mounted a 24-hour series of raids aimed at destroying radio installations and damaging airbase facilities on Butaritari and Betio.

One direct result of these raids was the evacuation of all land-based aircraft from Betio; this was a temporary move, and the air group's ground detachment stayed behind. Air-search operations were to be made by Makin's amphibious air group.

Japanese carrier air groups, which were to have rushed to the aid of the ground defenders in the event of an attack, had been butchered in the Solomons, and the Imperial Navy had decided to forego such a response. Thus, there would be no effective air deterrent in the Gilberts.

One direct result of the raid was the construction of a large, formidable bombproof bunker on Betio to serve as Admiral Shibasaki's new command post.

It is also possible that the September raids were responsible for the execution of as many as two dozen Europeans who had remained in the Tarawa area from the start of the war. It appears that these people had been rounded up in late 1942 or early 1943 and forced to work on the Betio defenses, chiefly on extending the main pier 300 yards to the edge of the reef. The story, possibly apocryphal, is that these men had cheered the

American bombers on, standing exposed and enthusiastically waving at the first Allies they had seen on the offensive. The Japanese apparently thought the Europeans were passing messages by some clever code, and the decision was made to put them to death.

It is known that none of the European men who had stayed behind lived in the Gilberts by the beginning of November, 1943, and none survived the war. The only Europeans living in the Gilberts were Catholic nuns, who were not disturbed.

If Admiral Shibasaki really had boasted that a million men could not take Betio in a thousand years of battle, there was only one possible way for him to prove such a boast.

Part II
THE FIRST DAY

6

Nightfall, Friday, November 19, 1943.

Everything was set to go. Weapons had been cleaned and oiled, combat gear had been neatly packed, ammunition had been issued, intelligence reports had been brought up to date, letters home had been written.

After the sun set behind the western horizon and the quarter moon appeared, the only job left for 2nd Marine Division's 20,000 men, and particularly the nearly 3,000 Marines of the three initial assault battalions, was to attain some final spiritual communion.

The officers who would lead the assault units could do no more than offer their good wishes and a few high-flown sentiments. Their words were not going to save lives, but there was reason to believe that the spirit they might instill would result in a few more yards on the morning's bloody beaches.

On that last evening aboard ship, LtCol Herb Amey preceded his final briefing to the officers of his 2nd Battalion, 2nd, with a few extemporaneous remarks: "We are very fortunate. This is the first time a landing has been made by American troops against a well-defended beach, the first time over a coral reef, the first time against any force to speak of. And the first time the Japs had the hell kicked out of them in a hurry."

Herb Amey truly believed that the morning's fight would be over almost as soon as it began, a victory for his side.

Only a few hours earlier, Amey had been kidding with the 2nd Regiment's Catholic chaplain, Father Frank Kelly, an old friend and fellow Pennsylvanian. When the priest asked Amey, a Protestant, if he minded a good "right-handed" burial, Amey laughingly replied, "But, Father, you've got it all wrong. You're the left-hander! And don't worry about it."

Aboard *Heywood*, Maj Henry Pierson Crowe, commanding

the 2nd Battalion, 8th, explained to his officers that Amey's battalion was going into Beach Red-2, and that Maj John Schoettel's 3rd Battalion, 2nd, was going into Red-1. Then, staring levelly at his 35 officers, Crowe said, "And for the third beach—that's Beach Red-3—they've picked this battalion. And you all know me!"

They certainly did know Jim Crowe, an old-time enlisted Marine who had been a warrant officer as late as 1940 and who had earned himself quite a reputation at Guadalcanal. The fiery redhead, who sported a wonderful waxed handlebar moustache, was one of the saltiest battalion commanders in the Corps. There was not a single officer present who did not believe that Jim Crowe had gone to considerable trouble to secure a lead-off position for his battalion. They knew him, all right.

In the hours and days ahead, Jim Crowe was to find supreme frustration, and equal amounts of glory.

During those last hours of final briefings and farewells, Division Commander Julian Smith spoke to his Marines in a proud, fatherly vein: "I know that all of you are well trained and fit for the tasks assigned to you. You will quickly overrun the Japanese forces; you will decisively defeat and destroy the treacherous enemies of our country; your success will add new laurels to the glorious tradition of our Corps." In closing, Julian Smith invoked a blessing from the Almighty and cast the fates of his young Marines to Mars. He had done everything in his power to prepare them for this venture, and his was now a waiting role.

Late that evening, Father Frank Kelly received an unexpected caller, Col Dave Shoup, upon whose shoulders had rested the responsibility for planning the Betio landings and upon whose shoulders would rest the responsibility for leading it. Shoup came right to the point. "Padre, I want you to pray for me."

"What sort of a prayer, Colonel?" The priest was a bit nonplussed, for Shoup, like Herb Amey, was a Protestant.

"I want you to pray that I don't make any mistakes out on that beach; no wrong decisions that will cost any of those boys an arm or a leg or a hand, much less a life. I want you to pray for that, Padre."

• • •

The first serious action to take place near Tarawa began at 1930, when Radarman 2nd Class Jack O'Brien, of destroyer *Ringgold*, picked up a "skunk," a surface target, on his radarscope. An alert was sounded, and The Flag, the force command, ordered *Ringgold* to join with destroyer *Gansevoort* and light cruiser *Santa Fe* to investigate.

As *Ringgold* proceeded at flank speed, the target switched on searchlights to probe the darkness. She must have had radar of her own.

Cdr Thomas Conley, *Ringgold's* captain, ordered his torpedomen to fire two fish. One exploded on its own, and the other turned back toward *Ringgold*. Conley shoved his helmsman aside and spun the wheel, neatly turning his destroyer. The torpedo passed through *Ringgold's* wake, close astern.

Next, fearful of firing his remaining torpedoes, Commander Conley requested permission to open with gunfire. The message was not acknowledged, so, while the target was still available, Conley ordered his guns into action. *Santa Fe* and *Gansevoort* joined in.

Radarman Jack O'Brien saw a definite hit, then watched the contact disappear from his radarscope. As far as *Ringgold's* crew was concerned, the destroyer had sunk an enemy vessel.

At 1930, the radarman on duty aboard fleet transport submarine *Nautilus* picked up a skunk. *Nautilus*, which was carrying 75 Marines charged with reconnoitering and seizing Abemama Atoll, was running on the surface to recharge her batteries. It was the submarine's second mission to the Gilberts; fifteen months earlier, she had carried a company of Carlson's Raiders to Makin.

The skunk was soon joined by two others, one the same size and one larger. *Nautilus's* captain assumed they were friendly and ordered searchlights switched on for recognition.

The lookouts saw two flashes, then heard an explosion. The captain ordered his ship to crash dive. The bridge was cleared and the descent began. A moment before the top of the conning tower slid beneath the waves, *Nautilus* sustained a hit and plummeted 50 fathoms before control could be regained.

Although her conning tower had been holed and she was taking on water, she survived and her mission was not affected.

• • •

Heywood's Boat Group Officer, Lt Galen Brown, was privately sweating out the reef. Months earlier, during practice landings at Hawkes Bay, Brown's LCVPs (light landing craft) had been brutally chewed up on New Zealand coral, and he had been lucky to salvage all of them. Warned about Betio's coral ring, Brown had discussed his concern with Jim Crowe, who told him to stay well clear of the reef if there was not sufficient water. That way, even if Crowe's battalion had to wade ashore, Brown would be able to supply it and evacuate casualties.

The Navy cooks began preparing breakfast at 2000 on November 19. At 2200, the first meal shift aboard *Zeilin* was ordered to lay up to the messing deck for steak and eggs, a New Zealand custom that was about to become the traditional last breakfast for action-bound Marines.

Pfc Arnold Gladson, a 37mm antitank gunner with Weapons Company, 2nd Marines, sleepily climbed from his bunk and dressed for breakfast by sprucing up his slept-in dungaree utility uniform. Like most Marines, Gladson was pleased to hear that the job would be completed by early afternoon. He had been at Guadalcanal for five months.

Gladson joined his gun platoon in the troop messing compartment and got in line for his steak and eggs and coffee. Within minutes one nearby Marine was moved to comment on what every other Marine already knew or expected: "These goddamn eggs taste like they're four years old!" No doubt, but they were the first eggs any of them had seen in over a month, so they ate. Nobody knew yet what a mess steak and eggs can make of a stomach wound.

Aboard *LaSalle*, 17-year-old FM1 John Lane, a member of I Company, 8th, had forsaken sleep, his mind alive with the taste of previously unknown feelings. Lane, who had quit high school to enlist, felt that the time had arrived for figuring out where he stood in the universe. He found a secluded spot topside and sat down to try in the innocence of his youth to conceive of what the day ahead might be like and what it would mean to be no longer living. He ran the full line of horrible conjurings but became increasingly dissatisfied. A bit frustrated by the hitherto unknown vagaries of his mind on the loose, young Lane decided to return to his bunk for a final crack at some sleep.

· · ·

Veteran *Time* correspondent Bob Sherrod was roused at midnight and told to lay up to the troop officers' messing compartment. He sleepily shrugged into his clothing and joined Herb Amey's staff for steak and eggs, fried potatoes, and coffee. Sherrod ate and shot the breeze with Amey's staffers, then rushed to his stateroom to finish adjusting his gear.

Below decks, many enlisted Marines were catching the final moments of fitful attempts at sleep. The troop-berthing spaces were unbearably hot, but the rumors were even hotter. Few of the troops gave them much credence at first, but as they made the rounds and were heard again, often with clever embellishments, even the most optimistic Marines began taking them seriously.

Bob Sherrod was making his way topside when General Quarters was sounded. It was 0215, Saturday, November 20, 1943. D-Day.

Father Frank Kelly conducted a final Mass in *Zeilin's* small, dimly lighted troop officers' messing compartment. The room and adjacent passageway were overflowing with Marines of every faith. As Kelly recited the Mass, Dr. Ed Welte, Amey's battalion surgeon, whispered the order of hymns to the ship's organist, a Protestant who had been loaned to Father Kelly for the occasion.

In the midst of the crowd, Cpl Jerry Kubinski, a squad leader with E Company, 2nd, was having a novel experience. The 29-year-old Guadalcanal veteran, who had grown up in a Polish parish in Philadelphia, was reciting his first Mass in English.

For many there, it was the last communion.

Aboard *Zeilin*, 1stLt William Deane Hawkins called his specially-trained 36-man Scout-and-Sniper Platoon for a final briefing. Elements of the platoon, with a team of assault engineers, were to land 15 minutes ahead of the assault companies and reduce defenses along the 500-yard-long pier running from the lagoon reef to Betio's north shore.

Hawkins had failed to pass Air Corps and Navy physicals after Pearl Harbor because of a large, ugly burn scar he had acquired as a toddler, so he had turned to the Marine Corps. He had been commissioned in the field at Guadalcanal while serving with the 2nd Marines Intelligence Section. Following Guadalcanal, in New Zealand, Hawkins had chafed under the rigors of commanding a desk and had finally wangled command of the Scout-and-Sniper Platoon. Under Hawkins's unrelenting leadership, the platoon became by far the best trained outfit in the division, a fact which Deane Hawkins never let his men forget.

Hawkins, a loner, was so confident in his own abilities that he unashamedly told fellow officers of his conviction that he would win a Medal of Honor in combat. The men he told had the eerie feeling that Deane Hawkins was not bragging, just level-headed certain that he would rise to the occasion.

Anyone listening to Tokyo Rose that night would have been a bit shaken. The Japanese propaganda program told the world that a division of unfortunate Marines was being sent to Betio.

Capt Joe Clerou was in a good humor that night. He knew that the landings would be easy; he had been assured of it. All the lessons he had helped bring home from Guadalcanal had been taken into account, particularly in terms of his specialty, supply. Clerou commanded F Company, 2nd Battalion, 18th Marines, a shore party unit assigned to take care of the immediate needs of the 8th Marines. Since Clerou's 2nd Platoon would be providing assistance to one of the assault battalions—Crowe's 2nd Battalion, 8th—he had elected to travel with it aboard *Heywood*. Clerou's other two oversized platoons were on other ships with the 1st and 3rd Battalions, 8th Marines.

Following the final briefing, Clerou was joined topside by 1stLt Sandy Bonnyman, assistant commander of 2nd Platoon. Bonnyman, like Clerou, was a Guadalcanal veteran. Unlike Clerou, however, he need not have been in the service; he was married, the father of three, and owner of several copper mines in the Southwest, an essential wartime occupation.

Bonnyman kept refusing a $10 debt Clerou tried to pay off, the result of the captain's short supply of liquor money during the last liberty in Wellington. At length, Bonnyman said that he would take Clerou's brand new jungle boots as repayment. Clerou refused, but laughingly assured his subordinate, who was several years older than he, that the boots could be collected off his dead carcass if the landing was livelier than advertised. Sandy Bonnyman agreed with a chuckle and a handshake, then left to rejoin his platoon.

Aboard *Middleton*, Pvt Joe Murray, a BAR-man with L Company, 2nd, spent much of the night cadging lemon extract from the ship's cooks. Since this was the 18-year-old Philadelphian's first prospect of battle, he wanted a supply of anything alcoholic, even the mild fruit extract.

Most of the rifle units aboard *Middleton* had to spend a little time obliterating traces of mischief. Members of I Company, 2nd, had gone to considerable lengths fashioning spigot handles for the freshwater showers, which the Coast Guard crew ran at odd and infrequent intervals. The hardware was carefully stowed in anticipation of use later in the week. And the holes the troops had cut into air ducts to reduce the chance of suffocation in the stuffy holds had to be covered.

In *Middleton's* wardroom, the officers of the 3rd Battalion, 2nd, were breaking up following their final briefing. In the rush to gather maps and loose papers, 2ndLt Jim Fawcett of K Company came away with an aerial photo belonging to a fellow platoon leader, 2ndLt Mike Hofmann. Although Fawcett immediately noticed the error, he decided to keep the photo until after the operation, then give it to his friend as a memento of their shared baptism. There would never be a chance.

Fawcett next talked another K Company platoon leader, 1stLt Ott Schulte, into a few quick hands of gin rummy. By the time the two officers had to rejoin their platoons, Fawcett had successfully fleeced Schulte of $20. After a comradely handshake, Fawcett said, "And remember what Paul said about collecting debts from the dead. I don't want to have to do that." As the two friends separated, Schulte stuffed a cigar into his pocket along with a candy bar; he figured he would give the "pogey bait" to nonsmoker Fawcett on the beach following the successful landing while he enjoyed the cigar. But the two would never meet again.

Unbeknownst to most Marines, the circling transports had come about to a heading that would take them right up to the reef surrounding Tarawa Atoll.

• • •

PlSgt Jack Hernandez, of K Company, 8th, was privately overjoyed at the prospect of an easy landing. He had been in the Marine Corps for five years and had seen enough action on Guadalcanal to last a lifetime. Still, there was a job to be done. Hernandez's battalion was to secure Bairiki. As the minutes ticked off, a call for troop leaders got Hernandez's platoon out from under his watchful eye for a few minutes, more than enough time for imaginative Marines to get into trouble.

General Quarters was sounded moments after Hernandez was called away, and the troops began hitting the deck to prepare. One inevitable late riser lost the advantage of his extra sleep by having to move twice as fast as his companions. Somehow, the spoon on one of his hand grenades got hung up in the wire mesh support of his bunk. Sgt Leonard Wynn, a battalion communicator attached to the platoon, was just entering the compartment when the grenade exploded, cutting down the men on either side of the hatchway. Wynn escaped unscathed, but eight Marines were wounded, a quarter of the platoon.

Shortly after Task Force 53 stopped close by the reef protecting the open side of Tarawa Lagoon, preparations began for the debarkation of the assault waves. No one knew it, but the transports stopped south of the desired spot and began launching landing craft and amphibian tractors.

At 0320, a terse order from The Flag resounded through the troop holds of *Zeilin, Middleton,* and *Heywood:* "All Marines lay topside to your debarkation stations."

Aboard *Heywood,* civilian correspondent Richard Johnston stopped a young Marine and asked the boy if he was afraid. The reply, typical at that early hour: "Hell no! I'm a Marine!"

Among the first troops to gain a position topside aboard *Heywood* was Sgt Ernie Butner, a veteran communicator with Maj Jim Crowe's headquarters. Butner was more heavily encumbered than most Marines. In addition to his carbine, 100 rounds of ammunition, C-rations, canteen, change of socks, toilet articles, a few personal possessions, entrenching tool, gasmask, and steel helmet, he had a heavy TBX radio component strapped to his back. In all, Butner's weight was up by at least 75 pounds. He was not looking forward to getting dumped in deep water.

Butner's fears were initially insulated by the knowledge he

had acquired concerning Japanese defenses and Betio's limited terrain. He felt confident, but that confidence was dampened a bit when he saw Navy corpsmen stacking litters and medical supplies a few feet along the deck on which he was standing.

The night was clear, and sounds had an odd way of traveling through the stillness. Capt Thomas Fitzpatrick, master of *Zeilin*, had just shaken hands and wished Godspeed to LtCol Herb Amey when his ears picked out the squeal of boat falls passing over the sheaves of the boat blocks; *Zeilin's* first bank of landing craft was being lowered into the water.

Zeilin was a transport steeped in Marine Corps history, for she had been named after a mid Nineteenth Century Commandant of the Marine Corps, Jacob Zeilin. As the first boats were set gently into the water, *Zeilin's* crew paid their respects to the dungaree-clad warriors who would ride them to battle. All other sounds were momentarily drowned out as the strains of "The Marines' Hymn" blared from *Zeilin's* loudspeakers.

The 42 men comprising 1stLt Ott Schulte's 1st Platoon, K Company, 2nd, left *Middleton* at about 0330 aboard an LCM, a tank landing craft, but soon transferred to the three amtracs that would bear them to the far left flank of Beach Red-1. Under Schulte's temporary command was K Company's mortar section, with which the weapons platoon leader, 2ndLt Tom Becker, was to establish a base of fire to support the company's advance inland. Second Lieutenant Mike Hofmann's 2nd Platoon was to land on Schulte's right with Becker's light machine guns. Finally, 2ndLt Jim Fawcett was to bring his 3rd Platoon in three minutes behind Schulte and Hofmann and go to the support of the lead platoon with the best prospects of advancing. Three minutes after Fawcett's platoon landed, Capt Jim Crain, the veteran company commander, was to touch down near the center of the company sector with his headquarters group and a medium machine gun platoon from M Company, the battalion weapons unit. On Crain's right, I Company, 2nd, would be similarly landed from tractors. Later, L Company would debouch from LCVPs at the beach or on the reef, depending upon tidal conditions, and move to help exploit the most exploitable gains of the lead companies. Battalion weapons and regimental support units assigned to the battalion would follow L Company. The battalion command group would be in a "free" boat which could land anytime, anywhere, at the discretion of the battalion commander.

The formation that would hit Red-1 would be duplicated on Red-2 and Red-3: four reinforced rifle platoons in the lead; two reinforced rifle platoons in the second wave; company head-quarters and supports in the third tractor wave; back-up rifle company in the first boat wave; and supports and command groups somewhere between the second and fifth waves.

Father Frank Kelly and his Protestant counterpart, Rev. Norman Darling, left *Zeilin* early with Col Dave Shoup and various key headquarters personnel. The padre was carrying his Mass kit under one arm and a bundle of candy and toilet articles under the other. The first would be put to immediate use if the landing went as planned, for a Mass of Thanksgiving; if the beaches were bathed in blood, the candy and toiletries would help boost morale around the aid stations.

As the assault waves slowly circled in the water awaiting orders from The Flag, every Marine not otherwise occupied lined the rails of their ships to watch the unfolding spectacle.

The men of Combat Team 8, aboard *Sheridan, Monrovia,* and *LaSalle*, would be fed into their boats soon. All of them knew that if there was opposition on the beach they would have to be sent in. For the moment, however, they were in reserve, contemplating a few days of hard labor cleaning up after the naval bombardment. All the men of the 8th Marines could do for the time being was sweat things out, something the 4,000 men of Combat Team 2 were doing all the more, although few would voice their concerns.

The Word would come, all in good time.

7

The Japanese fired the first shot.

As American naval gunnery officers counted off the last minutes before they were to unleash their own bombardment, the *rigosentai* crew manning one of the large coastal defense guns covering the lagoon lost nerve. An eerie red star cluster burst over the lagoon at 0441, its glowing fingers probing the blackness for a worthy target.

The battle for Betio began, then paused.

The star shell was followed by a silence more profound than anything anyone could recall. The Japanese did not fire again, nor did any American warship. Each side coldly stared back at the other over the black lagoon.

Aboard battleship *Maryland*, The Flag was in pandemonium. This one action on the part of Admiral Shibasaki's guncrew meant that at least one large-caliber weapon was still guarding the lagoon. Previous bombardments had missed at least that and, very likely, a great deal more. But every assurance had been given that MGen Julian Smith and his division would be well served by RAdm Harry Hill's gunfire section. The final softening-up fire was set to begin within 30 minutes.

At about 0505, the crews of many medium- and large-caliber guns on Betio's lagoon shore were ordered to prepare to fire on the American fleet. Two minutes later, at 0507, the order to commence firing was giving. Targets were the ships nearest Betio.

LCdr Lou Fabian, the amphibious squadron beachmaster, was in one of *Zeilin's* boats moving on the narrow lagoon entrance when the first shell hit about 300 yards away, between his boat and the transport. The startled 40-year-old Annapolis graduate and former Bank of America executive took a quick look at the island and saw flashes all along the beach. As did

41

many senior officers in the area, Fabian told his coxswain to move out in a hurry, then looked back to see *Zeilin* already heading for safer waters.

The Japanese fire went unanswered for 35 long minutes. Then, at 0542, *Maryland* swung her 14-inch main batteries to lay on Betio, and the flag communicator growled, "Commence firing!" The first few tons of 14-, 8-, 6- and 5-inch shells were sent into the blackness. In the next moments, Japanese fire appreciably dropped off.

Aboard *Zeilin*, 2nd Regiment communicators were gathering to await the boats that would take them ashore along with Colonel Shoup and the regimental staff. As the crowd edged toward the rail, a huge battleship cut loose with her main batteries. A wrinkled old Navy chief—he looked like he was at least 60—slipped through the crowd for a look and perched himself on the rail. The old salt clenched his pipe between his teeth, smiled, and proudly exclaimed to the young pups around him, "That there's the *Colorado*. She was at Pearl Harbor." With that, *Colorado* cut loose again, sending over a shockwave that lifted the old man from his roost and dropped him into the drink. Minutes later, the sodden old chief climbed over the rail into the midst of the bemused communicators. He shook his boney fist and yelled across the water to the 3,000 men in *Colorado*, "I hope all you bastards wind up in the Submarine Service!"

Lt Galen Brown, who had been endlessly worrying about the effect of the reef on the boats under his command, was nowhere near the reef and was having considerable troubles. When the Japanese guns on Betio opened fire, the transports moved back out to sea to a point seven miles from the beaches. From there, landing waves would proceed through the reef channel and make the 3½-mile run through the lagoon to the beaches. It was an adequate plan for minimizing damage to the transports, but the boat crews were something less than ecstatic. Betio could not be seen from the transport area so, as far as Galen Brown was concerned, the boats and tractors were in open sea. Brown had 15 tractors and several boat waves to shepherd to Betio, and he couldn't even find the place. His only clue as to heading was a huge pillar of smoke from somewhere over the naked horizon.

Just as Brown thought he had the heading right, he had the sensation that he was caught in a fast current, drifting off course. Actually, the Japanese had found the range, and the transports, Brown's only frame of reference, were moving still farther out to sea.

When Brown stopped his boat to count the tractors, he came up with only 13 of the 15 in his care, so he ordered his coxswain to race ahead in the hope of finding the lost sheep. When he later reorganized the tractors into three waves, he found that he again had 15; there was no way to tell if they were all his or, if so, where the lost vehicles had gone to or come from.

The schedule was completely shot.

In a landing boat approaching the lagoon, Pvt Vince Michalski, a machine gunner with H Company, 2nd Battalion, 8th, heard one of his companions explain how some Army heavy bombers were on the way from Hawaii to plaster Betio with 2,000-pound "daisy cutter" antipersonnel bombs. That was about as credible a story as anything Michalski had heard in the preceding week, so he sat back to await the arrival of the miracle bombers.

Maryland ordered all the warships to cease firing as the far-off carriers were sending in airstrikes, which were supposed to be approaching the atoll. However, the carrier planes did not arrive on schedule and the ships did not resume the bombardment.

Pfc Arnold Gladson glanced to the east and saw the first faint glimmer of sunrise. Sitting high on the engine housing of his boat, the antitank gunner was trying to catch a glimpse of the low-lying island, dead ahead. All he could see were columns of thick, black smoke.

Gladson was impervious to the things around him, so intense was his concentration, until he heard a long, loud whistle grow ominously longer and louder. There was no time to duck, only to turn. A large shell detonated 50 feet astern and threw a heavy spray into the boat, giving the boatload of Marines its first real scare of the day. The remainder of the ride to the beach would be made with Arnold Gladson behind and below the thin plywood gunwales. A parting glance showed the gunner that the hitherto clustered craft had spread out.

Cpl Jerry Kubinski, whose squad was bound for Red-2 in the lead wave, was eager to get things going. He felt unafraid. It was to be a milk run. He barely noticed that he was anxiously threading his rosary and muttering short prayers in Polish.

Pvt Joe Murray was about as set as he would ever be. His quest for lemon extract had been successful, but he became increasingly unglued until he thought about how many Guadalcanal veterans he could look to if there was a fight. Meantime, Murray had a more immediate problem: his steak-and-eggs breakfast was not mixing well with the lemon extract.

American warships opened at 0606 with even heavier fires than earlier, and the Japanese guns on Betio's north shore were almost completely subdued. The long-overdue Navy fighters and bombers were presumably on the way.

A young Marine aboard *Monrovia* was moved to comment, "Hell, look at them firing on that island. There's so many shells being fired there won't be no island left to walk on."

The fire was indeed great, but in the clearing light a few men at widely dispersed points noted a serious defect in the Navy's much vaunted technique of close-in fire. In a tractor low in the water, a Marine platoon leader counted fewer explosions on shore than shells being fired. Looking more closely, he saw faint shadows fall, then rise from the spit of land dead ahead. A green mortar ammunition carrier on one of the transports noted the same curious effect; each time he expected an explosion at a point on the island, it came far beyond that point, over the water on the seaward side.

In fact, shells fired from close-in caromed off the low dunes and harmlessly exploded over water to seaward. Many shells did find targets, but the effect of the many tons of steel fired at the island was vastly diminished.

Lt(jg) Fred Whaley, piloting one of two fabric spotter planes high over the lagoon, was calling the shots for the Navy gunners while, in a similar plane nearby, LCdr Robert MacPherson gave a running commentary on the progress of the assault waves. Comments by both observers indicated that the view, at least, was impressive.

Sunrise was at 0612. At 0615, all ships ceased firing to make way for Navy fighters and dive-bombers, which bombed and strafed the beaches on the lagoon side of Betio, then withdrew.

The Flag announced W-Hour at 0620; naval gunfire would continue unabated for 60 minutes against area targets, then another 60 minutes of unrelenting gunfire would seek specific targets at the water's edge. This phase, Phase II, would be followed by a final airstrike in direct support of the landings at H-Hour, which was set for 0830.

At 0646, *Pursuit*, a small minesweeper that was to act as the control vessel at the assault Line of Departure, entered the lagoon under sporadic fire from Betio, but sustained no hits. Upon breaching the passage, she launched a whaleboat to lay smoke to cover her maneuvers.

Fourteen minutes after *Pursuit* passed through the barrier reef, minesweeper *Requisite* entered the lagoon without mishap in the face of intermittent fire.

The third ship to approach the passage was *Ringgold*, one of two primary support destroyers assigned to take on beach targets at close range. Every precaution had been taken to get the big destroyer through the narrow passage, for she could seal it if she ran aground. Despite having a longtime resident of Tarawa Atoll at the helm, *Ringgold* shuddered to a momentary halt, then started up again. She made it through but left her sonar gear on the coral.

In the moment she was stopped, *Ringgold* took a hit from shore-based artillery. A dud entered the hull below the waterline, damaging electrical and power systems. One of the seamen in the damaged compartment cradled the dud in his arms and ran topside to drop it overboard. Meantime, Lt Wayne Parker, who had been unable to find a more suitable material for plugging the hole, pushed his rump into the void and kept it there until someone arrived with bedding; he was to receive a rather uniquely worded Navy Cross citation. Although the inflow of water subsided, it could not be stopped until a volunteer went over the side—the exposed shoreward side—to weld on a patch.

With her power temporarily out, *Ringgold* drifted gently

back against the reef, dead in the water, a perfect target. The second hit, also a dud, struck her amidships. It plowed through a 40mm magazine, ricocheted off the torpedo mount (where it bent a hunk of steel over a live warhead) and plunged through the sickbay, where it destroyed most of the ship's ready medical supplies. After nosing through a bulkhead into the Emergency Radio Shack, where it narrowly missed a radioman's head, the still-lively shell spun in amongst the 20mm gun battery, where it bowled men over in all directions. Then it disappeared.

Several rounds from shore burst over *Ringgold's* fantail and high up by her mast, shutting down the radar.

Ringgold had not sustained one casualty.

Pursuit secured fire at 0715 and made for the Line of Departure. She switched on her main searchlight battery at 0726 to serve as a beacon for the assault waves. As she began tracking the lead tractor waves, she found that they were 26 minutes behind schedule because a headwind had halved the amtracs' top speed of four knots.

Still elated from his briefings, Capt Joe Clerou, the pioneer company commander with Crowe's battalion, approached Betio whistling a ditty called "Sleepy Lagoon." The selection was not wholly appropriate in the midst of the cacophonous cannonade going on over Clerou's head, but it was the most fitting song he could think of. Two hours later, the pioneer officer would be whistling another tune: *Ave Maria*.

As the assault waves began passing through the chokepoint at the reef, *Ringgold* got up enough power to free herself, then moved eastward to a point off Red-3, where she fired her 5-inch, 20mm and 40mm guns directly over the assault waves and into the beach. In the meantime, Japanese mortars were trying to range in on the tractor waves.

As loudspeakers ordered the 3rd Battalion, 8th, over *Monrovia's* sides, FM1 John Lane was struck by a curious insight. Although he had listened attentively at various shipboard briefings, he could not recall the name of the island that was the center of so much mad activity.

As Pvt Bob Lutz struggled to *Monrovia's* rail with a heavy load of 81mm mortar ammunition, he grabbed an inflatable lifebelt as an added precaution. Lutz checked the mechanism that would break open a pair of carbon dioxide cartridges pressing into his belly and made certain that the folds of rubber were firmly secured by a row of snaps. As he climbed carefully over the rail and down the cargo net, he began to find breathing a difficult chore. He chalked that up to excitement and exertion, but thirty feet above the bobbing deck of his LCVP, the mortarman was virtually without air, and he heard an alarming *hiss* coming from his midriff. With snaps in place, the belt had expanded inward. As Lutz grew weaker, he used the last of his energy, balance, and presence of mind to fumble for his trench knife and cut gashes into the ballooning belt. Too weak to ask for help, he dribbled downward into the boat, convinced that he had successfully weathered his worst ordeal of the day.

LCdr Robert MacPherson, the air spotter charged with keeping track of the boat waves, advised The Flag at 0730 that the first wave could not possibly reach Betio by H-Hour. RAdm Harry Hill authorized a 15-minute delay, pushing H-Hour back to 0845—as if he had any control over the speed of the tractors and boats. The bombardment was extended to 0835.

At 0740, continuing reports from *Pursuit* and MacPherson clearly demonstrated that 0845 was still too early, so Admiral Hill added another 15 minutes. The first wave was still over 3,500 yards from the beach.

The leading elements of the moderately dispersed first wave crossed the Line of Departure at 0824. *Pursuit* flashed news of the event to *Maryland*. At that moment, control of the fighting passed from the fleet commander to the ground force commander, and particularly to battalion commanders Crowe, Schoettel, and Amey and their nearly 3,000 subordinates.

The struggle for Betio had truly begun.

8

A solid quarter mile in front of the lead tractor wave, three LCVPs stormed toward the end of the 500-yard-long pier marking the boundary between beaches Red-2 and Red-3.

In one boat was a five-man team from A Company, 18th Marines, specially-trained assault engineers commanded by 1stLt Gordon Leslie. In the second boat was GySgt Jared Hooper and two sections of the 2nd Marines' Scout-and-Sniper Platoon. The third boat carried the other two Scout-and-Sniper sections under the command of 1stLt Deane Hawkins. The engineers and scouts had been in their boats for five hours.

On approaching the reef, Hooper's boat broke away from the others and began circling. It was prepared to go to the aid of Hawkins or Leslie or to move directly to Red-2, depending on how much opposition was stirred up at the pierhead.

The lead boats made their moves as small-arms fire peppered the high plywood gunwales and steel bow ramps. Leslie's boat made its run from west to east, stopped long enough for the lieutenant and four engineers to disembark, then pulled off to circle in readiness. As Hawkins's boat moved north to south, the platoon leader ordered his men to remain with the boat until the pierhead had been secured, then he leaped onto the eastern arm of the pierhead.

It was 0855.

An instant after gaining the pierhead, Hawkins joined the engineers and led them southward just as a volley of mortar fire from the island dropped into a gasoline dump where the eastern arm joined a seaplane ramp. The gasoline was ignited, but no Marine was injured.

The four enlisted engineers began working over two small buildings at the head of the pier with a flamethrower and TNT blocks as Hawkins and Leslie covered them with carbine fire.

The buildings were set afire, and the two lieutenants led the engineers southward again along the exposed plank decking.

Within two minutes of Hawkins's dramatic leap to the pier, his boat circled back and dropped a three-man fire team under Cpl Leonce Olivier. The team moved several yards down the pier and took cover behind a low step-up on the deck. The three scouts each fired several rounds in support of the advancing engineers, but Olivier discovered that he was doing a whole lot more praying than shooting.

The entire end of the pier was honeycombed with sniper and machine gun nests. Many Japanese light landing barges alongside held individual snipers. Hawkins continued southward, taking potshots into every boat and accounting for at least six Japanese. A few yards behind him, Gordon Leslie and his assault team burned and blasted the pier decking to get at a half-dozen hidden machine guns. In a bit over five minutes, the six supercharged Marines obliterated all opposition from the tip of the pier to a point 20 or 30 yards toward the island.

It has been Hawkins's original plan to land the remainder of his boatload of scouts as soon as the seaplane ramp was secured. However, the fuel-dump fire was out of control and impassable. Except for Corporal Olivier's fire team, no one else had been landed. Hawkins signaled the boat's coxswain to try to run down the boat passage, all the way to the beach.

Fortunately for all concerned, the boat ran aground about 150 yards south of the pierhead, so the scouts ordered the coxswain to carry them back to a point where they could disembark. By that time, Lieutenant Leslie had withdrawn his team to the seaplane ramp to wait for a ride to the beach, and Hawkins and Olivier's fire team leaped back into their own boat as it backed past their position south of the pierhead.

Moments after Hawkins rejoined his men, the boat came under fire from an unseen machine gun. Hawkins was convinced that he had missed an emplacement under the pier, so he ordered the coxswain to make a full circle off the western tip of the seaplane ramp. No one could see a thing, and the fire persisted.

The boat circled four times in all before Hawkins decided that the fire was coming from Red-2. He could do nothing about that so he concentrated on finding a way to the beach.

By that time, the initial assault waves had landed.

Minutes after regrouping at the pierhead, Leslie's engineers were picked up by their own LCVP, which also tried to get down the boat passage. The engineers also got hung up and had to back off. Once back at the pierhead, Leslie was fortunate in being able to flag down an amtrac returning empty from the beach. All the engineering team's leftover gear was tossed aboard, the engineers jumped into the troop compartment, and the Marine driver was ordered to return to the beach in a hurry.

The pier was clear.

9

On the extreme right flank of the amtracs crossing the Line of Departure, 24 Marine-laden vehicles adjusted their headings and moved in staggered lines toward Red-1: The first wave of Maj John Schoettel's 3rd Battalion, 2nd, was attacking.

Six minutes after crossing the Line of Departure, the troops bound for Red-1 watched a long line of Navy fighters and dive-bombers make repeated runs on the beach. Moments later, after the first aircraft had already climbed to begin their second passes, the sounds of the bombing and strafing reached the tractors, which still had another 5,000 yards to go, another 30 minutes. It was 0830. The troops were still highly confident.

There was no fire from the island, at least none that the men in the tractors could perceive. Dense billows of oily smoke obscured the view for most Marines, but some, like 1stLt Ott Schulte, were able to see American shells carom across Betio.

On Schulte's right, nearer the center of Red-1, 2ndLt Mike Hofmann's 2nd Platoon, K Company, 2nd, was set to deploy on the beach and advance in line with Schulte's 1st Platoon. And 2ndLt Jim Fawcett's 3rd Platoon, trailing by three minutes, was to go to the assistance of the most advanced company unit.

To the right, beyond Hofmann's platoon, I Company was set to move in on Betio's northwest point, where Red-1 ends and Beach Green begins. I Company's primary target was a pair of big 14cm naval-type gunmounts directly behind the point. The guns, which could cover the Red beaches or Green, fell directly in the path of I Company's 2nd Platoon.

Behind the initial assault waves, aboard LCVPs, and LCMs, L Company, with M Company's 81mm mortars attached, idled in to await definite orders to land.

Intelligence figured that most of the opposition would come

at the beach. After that, it would be clean running to the south shore, where the battalion was to reconsolidate and turn to for mopping up.

At 0854, six minutes before H-Hour, all ships' fire ceased, and aircraft made their final passes on the beach. Reports from the aerial observers were optimistic. Little opposition was predicted. But to the men in the first line of amtracs bearing down on Red-1, the story was quite different in two respects.

At a point some 700 yards from the beach, the hulking tractors were bounced around as they waddled unevenly onto the reef. That meant that *there was not enough water for the boats*! There was no way to warn L Company. Next, just as the tractors hit the southern edge of the reef, Japanese infantry weapons and artillery began firing.

First Lieutenant Ott Schulte saw that fire was coming from a machine gun emplaced aboard a derelict steel hulk on the reef about 200 yards to the left; this was *Niminoa*, which had been run aground two years earlier by her British master.

Of the 18 Marines in LVT-124, only three were standing: Schulte and two riflemen manning the forward-firing .30- and .50-caliber machine guns on the troop compartment's forward bulkhead. As the tractor continued its dogged two-knot run toward the beach, it nosed into the most dangerous, most exposed part of the journey. Red-1 sits almost completely within a shallow U-shaped concave arc. To reach the beach at the base of the U, the tractors had to pass between heavily manned points on either side. When targets on the beach became distinguishable from 200 yards out, Schulte ordered the machine guns to open fire. That fire was returned from four sides: the beach, dead ahead; the derelict hulk, left rear; and the two points of the U, left and right. One of the numerous bullets struck Schulte glancing blows on the right shoulder and wrist as he directed his own guns.

The instant Ott Schulte was hit, his tractor went out of control; the driver had taken a slug in the pit of his stomach. The assistant driver took over control and brought the amtrac back on course.

Schulte's gunners should have been replaced twice over. Pfc Edward Flaherty was wounded in the testicles, right foot, and left hand, and he suffered painful powder burns about both eyes. He steadfastly refused to relinquish control of the .50-

caliber gun. Pfc Carl Rustin, manning the .30-caliber, took slugs in both hands and hips, but he too refused relief.

The last 100 yards were the worst of it. The Japanese had the range down pat, and it was hard to miss a waddling, hulking amtrac. The quarter-inch boiler-plate armor the crews had jury-rigged in New Zealand was useless against 13mm bullets.

At 0910, the first troops from I and K Companies hit the beach, the first Americans to set foot on Betio proper.

Because of the intense fire from the shore, Ott Schulte's entire platoon was forced to diverge eastward in order to gain the beach. As soon as LVT-124 landed on the beach, the wounded platoon leader geared himself for a jump to dry ground, but he saw that none of his men was moving. As he conjured up a picture of Japanese running out onto the beach to chuck hand grenades into the packed troop compartment, he screamed at them, "Jump out or a grenade'll get us all!"

The men remained motionless, frozen by shock and fear.

Though Schulte feared his wounds might be clouding his judgment, he felt he had precisely one option. He yelled, "Follow me!" and vaulted to the sand, then scrambled for cover before he looked back to see Marines spew from the three tractors. Schulte bellowed orders at his noncoms to get an advance going.

As Ott Schulte lay behind a low hummock along with his radioman, he felt the gears of his mind clang to a weak, painful halt. He was unconscious before his eyes finished closing.

Only ten yards to the right of the spot where Schulte touched down, 2ndLt Tom Becker was bringing in K Company's three 60mm mortars. Moderate machine gun fire struck Becker's tractor as it waddled out of the surf just to the left of an active pillbox. Becker, the first man over the side, landed on his feet in the soft sand and was shot dead.

The second man out of Becker's tractor was Sgt Bill Lindblom, a mortar squad leader, who emerged unscathed and ducked behind the first cover he could find. The next three Marines were wounded in quick succession. With Lindblom's assistance, these men were moved behind the seawall and given first aid. Nearby, the remainder of K Company's 60mm mortar section went to ground.

The shades of darkness slowly cleared from Ott Schulte's mind. He opened his eyes and found himself staring at a pair of boondockers (low-cut sueded pigskin combat boots) only inches from his nose. The dazed officer reached up with his good left hand and pulled at the nearest of the heavy shoes. No response. He shook the foot again. No response. So Schulte slowly dragged himself forward and stared into the face of his dead radioman.

As 2ndLt Jim Fawcett's tractor began the last lap, the 24-year-old Washingtonian's gaze fixed upon the amtrac carrying 2ndLt Mike Hofmann and elements of K Company's 2nd Platoon, which was caught in a murderous crossfire as it bounced up onto the sand. Fawcett watched expectantly as Hofmann's riflemen vaulted to the sand and dropped to the beach. He began counting off leaping Marines, hoping beyond hope to reach 16 or better.

The count quickly climbed to eight, then stopped.

Fawcett peered more intently and thought he saw signs of life aboard the tractor. Then a familiar figure stood up straight and tall and latched onto one of the forward machine guns. Mike Hofmann was covering his rifleman.

Fawcett began a slow mental chant: "Get out, Mike! . . . Get out! . . . Get out!" With an eye on his own steady progress, Jim Fawcett prayed that the tractor in front of his would be emptied before the Japanese took yet more violent action.

Then, in the instant before Fawcett's tractor hit the sandy shelf, Mike Hofmann's entire tractor disappeared in an immense cloud of smoke and steel splinters.

Jim Fawcett's tractor hit the beach.

As Fawcett's mind raced over a hundred disjointed impulses, the mustang officer tried to sort out a plan of action. Then it struck home that he had to decide which of the lead platoons was in the best position to exploit an advantage. He could not even find Schulte's 1st Platoon, and he knew that there was a great gap where Hofmann's 2nd Platoon ought to be. So Jim Fawcett elected to move head-on.

Most of the men crouching on the left side of Mike Hofmann's smoldering tractor were fearful and badly disorganized. Two of Fawcett's squads were intact, but there was no news from Sgt Millard Odom's squad. An awesome sheet of bullets was passing over Fawcett's head, but casualties were surprisingly light. There were about 35 men on hand, including survivors of Hofmann's platoon.

Less than five yards from Fawcett, on the far side of Hofmann's tractor, Sergeant Odom and five of his riflemen were desperately searching for a way off the beach. About half the squad had come in behind Lieutenant Fawcett while, in the confusion of landing, Odom had ducked the wrong way. He had no idea where the platoon was.

Pfc Bernard Zerr looked over the top of the seawall and provided a running commentary for Odom and the others. When Zerr paused for a moment to ask the squad leader a question, he saw that Odom was kneeling less than a yard away with his head resting on a log in the seawall. Zerr asked his question twice, but got no reply. Odom, whose starched green dungaree utility shirt sported a neat little hole an inch or two below the left armpit, had taken a round through the heart.

The five leaderless Marines elected to sit tight a few yards farther to the right, out of the crossfire that had killed Sergeant Odom, and farther still from the rest of their platoon.

Lieutenant Jim Fawcett cursed his men back to life and rose to lead them over the wall. He was afraid beyond belief, but he knew that the men huddling behind the wall were prime targets for the machine guns on all sides, that they—and he—stood a better chance fighting on the move.

When Fawcett looked back to watch the platoon vault the seawall, he was suddenly transfixed by the most horrible sight he had ever witnessed. A man no more than four yards behind him was just coming over the wall. Head and shoulders rose into view, then the chest and abdomen. At that instant a shell burst directly on the exposed chest. There wasn't enough left of the Marine to roll in a strip of cigarette paper.

I Company, 2nd, was having mixed luck on K Company's right, where the U-shaped beach bends back toward the lagoon and then turns abruptly southward.

Although I Company's leading rifle platoons had little trouble gaining the beach, exits were blocked at the water's edge, and follow-up units were badly mauled. As the command tractor neared the beach, Capt William Tatom, the company commander, stood up in the face of sweeping gunfire for a look at his lead platoons. The veteran officer was standing for only a moment when he was pitched back into the troop compartment by a bullet in the forehead. He died moments later.

Command of I Company fell to 1stLt Sam Turner.

Second Lieutenant John Cannon, commanding I Company's 3rd Platoon, made the trip ashore with his mind full of new sights and sounds and feelings. A Marine for 23 months, Cannon was acutely conscious of the tension of every nerve and muscle, of pounding heartbeats, of the surging of his blood, of a stepped-up awareness of everything he could perceive, of fast-breathing men around him, of the bluest blues and the goldenest yellows and the reddest reds he had ever seen. Cannon's senses were by far at the highest pitch they had ever reached.

Standing behind John Cannon were a dozen riflemen from his 2nd Squad and four members of his platoon headquarters team. The troops had fixed bayonets at the reef and ducked low to avoid the bullets that were rattling into the bow of the tractor. They were exhilarated by the *boom* of ships' guns behind them and by the *carumph* of shells detonating on the beach ahead. They were yelling from pride and nerves and bravado. They were prepared to follow John Cannon wherever he led them.

By the time the second wave drew up to the beach, one of Cannon's three tractors had fallen behind. The two leaders landed abreast. There was no time to try to find the wayward squad; too much was happening too quickly.

The first thing John Cannon did was get the attention of his driver. He looped his arm up and out: Try to drive the amtrac over the seawall. The driver nodded agreement and turned his attention back to his driving. The high-performance radial aircraft engine roared full power and, as the driver lifted his foot from the clutch, the amtrac's entire weight lunged forward. The amtrac's nose drove upward as steel-cleated tread shoes dug into the coconut-log seawall.

Lieutenant Cannon and his men were toppled backwards to the rear of the troop compartment, packed solid by gravity, unable to regain their footing.

Every iota of horsepower strained for height. But it was no

go, and tons of steel plopped back onto the sandy beach. The driver turned to Cannon, who motioned: Go again!

Gears meshed and steel chewed into soft wood. The tractor bucked upward, higher this time than before. It seemed for a fleeting instant that one little nudge would tilt the steel body over the edge. But the combined weight of the engine and 17 men in the rear of the troop compartment worked against the lighter bow. The tractor toppled back, dropping a few of its passengers to the deck, buckling the knees of the rest.

Cannon turned to Cpl Hubert Luther, his 2nd Squad leader, and nodded: Go over the side. Luther put his hand on the gunwale, boosted himself over and disappeared from view. The rest of the riflemen quickly dropped to the sand. Then John Cannon jumped—and lost his balance as he hit the ground; the drop was longer by half than he had anticipated.

As Cannon dropped behind the wall with his riflemen, he peeled his eyes for the remainder of his platoon. Acting PlSgt Fred Farris had brought 1st Squad in only a few yards to the right, but there was no sign of 3rd Squad and no time to look. By then, the troops should have been advancing across the seawall, but they were milling about in confusion on the beach side. No one could negotiate the log barricade one-handed at a spot where it was better than five feet high; all hands were encumbered by one type of weapon or another, and no one was willing to sling a rifle before vaulting into the unknown.

John Cannon motioned his squad leaders to reform and led them to the spot where his own tractor had pulled down the top log. The platoon leader grasped his carbine in his left hand, reached up and pulled himself over, tumbling into a deep shell crater on the other side. A black blob registered at the periphery of Cannon's vision and he wheeled, firing half a clip into the body of an already dead Japanese. The green officer was surprised at how badly he felt about shooting a dead man. But he had not yet seen any fellow Marines die.

The tractor carrying John Cannon's 3rd Squad was stopped in the water about 75 yards from shore. The dozen men it was conveying dropped over the sides and began wading in under fire. Half veered to the left or right in hopes of finding less contested routes to the safety of the seawall. Pfc Jim Goldman went straight in. He was alone when he staggered out of the surf and stopped for a moment to rest. Other I Company

Marines came in behind him and moved to the seawall, but many others were shot down in the water.

When Goldman realized that the usual route *over* the wall would be too dangerous, he looked for a way *through*, and soon he found a very small opening. As he squeezed himself into it, however, his pack hung up on a steel cleat. After a moment of panicked pushing and pulling, the confused BAR-man ditched his belongings and wriggled forward into a shellhole. He decided to wait there until things settled down a bit.

No such luck. Moments after Goldman dropped into the shellhole, he discovered that his BAR was clogged with wet sand. Almost oblivious to the holocaust erupting practically over his head, he stripped the weapon for a cleaning. All the parts were carefully laid out, the sand brushed away, and ready to be reassembled when a Japanese mortar round burst on the lip of the hole. Goldman frantically dug through the scattered sand until he came up with all but one essential piece. As he took a breather to regain his composure, he spotted a dead Marine a few feet from his hole; the man was clutching a BAR in his dead fingers. Goldman then did something he knew was a bit strange while he was doing it: Rather than simply take the dead man's BAR, he removed a replacement for the missing part and pushed it into place on his own BAR.

Goldman then moved to his right, ready for action. He got ten yards before discovering the remains of a decapitated Marine. A class ring on the dead man's finger identified him as one of Jim Goldman's closest friends. Sick now, Goldman moved forward, alone among hundreds of men. His platoon was nowhere to be found, so Pfc Jim Goldman elected to fight his war alone.

Second Lieutenant Bill Cogdill, a recently commissioned Guadalcanal veteran commanding the medium machine gun platoon attached to I Company, 2nd, brought one section of his unit safely to the beach through a hail of Japanese shellfire. Cogdill's amtrac driver tried a number of times to breach the four-foot high seawall, but each attempt bounced the gunners against the steel bulkheads as the tractor slipped back. At last, Cogdill ordered all his men over the side. As he did, a burst of gunfire killed the tractor driver.

As Cogdill crouched behind the seawall, he spotted I Company's first sergeant lying wounded a few feet away. The noncom seemed in reasonable enough shape, so Cogdill turned to more pressing problems, which arrived in the form of a Japanese hand grenade, which detonated only inches from his body long before he could react. Barely cognizant of superficial wounds in his hands, legs, and face, Bill Cogdill ordered his gunners, many of whom were bleeding, to heave a few of their own grenades along the front. Then, after a quiet minute, the gunners rose and struggled through the loose sand on the inland side of the wall. Surprisingly, all the section's injuries were superficial.

Cogdill at first marveled at the extent of the destruction caused by naval gunfire, but his veteran's eyes soon saw that, although the open ground had been badly chewed up, very few defensive structures had actually been knocked out.

Second Lieutenant John Cannon cautiously peered over the lip of the shellhole in which he had found refuge. About thirty yards dead ahead were three buildings and what appeared to be a trench to the left. His best bet was the trench. Cannon led his 2nd Squad out of the hole and cautiously angled to the left into the fire trench, which veered in a southwesterly direction. It was as good an axis of advance as any, perhaps better because of the protection afforded by the trench.

Three of Cannon's men were already by the trench, one wounded and two covering him. The wounded man was quickly hauled into the cut, where a corpsman treated his wound; a bullet or shell fragment was lodged in his trachea. When all that could be done for the wounded man was done, the small knot of Marines moved out again. It was hard to see much, but it was evident from the volume of fire that Cannon was leading his group through a heavily defended area.

After cautiously advancing about 150 yards along the trench, Cannon spotted a small building sitting several feet above the ground on stilts. He wanted the building neutralized, but he feared a trap. Rather than risk the entire platoon, Cannon ordered one rifleman to toss in a thermite grenade. The grenade was thrown right through an open window, setting the house afire.

Farther on, Lieutenant Cannon decided that it was time to

pull out of the trench, which was taking him too far to the right and making it harder to maintain contact with friendly units. Cpl Hubert Luther, the 2nd Squad leader, was eviscerated by a stream of machine gun bullets as he stood to climb over a fallen log. The Japanese had turned a number of the guns guarding the southern beaches to contest the Marines moving from the north. That stopped Cannon's advance.

The noncoms staffing Cannon's platoon were not faring at all well. Three squad leaders were dead and two assistant squad leaders had been wounded. And the acting platoon sergeant and the right guide, the two senior sergeants, had already won a posthumous Silver Star and posthumous Navy Cross, respectively.

When the right guide, Sgt Roy Johnson, took over 3rd Squad at the beach, it was badly depleted as a result of straggling and casualties and had been stopped just south of the seawall by a Japanese tank, which was running back and forth along a track just beyond the first fringe of palm trees.

Sergeant Johnson studied the tank for a moment. Then, when the armored vehicle stopped to turn away from the squad, he ran across the open ground and leaped onto the behemoth's rear deck. Within moments, he had pried the turret hatch up far enough to squeeze in a grenade. The tank came to a sudden, final stop as the grenade blew. Johnson triumphantly leaped off the smoking chassis but was cut down as he sought cover.

Cannon's 1st Squad, which PlSgt Fred Farris had led ashore, was pinned by a machine gun a few yards south of the wall only moments after the platoon leader led 2nd Squad over the top. Farris peered over the lip of the shellhole in which he had gone to ground and saw that the gun was only a few yards away, protected by a double line of sandbags and manned by three *rigosentai*. He rose alone, charged across the open ground and, as he chucked a grenade into the emplacement, threw his weight in the direction of some meager cover. He was killed by the machine gun before he hit the ground. However, his hand grenade found its mark and the gun was destroyed, providing 1st Squad with a way off the beach. Fred Farris was just ten paces from the gun when he was shot.

Among the support units attached to Schoettel's battalion was the 3rd Platoon, A Company, 18th Marines, whose platoon leader was killed by shellfire before reaching the beach. As the first section dismounted several yards from the sandy beach and attempted to wade in, the section leader was mortally wounded and 14 demolitions men, a mine detector operator, and a flamegunner were killed or wounded. Thus, the 3rd Battalion, 2nd, lost what could have been a decisive means for dealing with the Japanese burrowed into dugouts largely impervious to gunfire. It was a crucial loss of strength at a critical moment.

Maj Mike Ryan's L Company was in LCVPs 500 yards from the beach and sustaining heavy casualties. To make matters worse, Ryan's company had no means for crossing the reef; it would have to wade in.

Although a great deal of the Japanese fire was mauling I and K Companies, much of it switched back to the lagoon to nip at the reinforcements. Weighted down by their heavy packs, ammunition, and weapons, the L Company Marines clumsily started for the beach. Within minutes, many of the wading men realized that speed was of the essence, so they began dropping gear. First it was demolitions, then packs, then ammunition and helmets and rifles. Everything that seemed to impede progress through the fireswept water was abandoned.

Members of the battalion 81mm Mortar Platoon threatened the coxswain of their LCVP until he agreed to try to get them over the coral barrier. The man rammed the coral and backed down, then rammed again, proving that he was not going to get into the beach. In the end, the LCVP was run completely aground, and its ramp was stuck in the up position, which obliged the mortar crews to drop over the high sides into the water.

Pfc Dirk Offringa, a 31-year-old ammunition carrier, vaulted the gunwale and safely landed in thigh-deep water. As Offringa looked around for his buddies, a sailor right over his head began dropping parts of a mortar over the side. Offringa managed to salvage a heavy steel baseplate, which he put to immediate use as crude, effective armor. As he waded to the beach with Marines dying all around him, Dirk Offringa deflected dozens of rounds that would have killed him, but suffered minor wounds from steel chips that were driven by the gunfire into his fingertips.

Capt Robert O'Brien, L Company's executive officer, had an exceptionally narrow escape when a round from the beach struck his cartridge belt and set off a chain reaction that fired every round of .30-caliber ammunition around his waist. O'Brien sustained numerous painful bruises, but there was no bleeding.

Capt Jim Crain of K Company established a makeshift communications center on the beach and tried to contact his rifle platoons and higher authority. He succeeded at length in contacting the battalion commander, Maj John Schoettel, and told him everything he knew of the events on Red-1. Then, since his exec, 1stLt Clint Dunahoe, was dead and the company command group dispersed, Crain moved inland to take charge of a leaderless medium machine gun platoon whose commander had been killed while dismounting his tractor.

While the disorganized and scattered remnants of I and K Companies struggled to move inland, the first survivors of L Company wandered ashore individually and in small groups. The company was totally disorganized. Second Lieutenant Joe Roach, the weapons platoon leader, arrived on the beach alone; he would not find a single member of his command until after the fighting.

Pfc Joe Murray and Pfc Drew Wilson reached the beach and collapsed behind the seawall, too exhausted to advance farther. Murray was awed by the thoroughness with which the Japanese had defended the beaches, right down to a one-man log emplacement he found built into the seawall. As Murray watched the men behind him struggle to escape death, he slipped into a total, momentary state of abject terror; he wanted to climb into the little one-man emplacement in the wall and shut out the sights and sounds of pain and death in which he had been immersed. But the fear quickly passed, replaced by an anger and bitterness he had not thought himself capable of feeling.

All over Red-1, men were making up their minds: They could succumb to their fears and remain behind the seawall, where they might escape unnoticed and unhurt; they could wait to regain their strength and composure and hope that the totally bizarre situation around them would become more realistic, easier to come to terms with; or they could charge off in quest of the unseen but sorely felt enemy and simply hope for the best.

All over Red-1, men were trusting to unknown leaders. They battered their way through obstacles wherever those obstacles appeared. They cursed and took unreasonable, unrewardable risks. They cried in pain or rasped long last breaths. Or they felt that certain awe creeping up the back ends of their minds, an awe that proclaims life where no one should be living.

Many men arriving on Red-1 spotted Capt George Wentzel, executive officer of M Company, the battalion weapons unit, as he stood helmetless, pipe-in-hand, atop the seawall, cursing and taunting the Marines who had sought safety there. The longer the stocky ex-college professor stood in plain sight, the more fire he drew, and the louder he cursed and yelled and insulted and ordered. The men around Wentzel kept telling him to get down, but he obstinately went about his business in defiance of the odds. At last, he took a round through the neck, dying before he wordlessly collapsed into the sand at the water's edge. Some in his audience took heart and moved on, but many saw George Wentzel's death as an omen, and those men stayed put.

Thirty yards short of the beach, L Company Marines sought cover behind a small sandbar, which appeared to be a good place for resting before breasting the final, heaviest test of fire. That's how it looked from the lagoon. The Japanese gunners had the bar zeroed in.

Something told Pfc Dirk Offringa to give the sandbar a wide berth, but a crewmate, Pfc Andrew Polmaskitch, made a beeline for it. Offringa yelled after his buddy and frantically waved, but Polmaskitch kept going. Offringa's voice played out just as Polmaskitch dropped behind the cover. Moments later, a horrified Dirk Offringa watched Andrew Polmaskitch rise directly into a stream of machine gun fire. Another gun caught the slumping body, which was held upright between the two streams of lead. The guns continued to fire until patches of clothing and flesh had been torn loose and hurled into the water. Then, their orgy over, the Japanese gunners switched to more profitable targets.

On the beach, Pfc George Atkins, a machine gun squad leader, was ordered to go after the Japanese guns firing on the sandbar. Atkins's seven-man squad, doubling as riflemen, immediately overran two gun emplacements, but the assault bogged down moments later, when Atkins was shot dead going after a third gun.

Pfc Milton Mayer took a slug in the foot within 15 minutes of reaching Red-1. Although there were two holes and a tiny drop of blood oozing from Mayer's boondocker, the wound did not appear to be serious. Buddies pleaded with Mayer to go to the battalion aid station, but he was the smallest man in the 81mm platoon, and the months he had spent building a reputation for toughness would have been wasted had he succumbed to his pain; this was first combat, and Milt Mayer had to prove himself. As the pain mounted, however, he was more easily convinced, and he finally agreed to see Dr. Glenn Warrick, the battalion surgeon.

As soon as Dr. Warrick saw Mayer's booted foot, he told the injured man that he could do nothing for him on the beach as all his instruments had been lost; Mayer would have to be evacuated to a ship. The gunner balked, offering to return to duty. As soon as he declared himself, however, his buddies insisted that he agree to evacuation, that he was lucky and ought to be thankful for the break. They capped it by declaring that no one doubted his courage. Mayer agreed to be evacuated and allowed himself to be helped aboard an outbound tractor. Mayer's buddies breathed a collective sigh of relief. As they watched him depart and began moving back to the seawall, a hugh explosion engulfed the departing amtrac, killing every man aboard.

The landing craft carrying the 37mm guns and light tanks assigned to Schoettel's battalion got hung up on the reef. Since there was no way to unload, the boats backed off, leaving the 3rd Battalion, 2nd, without any heavy weapons.

While the company commanders attempted to get an advance organized and moving on Red-1, nothing had been heard of or from the battalion commander. In fact, there was virtually no communication with the world outside Red-1. It was known that Major Schoettel had not landed, so Maj Mike Ryan, the senior man on the beach, passed the command of L

Company to his exec, the lucky Captain O'Brien, and took control of the beachhead.

At that moment, the battalion commander and his staff were in their LCM at the reef. Concentrated fire prevented them from disembarking and making for the beach.

The 3rd Battalion, 2nd, was isolated and unsupportable.

10

At 0917, seven minutes after the first amphibian tractors reached Red-1, 522 officers and men in the first three waves of Maj Jim Crowe's 2nd Battalion, 8th, were launched onto Red-3.

The slow-moving tractors had been hounded by fire from a brace of 70mm antiboat guns set well beyond the battalion's open left flank, near the tapering eastern end of Betio, when they came within 3,000 yards of the beach. However, this fire had been both sporadic and inaccurate and had resulted in few, if any, casualties. Lighter antiboat defenses, which struck the lead wave when it passed to within 500 yards of the beach, hit about 25 of the 150-plus Marines in the dozen leading amtracs.

The only close support vessels in action in the lagoon, destroyers *Ringgold* and *Dashiell*, were just beyond the reef off Red-3. They maintained a steady, constant fire against shore emplacements all along the beach, but, in truth, their 5-inch guns destroyed few emplacements. However, until they had to cease firing at 0910, they kept the Japanese down and disoriented. And, although they could no longer fire at the beach without very careful control, they could and did remain on station to fire on positions beyond Crowe's left flank.

All hands, down through squad leaders and most riflemen, had carefully memorized the battalion's mission and the missions of their respective units. Every man knew his spot. Upon reaching the beach, F Company was to form a two-platoon front and attack south and east. Its main objective was the command bunker of the 3rd Special Konkyochitai, and its western boundary was the Burns-Philp wharf, a stubby log affair about 75 yards east of the main pier. E Company was to press directly southward on a two-platoon front. A platoon of G Company was attached to E Company to form a link at the battalion center, and the remainder of G Company, embarked in LCVPs, was to land in the center and exploit early gains. Their final objectives were on the southern beaches.

Although practically at full strength, F Company's two lead platoons ran into trouble almost as soon as they began landing. They came in about 75 yards west of the objectives, which obliged troop leaders to back up to get a better perspective. And, there was no way over the seawall. As a result, F Company was forced to halt in place as soon as it left its tractors. As the troops ducked behind the seawall, dozens of hitherto unseen and unheard Japanese infantry weapons opened up all along the company front.

The 3rd Platoon, F Company, landed precisely three minutes behind the lead platoons and found its way barred, so it went to ground near the center of the company sector and behind the 1st and 2nd Platoons. The company weapons platoon, headquarters section, and a .30-caliber machine gun platoon from H Company landed within the next six minutes, appreciably adding to the mass of humanity on the beach but wresting no new ground.

On the right of F Company, the 2nd Platoon extended westward along the seawall and was able to tie in with units to the right by 0932. The entire platoon front was then shifted to the right, allowing 3rd Platoon to take over its share of the frontage. Light and medium machine guns were moved into the lines, and the 60mm mortars were set up on the beach.

Within ten minutes of landing, 1stLt Stacey Davis's 1st Platoon, on the company's left, had reorganized and wheeled to the left to seal the eastward flank. Then Lieutenant Davis ordered his platoon to attack due east along the narrow strip of beach to seize the Burns-Philp wharf. Japanese guns near the wharf easily broke up the attack, wounding Davis and forcing his platoon to backtrack to its original position.

E Company wasn't doing much better.

There was precisely one opening in the seawall along the entire expanse of Red-3. While the remainder of the leading waves went to ground behind the wall, two first-wave tractors gained a quick 30 yards before getting caught in an impenetrable crossfire. Thirty-odd riflemen thus gained the most advanced position on Red-3 in under three minutes, but it would be hours before that gain could be matched and it would be hours before those 30 Marines would be on a line instead of in a pocket.

The remainder of E Company got hit hard.

Maj Jim Crowe decided to go in early, before any of his assault units had hit the beach. As Crowe's "free" boat moved onto the beach, every man aboard stood to watch the last few minutes of naval and air bombardment. As soon as the fire was returned, Crowe ordered all heads down, then told the coxswain to zigzag. As the fiery major's men huddled on the deck, he alone remained standing, disdainful of the increasingly heavy fire.

Crowe intended to barrel all the way onto the beach, but his hopes were cut short when the boat rammed the reef 500 yards out. Despite the major's voluble protestations, the reef would not budge, and the crew refused to lower the bow ramp in fear of swamping. That was just as well, for the Japanese could easily have brought a gun to bear on the headquarters group. The furious redhead cursed the sailors and pesonally led his staff over the side.

Communications Sgt Ernie Butner, whose early resolve was badly shaken, leaped into the water and was pulled straight down by his heavy radio pack. When he realized that he was standing upright in more than ten feet of water, he walked straight ahead. Fortunately, the bottom sloped up to the reef, and Butner reemerged only a minute after going down. Others in the command group were less fortunate or had less presence of mind.

The bulk of G Company, 8th, slammed into the reef minutes after the battalion command boat. After overcoming the initial shock of solid contact, the platoon leaders ordered their riflemen and gunners into the water.

Lt Galen Brown, *Heywood's* boat group officer, watched helplessly as his command boat idled in about 500 yards off the reef. It took long moments before it registered on Brown that his worst fears had come true: none of his boats was able to top the reef, and hundreds of heavily laden Marines were dropping into the water, wading toward the beach in diminishing rows, fully exposed to horrendous fire from the shore.

Tractors outbound from Red-3 were already passing Brown's

boat, and he saw that they were filled with dead and dying men. Brown ordered his coxswain to ease up to one of the blood-spattered tractors, then disembarked his corpsman to care for the wounded. Next, Brown called in one of his boats which had a medical team aboard; corpsmen and a surgeon transferred into Brown's boat within minutes.

As the doctor worked over casualties taken from passing tractors, a nearby LCVP took a direct hit and sank within 30 seconds, leaving 25 heavily laden Marines struggling in deep water. Brown's crew managed to save three strong swimmers, one of whom had been sliced open from hip to hip. The seriously wounded Marine was laid across the command LCVP's hatchcover while the doctor yelled to Galen Brown, "Let's get farther out, where I can work without ducking bullets." Brown simply pointed to the bullet-spattered lagoon 1,000 yards farther out.

Capt Martin Barrett, commanding F Company, 8th, was suddenly aware that the intense Japanese fire was no longer coming his way in such unbelievable quantities.

Just beyond the reef, Sgt Ernie Butner was certain that the number of geysers in the water around him had increased within the past few seconds, and they continued to increase. Much of the fire seemed to be coming from automatic weapons emplaced under the main pier, to the right.

Maj Bill Chamberlin, Crowe's exec, was wading to the beach alone when he happened upon 2ndLt George Kern, the battalion communicator. Kern had been painfully wounded in the leg and was on his way back to the reef to find a ride out. There was little Chamberlin could do to help Kern, so he wished the lieutenant luck and saw him on his way. No one ever saw George Kern again.

The LCVP carrying H Company's 3rd Platoon, a .30-caliber machine gun unit, reached a point in line with and a few yards east of the main pierhead without undue difficulty, but was stopped there by the reef. Like G Company, to which the platoon was attached, the gunners took to the water and were badly torn up within minutes. As Cpl William McKibben leaped off the end of the boat's ramp to begin wading, there was a muffled roar. The men around McKibben watched him take one more step without his head. Pfc John Mohrlang was felled by another blast. As he backstroked to regain his stance, he saw one of his lower legs float by. His eyes locked on those of an ammunition carrier, but the other man just stared back and continued his mechanical pace toward the beach; the platoon had been told to leave casualties for rescue boats. Mohrlang was picked up within minutes, but the combination of shock and loss of blood eventually killed him.

As Sgt Ernie Butner neared the beach, he stared in amazement as the man on his immediate left floundered under the impact of a shell shard that tore out his stomach. Butner instinctively turned to help and was only an arm's length away when a familiar redheaded figure—Jim Crowe—waved a pump shotgun in his face and bellowed orders to keep moving, to leave the man for the corpsman. Butner turned and, staring straight ahead, walked on, terrorized and praying.

That anyone made it to Red-3 can be attributed in great part to destroyers *Ringgold* and *Dashiell*, which remained on station just beyond the reef, blanketing Crowe's front and far left flank with pinpoint fire.

As far as LCdr Robert MacPherson could determine from high above Betio, the stiffest resistance on Red-3 was coming from a huge sand-covered multistory building on Crowe's southeast flank. MacPherson, who had to handle his own radio because his radioman had been wounded by ground fire, asked that ships' fire be placed on the huge bunker, but the best he could draw was a simple acknowledgment of the message. No such mission would be fired.

Jim Crowe got himself on the air at 0940, within minutes of gaining the beach. The first message from Red-3 to *Maryland*: "Heavy opposition."

The Japanese had assumed that the initial assault waves would get ashore, so they planned to switch their heaviest fire early against back-up units. They reasoned that the fewer the men surviving the trip to the beach, the less opposition there would be to their mop-up efforts—thus the shifting of heavy fire from E and F Companies to G Company and support units.

On Crowe's left flank, Capt Martin Barrett and his weapons platoon leader were on their stomachs behind the seawall discussing the most favorable deployment of F Company's machine guns and 60mm mortars. Suddenly, a cylindrical object plopped down on Barrett's back. It was a Japanese grenade. Too startled to act, Barrett simply craned his neck for a better look, wondering the while why it did not go off. Although Barrett quickly realized he had been hit by a dud, he had no time to move out of range of another hand grenade. A second cylindrical object plunked down between the two officers, and it was no dud. However, Barrett quickly forgot about the slight wounds in his leg in the press of more urgent business.

Sgt Ernie Butner, thoroughly exhausted from wading to the beach, collapsed in the sand. Suddenly it dawned on him that he should be digging in. He slipped off his radio pack and personal gear and hurriedly tried to unknot the length of telephone wire with which he had cleverly secured his entrenching shovel. But his fingers would not do the job. Unable to free his shovel, the frantic communicator began scooping handfuls of soft sand. Much later he realized his hands had been cut by sharp coral pebbles.

Pfc Johnny Borich was the only man on Red-3 with a flamethrower. He and the other flamegunner from C Company, 18th Marines, had been consigned to the second boat wave. The other flamegunner was quickly and painfully wounded in the thigh and had to ditch his 70-pound fuel tanks in the lagoon before going on to the beach to seek medical treatment. Meantime, Johnny Borich had shaken his .45-caliber pistol— menacingly, he hoped—at the unseen Japanese firing at him from under the pier. He waded through the fire, arrived ashore unmarked, and sat down to catch his breath. While Borich was resting, a demolitions man from his engineer platoon threw a four pound block of TNT over the seawall into a medium-sized building on the eastern side of the inshore end of the pier. The charge blew tons of Japanese torpedo warheads and Johnny Borich was knocked cold by the monstrous concussion. He came to minutes later and discovered that his hearing was badly impaired; his ears would be ringing for days.

As Borich was trying to clear his head, Jim Crowe stalked into view and ordered everyone over the wall. Borich followed along as a group entered a small covered bunker about 15 feet long. Behind the protection of stout log walls, the flamegunner removed his gear to check it for damage. He had just disengaged himself from the cumbersome rig when two hitherto motionless Japanese lying in a heap in the corner began stirring. The flamethrower roared briefly, and a sweet-sick smell of charred flesh engulfed the startled Marines. Pfc Johnny Borich never took chances.

Sgt Elmo Ferretti's assault engineer squad was supposed to land in the third wave about 100 yards east of the Burns-Philp wharf and move to the support of an F Company platoon assault on the Japanese command bunker. The engineers landed ahead of schedule and 30 yards west of the main pier.

The engineers were heavily laden. Each member of the three-man demolitions team carried two sacks full of prepared charges in addition to his explosives-filled chestpack, backpack with personal gear, weapon, and all the other normal accouterments of war. It became evident that the squad had landed in the wrong place as soon as it reached the seawall, although no one dreamed it was nearly 150 yards from where it should have been. Cpl Harry Niehoff, the demolitions team leader, was ordered to take the point. He made a quick sally to a deep shell crater, got some idea of where he was, and crawled back to the seawall just as the torpedo warhead dump blew up nearby; it rained sand and rocks and wood and metal and bleeding meat for a full minute. As the dust settled, the squad began moving eastward again, but it was intercepted by Maj Jim Crowe and TSgt Don Baker, the senior engineer noncom on Red-3. Crowe pointed to a small pillbox that was giving his troops a bad time. The engineers quickly spotted a small embrasure and noted that the objective was sitting squarely between two larger covered emplacements. A tough job.

Corporal Niehoff dived over the seawall and zigzagged to avoid being shot. When he was halfway to the objective, he heard the leather-lunged battalion commander yell, "Be careful! He already shot five men." His confidence obliterated, Niehoff moved double-quick and came up beside the objective, barely conscious of the covering fire or the fact that Technical Sergeant Baker had hurled a charge that kicked up enough sand to cover his approach.

The engineers had rigged TNT blocks into bundles of four held together by electrician's tape and armed with fuses of varying lengths, usually four to six seconds. Each demolitions man was puffing away at a cigarette or a cigar, even nonsmokers, as these were the surest means for igniting fuses. Niehoff's charge had been in a sack for several days, and the end of the fuse was frayed and some of the powder train was lost.

It took Harry Niehoff precious moments to ignite the fuse and keep it going, but when it started flaring and Niehoff tried to push it through the embrasure, he found that the charge was too big for the opening. Niehoff dropped the charge and dived for a nearby coconut log just as it blew up—and enlarged the embrasure. A Japanese rifleman emerged from the dust to shoot the little finger off a covering rifleman while Sergeant Ferretti stuffed a second charge through the enlarged embrasure. The pillbox blew and the engineers headed east.

Crowe's battalion did not begin taking ground beyond the seawall until 1015.

Crowe sent his exec, Maj Bill Chamberlin, to the east flank to get information. In the process, Chamberlin assumed control of the sector and set himself the task of anchoring the open left flank. In order to succeed, he had to send troops at least as far south as a log revetment at the edge of the airfield.

Time was of the essence, so Chamberlin grabbed the first warm bodies he could find, a 60mm mortar squad, and drove them over the seawall. The mortarmen were eager to get their gun into action, but they registered shocked looks of dismay as the major barked orders at them and quickly explained the situation. The gunners reluctantly ditched their mortar and advanced while Chamberlin broadened his search for larger groups to send south. He teamed a rifle platoon and G Company's weapons platoon, which were just arriving from the right, with an F Company rifle platoon and ordered this sizeable force to attack southward to the edge of the airstrip, then drive eastward as far as possible.

The three platoons immediately drew heavy fire from directly east of the revetment position and almost due south of the Burns-Philp wharf. The fire came from an enormous covered ferro-concrete bunker several stories high, supported by many machine gun emplacements. Also, the Marines were struck by heavy fire from a pair of pillboxes covering the northeast and southeast corners of the covered bunker. Although they took some ground and set a number of buildings afire, the three platoons were stopped and eventually were forced to back up to positions in line with the log revetment. The gains were minimal, but the flank was sealed.

First Lieutenant Robert Rogers's E Company, 8th, on the battalion's right, was also taking ground. After a G Company platoon established a base of fire along the seawall, Rogers's riflemen advanced southward along the entire company front and cleared numerous snipers and pillboxes. Following numerous hard fights with diehard defenders, several E Company squads managed to reach the company's objective—the northeast airport taxiway—by 1050. The line, however, was not fully consolidated, and the small groups that actually reached the taxiway were forced to take cover from intense fire from across the open area. As soon as the advance bogged down, the G Company platoon mopped up behind E Company.

There was a major gap in the front that had to be plugged. E Company had made significant penetrations on the right, and elements of F and G Companies had pushed southward on the left, but little or no ground had been taken in between. There were no regular line units to spare; G Company had been parcelled out all over the beached, E Company was fully committed on the right, and F Company was in a number of heavy fights on the left. When 1stLt Orlando Palopoli, the F Company exec, realized the importance of refusing the dangling flanks at the center, he worked his way back to the beach and collected every straggler he could find: a team of pioneers, engineers, mortarmen, machine gunners, and the odd headquarters warrior. These he led over the wall and rapidly advanced to the taxiway. Flank extension to the right welded a link with E Company, but units to the left were too far away to be reached, so Palopoli bent his left flank northward and ordered everyone to dig in. Nothing more could be done until more troops arrived on Red-3.

Maj Jim Crowe paraded along the beach, disdainful of the bullets being fired into his CP by unseen snipers, defiantly brandishing his pump shotgun, cussing and jeering at his hero-worshipping young riflemen as cowards and braggarts unworthy of the name *Marine*. It was quite a show, and it bolstered flagging pride and fortitude in many who witnessed it.

Except for the shortage of manpower, the rapidly climbing casualty rate, and the spirited Japanese defensive effort, the situation on Red-3 was well in hand.

11

Twenty-seven minutes after Lieutenants Hawkins and Leslie stormed the pierhead, E and F Companies of LtCol Herb Amey's 2nd Battalion, 2nd, began hitting Red-2.

The ride to the beach was every bit as harrowing as that experienced by the 3rd Battalion, 2nd, to the left. Amey's tractors were obliged to pass alongside the main pier. Japanese machine guns and small arms struck them at a point about 50 yards south of the pierhead and all the way to the beach. The Japanese exacted a heavy toll.

The E Company platoon on the battalion's extreme right took a fantastic amount of fire from the Japanese strongpoint at the boundary of Red-1 and Red-2, and many of the men in the platoon's three tractors were hit by ricochets. Fortunately, the platoon's three amtrac drivers were able to land quite close to the assigned sector within seconds of one another. As they did, however, the fire suddenly intensified, and many Marines were immediately killed as they disembarked. The platoon leader ordered his men to the seawall. He was gunned down as he led the way. The survivors fought a fierce battle over possession of a spacious bomb crater near the water. On gaining the position, they regrouped and surged over a small strongpoint, destroying the defenders. Immediately, the incoming fire became even more intense, and the platoon was forced to cede its gains. The survivors returned to the bomb crater with their wounded and went to ground.

A four-man flamethrower team, two gunners, and two assistants, were all that remained of a 21-man tractorload of engineers destined for the center of the beach. The engineers were forced into the water when their amtrac was stopped a few feet on the lagoon side of a barbed-wire barrier guarding the beach. Japanese machine guns completely obliterated the section as it struggled in the water. The four surviving engineers flagged down an empty amtrac and frantically loaded the injured aboard under fire. Since their flame gear had been lost, the four climbed aboard the tractor for a ride to the nearest ship.

Two additional squads of the 1st Platoon, A Company, 18th, 1stLt Gordan Leslie's unit, were totally destroyed as they attempted to land in support of E Company.

Well below the steel sides of one E Company tractor, Cpl Jerry Kubinski's rifle squad was on the verge of panic. Bullets from the pier on the left and the beach dead ahead beat an unending tattoo on the tractor, but no one was hit. When Kubinski felt the tractor finally bottom on solid ground, he followed another Marine over the side. Since he had not had time to survey the situation, he was startled to find himself standing chest-deep in the surf. The water helped to dissipate the 29-year-old veteran's shock, and he staggered to the beach to find his squad intact and fully equipped but for one lost helmet.

Kubinski's platoon leader, an officer who had won his gold bars in the field on Guadalcanal, successfully gained the beach but was engulfed in the detonation of a round from a distant medium-caliber gun. The remainder of E Company's officers suffered similar fates. Of six, only 2ndLt Carl Mesmer lived through the first minutes ashore.

F Company, 2nd, landed next to the pier.

PlSgt Randall Johnson of 1st Platoon, who commanded an amtrac carrying a rifle squad and a squad of engineers, had his substantial reputation riding on how far inland he could get before leaving his amtrac. He shared a boast and a bet with PlSgt Art Maher of 2nd Platoon: First man on the southern beach won.

Much to Johnson's amazement, he immediately found a gap in the seawall and continued southward, even though tractors on all sides were being knocked out. Johnson felt sure he would win the bet until the engine stalled about 50 yards inland, a few feet shy of the northwest taxiway of the Japanese airstrip.

Platoon Sergeant Johnson had just ordered his men over the

side when the engine sputtered back to life, so everyone remained aboard to see what was going to happen next. By that time, Johnson realized that he had far outdistanced friendly forces, so he reluctantly ordered the driver to return to the beach. Japanese fire was pounding in from all sides as the tractor swerved on its tracks and dashed toward the beach. It got less than twenty yards, then nosed into a deep, conical shell crater. There was nowhere to go and no way to get there, so the two squads and the tractor crew bailed out and ran for the beach. Most of the troops survived the mad dash, and others ducked into craters and behind cover all along the way.

The two tractors bearing the rest of 2ndLt Ray Marion's 1st Platoon, F Company, 2nd, became targets for a Japanese mortar section as soon as they crossed the reef. Fortunately, the steady progress of the tractors probably ruined the aim of the mortarmen. The squad in Marion's tractor suffered its first casualty halfway between the reef and the beach when a 13mm bullet penetrated the bulkhead and killed a rifleman. Lieutenant Marion, who was standing between the forward machine guns, lifted his binoculars to his eyes and spotted the muzzle flashes of several Japanese machine guns, dead ahead. He yelled, "Duck!" to his two gunners and threw his own body to the deck. The warning went unheeded, and both gunners were shot to death within a second. The platoon leader rose just as the driver and his assistant were shot to death, causing the tractor to veer out of control into a concrete tetrahedron and turn over, thus exposing all hands to the heavy fire from the beach. Ray Marion ordered his troops into the water. Four Marines and a corpsman responded. They were all that remained unhurt of the 21 men who had crossed the reef with Lieutenant Marion. Moments later, a squad leader's body floated past Ray Marion, who saw that a ghastly hole had appeared in the man's head. In another second, the two remaining riflemen were severely wounded.

Overcome by shock and grief at the loss of so many of his Marines, Ray Marion flagged down an outbound amtrac and ordered its gunners to fire cover while he attempted to save the wounded men in the red-tinged water all around him. Several of Marion's riflemen were hoisted aboard the covering vehicle, but mortars on the beach found the range and knocked Marion senseless. He would come to hours later aboard ship.

F Company's 2nd Platoon had to abandon all three of its

tractors well short of the beach. Led by 2ndLt Joe Barr and PlSgt Art Maher, the platoon took to the water 50 yards out and made for the small boat cove at the base of the pier, where it immediately fragmented as individual Marines sought needed cover.

As soon as Platoon Sergeant Maher reached the boat cove with several riflemen, he was knocked off his feet by a gargantuan eruption. Up and down the beach, men fighting for cover were felled when the torpedo storage dump blew up. Maher, who was very close to the blast, lost consciousness an instant before thudding into the sand.

Capt Lefty Morris, F Company's skipper, was rushing to the beach several minutes behind his rifle platoons when his tractor was blown out of the water about 125 yards west of the pier and 20 yards from shore. Only four men survived the blast: Morris and two assault engineers under SSgt Bill Bordelon, an extremely resourceful young man who had helped organize the engineer assault teams after Guadalcanal. The four men put their heads down and waded to the beach.

Captain Morris ran to the left to find his company and Staff Sergeant Bordelon sprang to action where he was. A quick search of the beach netted a sackful of TNT, from which he fashioned two powerful charges. As soon as Bordelon located a target, he arranged to be covered by nearby riflemen and charged over the seawall. He quickly blew out two pillboxes. Then he returned to the beach, fashioned another charge, and went after a third emplacement. The machine gun in that pillbox wounded him slightly and forced him to seek cover.

Moments after PlSgt Art Maher came to, he found that he was deaf and all alone. He padded forward to see if a nearby building would provide adequate cover, but he found that it was another torpedo storage dump, and he moved out to look for a safer place. By that time, one ear had cleared and he could hear the sounds that accompanied all the horror he was witnessing. Maher was in a state of shock. He could plainly see that everything was going wrong and that F Company had been badly torn up just getting ashore. Worst of all, he could not see the enemy, only the havoc the enemy was wreaking upon the attackers. Art Maher picked his spot and decided to try to take a few of the Japanese with him when he died.

• • •

Most of G Company, 2nd, landed in tractors at 0830, three minutes behind schedule. The platoon that was to have supported E Company on the right took such powerful fire from the Japanese beach boundary strongpoint that all three of its tractors veered farther and farther west to get out of the fire. Before long, Red-2 was left far behind. The platoon finally landed on the northwestern tip of the island, behind the 3rd Battalion, 2nd.

The remainder of G Company suffered heavy casualities as it seized a shallow perimeter behind the seawall. Contact with E and F Companies on either flank was tenuous. The company commander and nearly all the officers were at least slightly wounded, and many enlisted men were injured, some critically.

Landing craft bearing needed support units and command teams were milling about in confusion at the reef. Unlike his fellow battalion commanders, LtCol Herb Amey had decided to sacrifice firepower for manpower by holding his machine gun platoons in boats while sending G Company in early aboard amtracs. Conditions peculiar to Red-2 made Amey's strategem a lucky guess, for landing G Company in the center prevented the Japanese from exploiting the otherwise isolated positions of E and F Companies, which would have been easily overwhelmed by counterattacking infantry.

LtCol Herb Amey had split his command group in half and placed it aboard two boats to obviate the loss of all the battalion's key personnel in a single catastrophe. Amey was in an LCM just beyond the reef, and his exec, Maj Howard Rice, was in an LCVP a short distance away. By prior agreement, Amey's command group would try to get to the beach first.

Amey saw early that things were going badly on the beaches, so he decided to get in as early as possible to take control and report his needs to regimental and divisional headquarters.

Amey's boat fouled on the reef as soon as it turned shoreward. As Amey looked for a solution, he immediately spotted a pair of amtracs putting distance between themselves and the beach, and he hailed them in close to begin transferring his command team. Amey was in good spirits, despite the obvious setbacks on the beach and the fire that had just started erupting around him. A moment before he boarded his tractor, the 29-year-old Pennsylvanian turned to Associated Press correspondent Bill Hipple and said, "I guess you got a story. Guess the Japs want a scrape." He sounded elated.

Amey had 13 officers and enlisted Marines with him when his tractor cast off, including LtCol Irvine Jordan, an observer from the new 4th Marine Division. Immediately, the two tractors separated as they maneuvered to avoid fire.

The battalion commander's tractor fouled on barbed wire 20 yards from the beach. There was no way through, so Herb Amey ordered everyone over the side. The bullets were coming thick and fast. The command group waded several yards beyond the protective side of the tractor. They were hit by heavy machine gun fire just as they reached the wire and were preparing a passage. As correspondent Bill Hipple wheeled to avoid the incoming rounds, he saw the man next to him go down. It was Herb Amey, and he was dead.

The survivors made for the lee of the tractor and used it for cover as they passed through the barrier and waded ashore.

It was 1000. In just 30 minutes, the 2nd Battalion, 2nd's three rifle companies suffered over 30 percent casualities, over 50 percent of the battalion's rifle-company officers were dead or wounded, organizational integrity was destroyed, most of the combat engineers assigned to the battalion were killed or wounded, and the battalion commander was dead.

In the battalion's second command boat, Maj Howard Rice was doing his level best to get ashore. Minutes before Rice's boat was due to land, however, it was approached by a Navy control boat. The Navy officer in charge shouted a brief account of the fighting ashore and told Rice to stay in his boat until a tractor could be found. The men in Rice's boat could hear and see fire all along the distant beach and all over the lagoon.

When a tractor finally came alongside the boat, Major Rice hurriedly designated the people he wanted to accompany him ashore. He left Capt Ben Owens, the battalion operations officer, and several other officers and enlisted specialists.

Rice made directly for Red-2 through heavy fire. As the driver attempted to find a clear, safe path, he began edging westward, which only made matters worse. The amtrac continued to veer still farther to the west, passing through cones of fire from strongpoint after strongpoint, angling farther and farther west, farther and farther from its objective. At last,

Major Rice bowed to the inevitable and ordered the driver to make all deliberate speed for the northwest point of the island. The 2nd Battalion, 2nd's command group would simply have to march overland to regain contact with the battalion.

Meantime, Capt Ben Owens and the men Rice had left in his boat continued to idle back and forth at the edge of the reef. Owens had no reason to be overly concerned, for three-fourths of the battalion headquarters had started for the beach, and there was no reason to assume that no senior officers had arrived there. Captain Owens did not know it, but he was the only staff officer of the 2nd Battalion, 2nd, who had even a remote chance of assuming control of the badly hurt battalion.

Scores of LCVPs and LCMs were milling and swerving all over the area near the Line of Departure. Their crews and passengers were unwilling or unable to get clearance for the ride to the beach.

Aboard one such boat, 37mm gunner Pfc Arnold Gladson succumbed to the desire to see what was going on and lifted his head just in time to see the boat ahead disintegrate under a direct hit. Gladson was about to duck anyway, when a stream of 13mm bullets from the beach skimmed overhead. He recoiled to the deck, where he saw that one of the gun chiefs was leaning against a rubber tire obviously engrossed in a comic book.

Second Lieutenant Lawrence Vlach, whose H Company .30-caliber machine gun platoon was in an LCVP stopped at the reef, was anxiously looking for several empty amtracs. As Vlach's coxswain patiently circled just beyond the reef, Japanese artillery began getting the range. The boat was close to *Niminoa*, the grounded hulk, so Vlach ordered the coxswain to heave to on her lee side to ride out the mortar storm. As the boat came abaft the hulk's raised fantail, its bottom scraped and forward motion ceased. Vlach immediately ordered the coxswain to advance to full throttle, but the bow ramp fouled on the hulk's fantail.

While the coxswain tinkered, the platoon leader had one of his sergeants support his legs while he shinnied up the bow ramp to take a peek into the rusting ship. Two Japanese riflemen were holed up in *Niminoa's* bows. Vlach, who had been a Marine since 1927, needed no prompting. He raised his light M2 carbine and snapped off several rounds at the snipers, killing both. Immediately, three *rigosentai* Vlach had not seen accosted him as he was about to drop back into the LCVP. A lively exchange ensued, and Vlach again emerged the victor. Just then, the coxswain's foot slipped off the gas pedal and the boat bounded away from the hulk, dropping Vlach to the deck. He would not know it for hours, but he had taken minor wounds in his shoulder and collarbone. Although Vlach was game for another go, his coxswain was ordered by a senior officer to make way for another boat, which strafed *Niminoa* with its machine guns.

Lieutenant Vlach flagged down a passing tractor and ordered one of his two .30-caliber gun sections to take possesssion of it and land. The second section, with Vlach, boarded a second amtrac minutes later.

Vlach heard from *Niminoa* once again, when he was about 250 yards from shore. This time, a mortar round from the rear hit the amtrac and all the men in it, killing several and wounding everyone else. Lieutenant Vlach simply ordered the driver to keep going. He and his survivors landed at 1017.

Vlach's other section was driven off course to the left and forced to land on Red-3. The gunners trudged westward until confronted by a huge concrete pier section. Several of the men safely wriggled beneath the barrier but many of those who went over the top were killed or wounded. The survivors stopped where they were.

Although Lieutenant Vlach and his entire machine gun section were casualities, they refused to be stopped. Immediately upon reaching the seawall, Vlach saw a large group of Japanese in the open, shifting from right to left across the Marine front. He ordered the guns into action, and the stunned survivors of his section mercilessly flayed their enemies with hundreds upon hundreds of steel-jacketed rounds.

Lieutenant Vlach's section was the first and, for a time, the only medium machine gun unit to reach Red-2; H Company's other two platoons had been driven off course to Red-1, where they were fed into the lines of the 3rd Battalion, 2nd.

Maj Hal Throneson's H Company gun platoons had all been doled out to the rifle companies, so the former Raider and veteran of the defense of Midway began his trip to Betio with Herb Amey's command group. One of a few fortunates from that group to land without mishap, Throneson made a quick survey of the situation and noted that the heaviest weapons on Red-2 were what remained of the nine 60mm mortars belonging to the rifle companies. It was so evident that the battalion 81mm mortars were urgently needed that Major Throneson dropped everything else to search for the best place to set them up. He stopped looking when he saw *Niminoa* high and dry on the reef, a stable platform far enough out for the guns to be able to pitch high-angle fire at Japanese positions only yards from Marine positions on the shallow beach. The pierhead was a good second choice.

Hal Throneson had no way of knowing that he was the highest ranking 2nd Battalion, 2nd, officer on Red-2, so he hopped aboard an outbound tractor and ordered the driver to take him to the spot beyond the reef where he had left the 81mm platoon's LCVP. However, he found that the guns were gone, driven off by fire from the beach, so he ordered the amtrac driver to keep looking.

SSgt Bill Bordelon was spoiling for a fight. He had already destroyed two pillboxes and had been hit going after a third. But he refused to be stopped before he had avenged the deaths of so many of his comrades and subordinates. He grabbed a rifle from the hands of a dead Marine and covered Marines who were trying to scale the seawall. As he fired, he was accosted by a Navy corpsman, who insisted upon having a look at the wound. As Bordelon angrily waved the man away, he saw a wounded engineer struggling in the surf and raced into the water to lend a hand. Before Bordelon reached the first engineer, he spotted another wounded engineer nearby. With one man under each arm, and under fire from Japanese small arms, Bordelon made his way back to the seawall. Although he was copiously bleeding from his untended wound, he got to work fashioning a fused charge of TNT for any of the plentiful targets nearby. When William James Bordelon crossed the seawall for the third time that morning he was killed by machine gun fire. He had earned a Medal of Honor.

The 2nd Battalion, 2nd, was in grievous condition. E Company had been all but extinguished, G and F Companies had been seriously harmed, and H Company had failed to arrive. There was not a single operable radio on the beach, and no one was on hand to take charge of the survivors.

But no one told the riflemen and troop leaders. In the opening hours of combat, small groups penetrated as many as 75 yards inland along a 300-yard front.

Help was on the way.

12

Col Dave Shoup was the most-frustrated man in Tarawa Lagoon. During the three hours since sunrise, Shoup's three initial landing teams had been strewn all across three beaches, the reef and the lagoon. All were fighting major, unremitting actions, and there was little the combat team commander could do to help.

Reports from the beaches were jumbled and confusing, each of them limited by the circumstances of the sender. Still, as reports filtered in from radios on the beach or crews and passengers in outbound tractors, Shoup was able to begin making some hazy sense of the overall situation. It looked desperate.

Of the three reinforced battalions, only Crowe's seemed in decent enough shape to get an advance going. The sporadic reports from Red-1 were the most jumbled, most confusing, most alarming; it seemed, however, that the 3rd Battalion, 2nd, had taken some ground. Of Amey's battalion, there was little news, and all of it was bad.

Dave Shoup had no idea that Schoettel's battalion had been reduced to 65 percent of its starting strength or that less than 25 percent of the battalion's supports had been landed. The colonel did not know that a rifle company on Red-2 had ceased to exist, or that the others had taken debilitating casualties. And he had only the vaguest inkling that Crowe's battalion was more or less intact but bogged down just beyond the seawall.

One thing had become urgently apparent to the Combat Team 2 commander as fragmentary reports from the beaches mounted: he would have to get at least one more battalion—the 1st Battalion, 2nd—into Betio and into the best possible spot for a rapid exploitation of even the minimal gains made thus far.

Red-1 seemed out of the running from the start. Not enough

was known of the situation, and the beaches were a bit out of the way. As the reef had been proven a major obstacle, the good wide beaches on Red-1 would be useless for landing needed material. It appeared, moreover, that the force on Red-1 was restricted to the western half of the beach, completely out of contact with the 2nd Battalion, 2nd.

Red-2 was no safe bet, either, but it was no worse a bet than Red-3. The beaches were okay, but the low water over the reef neutralized that possible advantage. Red-2 was next to the pier and it was the beach on which Dave Shoup had pretty much decided to come ashore; its central location resolved any questions in that regard. The inclination toward landing the 1st Battalion, 2nd, on Red-2 was bolstered by the apparent need to land another battalion of the 8th Marines; that battalion, the 3rd, might just as well go in behind Crowe on Red-3, where it could be effectively controlled by its own regimental officers in the event they landed.

The clincher was news from Crowe that the 2nd Battalion, 8th, had been held to minimal gains just south of the seawall and that it was faced with breaching what appeared to be the most extensive defenses on the island.

It *had* to be Red-2.

Maj Wood Kyle, a veteran of rugged fighting on Guadalcanal, was ordered at 0958 to begin moving his 1st Battalion, 2nd, to the eastern half of Red-2. Once he had regrouped the battalion, Kyle was to sweep westward to consolidate the gains of the 2nd Battalion, 2nd, then regroup again to carry out frontal attacks toward the south shore.

Confusion and partial disorganization began hampering Kyle's battalion as soon as the first line of boats closed on the reef. No one in the battalion had known that the way to the beach was barred by that reef of coral. A small knot of tractors arrived just as the proceeding was about to fall into total chaos, but there were 1,000 men in the battalion and enough room in the amtracs for only a few platoons.

Major Kyle's command boat pushed through the milling mass of landing craft. The battalion commander perched high on the ramp, trying to pinpoint his company commanders. He informed Capt Bill Bray of A Company and Capt Maxie Williams of B to begin feeding their riflemen onto the tractors and make for the beach; C and D Companies and the battalion headquarters would await the arrival of additional tracked transport.

The moment the word was passed, 2ndLt Bob Harvey, an A Company platoon leader, crowded as many men as he could onto one tractor and moved to the beach without waiting to join with the remainder of the company. Another A Company officer got two squads of his platoon aboard another tractor before the driver pulled away to avoid being swamped.

Singly and in pairs, additional tractors were brought alongside the milling boats, from which the troops surged aboard until there was no room. There was little chance of regrouping the companies into tractor waves, and not much point in it. The troops at least were exhibiting an exhilarating eagerness to enter the fight, despite horror stories passed along by the tractor drivers.

A and B Companies, 2nd, began succumbing to gunfire from the beaches as they made the final lunge toward Red-2, at about 1030. Most of the fire came from the right front, from the major strongpoint at the boundary with Red-1.

In the lead of the battalion, 2ndLt Bob Harvey's tractor reached the beach before many Japanese gunners realized the size of the reinforcement. The tractor came to an abrupt halt yards from the first strand of dry sand. As fresh, eager Marines clambered over the sides, Pfc Dick Clark, a BAR-man, distinguished himself by landing flat on his face in less than a foot of water. Spluttering and cursing, the green automatic rifleman struggled to his feet, poured salt water from his weapon, and dived for the seawall to rejoin his buddies.

The tractor carrying two squads of another A Company platoon had worse luck when it was caught in a crossfire just as it stopped to drop off the troops. The dazed Marines started a disorderly mass exodus to the beach which even the intense fire could not abate. Every man was hit.

Capt Maxie Williams, of B Company, had been through this sort of thing before. Sixteen months earlier, while serving as a platoon leader with his own B Company, Williams had been the first American officer—possibly the first American—to land offensively against the Japanese in the Pacific War. But that had been an uncontested landing near Guadalcanal, and this was Betio. Williams's quick peeks over the side warned him that his first task would be reclaiming lost and straggling squads before he would ever get an advance going. For the moment, Williams just wanted to complete his second combat landing intact.

Way over to Williams's right, segments of B Company were being ground up by a heavy concentration of automatic and medium-caliber antiboat fire from the beach boundary strongpoint. Several tractors, in fact, were being forced westward in the direction of Red-1, when the company exec decided to go with the flow of events and land wherever he could get his men safely ashore. In all, about 110 men, including a number from A Company, landed on Red-1, where they learned that the way to Red-2 was barred. All these men were absorbed into the 3rd Battalion, 2nd.

Maj Hal Throneson, of H Company, 2nd, failed to find his 81mm mortar platoon at the reef, so he caught a shorebound tractor laden with ammunition and several B Company weapons people. On the way to the beach, the floating ammunition dump developed mechanical trouble and could not be put into reverse. This bothered Throneson not in the least; he was intent on reaching Red-2, which was forward.

When Throneson glanced over the amtrac's side and spotted a knot of Marines cowering behind a group of concrete tetrahedrons, he leaned far out over the side and raised his collar to reveal a gold leaf hidden there. "Get into the beach! They need you people." Then, in words he had never consciously composed, he added, "You'll never get to heaven standing there."

An instant later, Major Throneson was hardly the picture of assurance. Precisely as the last word left his lips, he was bowled over backward by a bullet in the stomach. As he lay in the tractor's bilges, not quite believing that he had been shot, the weapons company commander allowed a merciful numbness to settle over his mind and body.

Capt Bill Bray of A Company was set ashore about 150 yards west of the main pier with elements of his company command group. When fifteen A Company riflemen landed nearby, Bray consolidated the two tractorloads of men and pushed over the seawall as far as the taxiway. Soon Captain Bray noticed that his small command was alone and unsupported, so he ordered everyone back to the seawall.

To Bray's far left, Capt Maxie Williams arrived among three tractorloads of troops. As the 24 men from two of the tractors dropped into the water, Williams among them, intense fire erupted against them. Nine of the 24 reached the beach, including Captain Williams. The third tractor, still packed with Marines, swerved around and headed back toward deeper water.

A and B Companies, 2nd—those small elements that had gotten safely ashore—were stopped at the seawall.

Only one minute after he ordered Kyle's battalion to land on Red-2, Dave Shoup made his first firm contact with the commander of the 3rd Battalion, 2nd. Major Schoettel radioed at 0959: "Receiving heavy fire all along beach. Unable to land." At that moment, Schoettel and his command group were near the reef, unable to move to the beach for want of tractors.

Schoettel got off a second message to Shoup at 1107: "Boats held up on reef off right flank of Red-1. Troops receiving heavy fire in water." The battalion commander was referring to his fourth wave, but did not clarify. Shoup's response was immediate: "Land Beach Red-2 and work west." Schoettel's ominous reply: "Have nothing left to land."

Shoup knew very well that at least several companies had landed on Red-1, so he turned to more pressing matters.

During the major portions of his exchanges with the beach and Majors Kyle and Schoettel, Colonel Shoup had been aboard a tractor bound for Red-2. With him, among others: LtCol Evans Carlson, the famous Raider who had led the Makin Raid; Maj Tom Culhane, the 2nd Regiment's operations officer; LtCol Presley Rixey, commander of the 1st Battalion, 10th, the 75mm pack howitzer unit assigned to support the 2nd Marines; and LCdr Don Nelson, the regimental surgeon.

As the command tractor waddled toward the left half of Red-2, it came under intense fire from Japanese machine guns and hidden antiboat guns, which forced it to pull up short at the pierhead. Shoup ordered the amtrac driver to attempt a passage down the eastern side of the pier, to Red-3.

As the tractor rounded the pierhead, it was joined by three LCMs, each carrying a Sherman M4 medium tank. Immediately, the tiny flotilla was taken under fire by a pair of 70mm guns. Two of the tank lighters were sunk and the third withdrew, shipping water and losing steerage. Shoup's tractor driver also prudently withdrew for another try down the west side of the pier.

The fire this time was less intense, but the tractor's abused engine sputtered and died halfway to the beach. Shoup shrugged and vaulted over the side, hitting the water in time to be buffeted by the blast of a medium caliber shell. Although the colonel badly wrenched his knee, he doggedly continued toward the beach, his command group following in his wake. Everyone safely reached the base of the pier at about 1030.

13

At 1018, nearly a quarter-hour before Col Dave Shoup's command group was able to reach Red-2, MGen Julian Smith, the division commander, decided that it was getting close to the time when he would have to release another rifle battalion to bolster his depleted forces ashore. The Division CP (Command Post), aboard *Maryland*, contacted Col Elmer Hall, the 8th Marines commander, and ordered him to begin moving Maj Robert Ruud's 3rd Battalion, 8th, to the Line of Departure. Once at the line, Ruud's battalion was to pass to Dave Shoup's tactical control.

Julian Smith made his first official report to MGen Holland Smith, who was at Makin, within the half-hour: "Successful landings on Beaches 2 and 3. Toehold on Red-1. Am committing one landing team from division reserve. Still strong resistance throughout."

Ruud's battalion, organized into six boat waves, immediately moved on the Line of Departure with K Company in the lead and L close behind. The first boats reached the line at 1103.

Light breezes sweeping across Betio from the lagoon dissipated the heavy smoke over the beaches and allowed the crew of a Japanese 4.7-inch dual-purpose gun mounted near the swept-back eastern tail of Betio to spot the incoming line of blue boats moving hard upon the reef. The gun captain ordered his waiting, tense gunners to adjust aim and . . . fire! *WHANG!* The sound of furious battle on three beaches was overriden by what one listener likened to a steel girder smashing concrete.

Aboard the westernmost boat, PlSgt Jack Hernandez was peering over the side, despite the crisscrossing lines of pink tracer only inches above his head. He watched as the easternmost boat ducked to a blurred halt and fell apart, dumping its entire complement into the lagoon.

A few feet behind Hernandez, communications Sgt Leonard Wynn also saw the boat disintegrate. And, as he looked on in awe, he heard a sound like a freight train pass overhead. The second boat in the line met precisely the same fate as the first.

Unnerved, the boatcrews of the three surviving boats stopped where they were, one commander gruffly stating, "This is as far as I go," as he dropped the ramp. Keyed up beyond normal levels, every man in the boat surged forward. The first men went off into between 10 and 15 feet of water, pulled down by their heavy gear. Few managed to paddle the short distance to the reef.

K Company's entire 1st Platoon, aboard the easternmost boat, stared incredulously as the thoroughly fearful Navy crew chief vaulted over the gunwale and splashed into the water. The coxswain then told 2ndLt John Adrian that he would not go farther because of shoals and fire from the beach. Adrian calmly leveled his carbine on the crewman and ordered him to proceed. At the same time, Platoon Sergeant Hernandez ordered a rifleman to lower the ramp. The coxswain watched open-mouthed as the Marines charged into chest-deep water.

Meantime, destroyer fire blanked the 4.7-inch gun.

Col Dave Shoup and LtCol Evans Carlson watched from the beach in helpless frustration as Ruud's first wave was chewed to bits. When the two men, and LtCol Presley Rixey, regained their composure, they frantically waved to attract the attention of the remaining boat waves, hoping to start them in farther to the west so they might gain some protection from the pier.

L Company began its run as the survivors of K Company waded toward the pier and the beach.

Cpl John Beck, a machine gun squad leader, was at the rear and to one side of his boat when it began the final lap; a rifle platoon and a 60mm mortar squad were forward. The entire complement had been ordered to stay low, and officers were busily enforcing the edict. It thus came as a complete surprise to all when the boat crashed into a solid object and holes began appearing in the plywood sides. The crew dropped the bow ramp. As John Beck caught his first look at Betio, the riflemen in the bows began collapsing under machine gun fire. The surge from the rear pushed the dead and dying into the water. By the time Beck reached the water, most of the men who had been in front of him were struggling under little pink clouds in the water. Beck and his gunners struck out for the reef, half walking and half swimming to the pier, where they sought cover and a brief rest.

I Company was aboard two LCMs far behind L Company when it passed *Pursuit*. As one of the LCMs passed the minesweeper's fantail, a small figure shouted orders through a megaphone: "Hurry up and land!" The two landing craft heeled over hard to starboard and moved toward the reef.

Bullets were clanging against the light metal innards of the boat when a dazed young Marine grabbed FM1 John Lane by the elbow and demanded above the din of the engines, "Lane, are they *shooting* at us? Are they shooting at *us*?" Lane, who was too frightened to respond, just stared.

Lane's LCM collided with another moving object only moments later. The excited Marine platoon leader commanding the boat looked back at the equally nervous coxswain and ordered, "Let the ramp down!" The crewman manning the stern machine gun looked crosseyed at the officer and tried to explain that the boat was nowhere near a safe landing place, that it had merely collided with the other LCM. The lieutenant sucked in a deep breath and, as his confused subordinates looked on, demanded again that the ramp be lowered. The coxswain shrugged and had it done.

The fear-charged Marines sprang into the water. From a dead stop to a dead run, Pvt Alvaro Mendes, an assistant machine gunner, took a flying leap and immediately sank from sight, pulled down by the weight of two ammunition chests he had tied to his suspenders to keep his hands unencumbered. He died.

John Lane, a good swimmer, found the water much too deep for comfort, so he dropped the package of flares he had been told to get to the beach. And, like many Marines around him, he deposited his helmet and pack in the lagoon. Unlike many others, he kept his rifle and swam a clumsy dog-stroke to shallow water; there is nothing more useless, he had been told, than an unarmed Marine in a firefight.

In the second I Company boat, still some distance from the reef, a sailor moved to the bow and began undogging the ramp. A 37mm shell exploded a few inches from his head as he reached for the last dog, and he staggered away, unhurt but badly dazed. Compassionate Marines supported him as he made his way to the stern, where he told the boat commander, a young ensign, that the ramp was free. The ensign released the ramp control just as a sheet of gunfire hit the boat. Forward-facing Marines felt the boat begin to drift out of control, and those at the rear turned to find that the crew had disappeared. All they could see was the pistol-pointing hand of the ensign waving over the edge of the armored crew compartment.

The men in the bow were taking heavy fire, and the lead ranks charged into the water, which was 15 feet deep. First Lieutenant Jim Motley, the I Company commander, tried to stop the rush, but half his men were already gone. The boat continued to drift out of control.

Meantime, the battalion commander, with the fourth wave, was approaching the reef east of Red-2, when the entire wave was stopped cold as Japanese machine gunners found the range. The volume of fire convinced Major Ruud that he had better back off, so the boats turned and were gobbled up by the incoming fifth and sixth waves, which also turned tail.

Dave Shoup radioed Jim Crowe at 1145: "Third Battalion is landing to your rear and catching hell." All Crowe had to do to find that out was turn and look!

Pfc Jim Gentry considered himself a seasoned combat Marine. He had been on The Canal. Until he began moving toward Red-3 at Betio, he thought he had already seen the worst of what would amount to 32 months overseas. He was one of the few men left in the 8th Marines who had formed the regiment and gone with it to Samoa in early 1942. Gentry, an ammunition carrier with M Company's 81mm mortar platoon, started out lucky. His platoon was largely intact and moving to the beach under light fire as men all around were crying and dying. The pier was afire, but the platoon was working its way down the boat channel and had yet to lose a man. The water in some spots was too deep to wade, so the mortarmen clung to the pier supports and half-swam the deeper parts. Gentry noted that the bottom was covered with what felt to his feet like sandbags but might well have been corpses. The air stank of death and putrefaction.

Lulled into trusting the bottom to hold to a steadily decreasing depth, Gentry stumbled into a deep hole as he neared the beach. Thirty yards farther on, the veteran realized that the small Bible he had been carrying over his heart was missing. He knew that he had dropped it where he had stumbled, so he turned and waded back to retrieve it. Just as Gentry bent to pick up the Bible, he heard a sharp report and felt a hot wave of pain pass across his back. He felt for a wound and came away with a blood-covered hand. A passing Marine mentioned that the wound looked terrible and had shreds of Gentry's dungaree shirt embedded in it. But Gentry felt fine. The bullet, fired by an unseen sniper, would have caught him square in the back had he not bent to recover the Bible; all it had done was cut a shallow trough down the length of his back. Jim Gentry treated the wound as well as he could and shakily, very shakily, lit a sodden cigarette and stumbled to the beach.

PlSgt Jack Hernandez took stock of his platoon as soon as he reached the pierhead. He had started in with 40 men, including a radio team, and he was down to 25, some of whom proved to be stragglers from other units. He had one rifle for every five men, and many men had no gear at all. Fire on the eastern side of the pier was far too intense at that moment to risk a move to Red-3 with a group of men so thoroughly beaten, so Hernandez led the men through a passageway under the pier and opted to move to Red-2. The slow-moving group arrived on Betio after what seemed an eternity. Too sapped to move inland under fire, the Marines dropped to the sand and sprawled out. They would remain where they lay for nearly three hours.

Cpl John Beck had to pick his way carefully through water filled with floating corpses to negotiate the last ten yards to the beach. Once there, he had to step around more corpses and, unbelievably, sleeping men. As soon as Beck found four feet of clear ground, he dropped, exhausted and bleeding from his encounter with the reef and the lagoon.

Agile swimmer John Lane approached the pierhead and, as bullets *sputted* around him, thought of a cribbage game on the beach to which he had been invited by an addict named Bishop. Gaining the pierhead, Lane happened to see a half-submerged body a few feet away; he did not have to pull the corpse over to see who it was, for a cribbage board was sticking out of one of the back pockets. Farther on, Lane watched two I Company Marines start a dash down the high exposed pier decking. They did not get twenty paces before being killed.

Lane joined up with a small group of Marines from I Company, 8th, at the spot where the pierhead split to form a shallow Y. The Marines began moving down the west side of the pier. When Lane stopped in a passageway under the pier for a brief rest, he watched another Marine begin to pass him. Just as the man came abreast of the passageway, he took a bullet in the back. The force of the impact spun him around, and a second bullet smashed his jaw. Next, a line of bullets passed over Lane's left shoulder. A nearby Marine pulled out a grenade and started after the gun, but an officer told him to belay lest he damage the vital structure. Moving right, away from the gun, the remnants of the group rapidly passed to Red-2. John Lane struck out alone for Red-3, where he encountered a howling redheaded maniac who waved a shotgun and screamed, "Keep your ass down!" Lane moved across the seawall into a large shellhole. It was as far as he would get that day.

The 3rd Battalion, 8th, had landed. Sort of.

14

The fighting on Betio's northern beaches was a rifleman's battle, in the hands of the several thousand individual Marines still capable of handling their weapons.

The battle was, from the very start, to be decided by the efforts of individuals, squads and platoons pitted against isolated Japanese snipers and gun emplacements. It was, from the very start, a matter of finding the enemy and digging him out. Win, lose, or draw, it was the sort of battle that defied plan or control. It rested solely in the hands of individuals and the luck they had in finding support or being in the right place at the right time and in the right frame of mind. It depended upon the prowess and willpower of the surviving troop leaders, many of whom were inexperienced. It depended a great deal on whether young officers could rise to the many challenges around them to show their Marines the way. It depended on how far the sights and sounds and smells of death could incite the ire of apathetic individuals.

It defied reason that so many men would throw their lives to the Fates for the sake of a few acres of ground on some remote island. The ground itself seemed worthless; it was too sandy to farm or support livestock, and there was not enough of it.

This was no battle. It was a free-for-all.

Almost as soon as Ruud's 3rd Battalion, 8th, began coming ashore on Red-2 and Red-3, Dave Shoup and his command group set out to find the CP of the 2nd Battalion, 2nd. Runners and passersby informed the colonel that LtCol Irvine Jordan, the 4th Marine Division observer, had assumed temporary command of the battalion and had established his headquarters in a large shell crater about 75 yards inland, 100 yards west of the pier.

Shoup's team proceeded under treacherous fire. Shoup's

primary concern for the moment was finding out what was going on. On reaching Jordan's CP, however, he found that his temporary battalion commander was himself in the dark. Shoup moved farther to the west and joined several regimental communicators beside a large wrecked hospital building 150 yards from the pier and only yards from the water's edge.

Ten medium tanks started from the reef toward Red-2 and Red-3. Two were sunk in their LCMs beside the pier, and seven made for Red-3 by crossing the reef. The eighth followed the pier to shore.

As 1stLt Lou Largey jockeyed *Cannonball* toward the beach, a shrieking explosion rocked the vehicle when it was hit in the bow by a medium-caliber shell. The driver quickly reversed and slewed around. When Lieutenant Largey saw that his command tank was responding well to the rough handling, he ordered his driver to turn back for shore.

While *Charlie, Condor,* and *Colorado,* Largey's three remaining tanks, made it ashore without mishap and joined the platoon leader off the beach, four of the five tanks from the 2nd Platoon, C Company, IMAC Medium Tank Battalion, reached Red-3 and regrouped to drive westward to Red-2.

Under orders from Jim Crowe, *Cannonball* led the way for *Colorado, Charlie,* and *Condor* in an attempt to cross the island. Within an hour of landing, *Condor* fell victim to an overzealous Navy divebomber pilot, who had been warned of Japanese tanks on Red-3 but who had not heard that American mediums had been landed. The crew bailed out. A short time later, *Charlie* lost a duel with a Japanese antitank gun. The same gun, or one nearby, hit *Cannonball,* which its driver deftly dumped into a burning underground fuel dump. Fortunately, both crews escaped. *Colorado* was also set aflame, but its driver raced to the surf, which quenched the flames. Lieutenant Largey gathered the 14 other tankers who had lost their tanks and began the long trek back to secure lines.

The 2nd Platoon, on Red-2, had equally abysmal luck. Immediately upon passing the base of the main pier, one of the four surviving tanks ran into a shellhole and sank to within a few inches of the turret top. Its crew drowned. Two of the surviving tanks moved to the front to support the infantry, where one lasted five minutes before running blindly into a shellhole. The third loss resulted from a Japanese magnetic antitank mine, which was placed on the hull by a man who knew he had seconds to live. The last tank withdrew behind the seawall, from which it supported the infantry with long-range 75mm fire.

In a little over an hour, the number of tanks on the central and eastern beaches had been cut from ten to two.

At 1045, 15 minutes after reaching shore, Col Dave Shoup contacted The Flag: "Stiff resistance. Need halftracks. Our tanks no good." The 75mm Halftrack Platoon of Weapons Company, 2nd, was ordered to the beach. Total strength: two.

The LCM carrying Number-2 Halftrack to the beach was sunk as it approached the reef. And almost as soon as Number-1 Halftrack reached the beach, it bogged down in the loose, sifting sand. The platoon leader ordered his crew to dig it out, but it would be hours before the critically needed 75mm gun could be used.

One of Colonel Shoup's primary headaches in controlling the battle ashore was the fact that his regimental communicators were running into the worst luck imaginable.

Pfc Bill Haddad, the platoon's fastest keypuncher, was aboard an LCM hung up on the reef with the long-range TBX radio team that would have been Regiment's best means of talking with The Flag. Unable to move, Haddad's team put the radio components together and started broadcasting to tell higher authority of its plight. The only friendly radio they could raise was the platoon's TBS, which was in an amtrac bound for the beach. Only minutes after contact was established, the amtrac was blown apart, and all aboard were killed.

Pfc Gordon Stevens and his three-man TBX radio team managed to flag down an outbound tractor, but its engine went dead after only 50 yards, and the radiomen helplessly drifted to the east. Yelling and waving at passing tractors netted only waves and shouts in response. The TBX was set up, as was a smaller set, and the communicators tried all frequencies without success as gunfire from the beach chased the drifting amtrac.

The only radio Dave Shoup had on hand was a small set run by Pfc John Gross, an exceptionally talented communicator who single-handedly organized a crude communications network throughout Marine-held Betio. Gross would operate without assistance for the entire first day.

Maj Hal Throneson had been carried back to the reef aboard the amtrac on which he had been shot, then transferred to an LCVP and started on what he expected to be a short ride to a nearby transport for emergency medical treatment. After what seemed an unreasonable amount of time afloat, the comfortable numbness that had sustained Throneson's hurt body wore off. He was not so much in physical pain as in mental agony, knowing only that he had been hit in the upper abdomen and left to wonder what the single round had done to his insides. Out of a morbid curiosity coupled with intense boredom, the weapons company commander spent a good deal of time probing the wound. He found one hole, but, since he could not locate a foreign object in his body, he nearly got hysterical looking for an exit wound. When he finally found the second hole, his relief was monumental.

After spending two hours aboard the LCVP, Throneson was gently transferred aboard a transport and placed with a group of wounded Marines to await his turn in the operating room. As he lay on the stretcher on deck, he noticed that the man next to him was a sergeant with whom he had shared duty in Iceland in 1941. The major lifted the man's blanket and saw a loop of entrails protruding through a large hole in the abdominal cavity. He learned later that the sergeant had been shot in the liver and had died from internal bleeding.

For a long time, and much to his surprise, Throneson felt virtually no pain. He was quite hot, however, and a bit discomforted by the wire litter on which he had been placed. Later, after being stripped for surgery, Throneson's discomfort as a result of the wire construction of the Navy litter would increase considerably. Perversely, the major fell asleep, only to be reawakened when carried into the operating room. He underwent the intense pain of a spinal and, while only too wide awake, was probed and prodded and rearranged. And sewn up. Maj Hal Throneson had suffered no great internal injury and would live to fight another day.

Father Frank Kelly was happy after four hours of circling beyond the reef to get word that he would be allowed to make his way to the beach. Going all the way in aboard an LCVP was out of the question, of course, but the Navy coxswain managed to drop the priest and his clerk, Cpl Dan Goetz, a former machine gunner, among the crates and men at the pierhead, from which they began walking lightheartedly toward the beach. No one had told the priest that the pier itself was a deathtrap; he and Goetz walked a charmed 200 yards, halfway to the beach, before gunfire drove them into chest-deep water. Chaplain Kelly was still carrying his bundle of goodies for the wounded and his Mass kit. By then, however, he knew very well that there would be no Mass of Thanksgiving on Betio this day. After dropping both bundles off at an aid station, Kelly made his way to Dave Shoup's CP, where he was a welcome but unnecessary guest. There was nothing an unarmed priest could do to turn the tide of battle, but he was certainly welcome to try.

In the hours before landing, PhM3 Harold Blank had been cocky. Now he was badly shaken and a little mad. He had been lied to from the outset. Betio was *not* a milk run. The constant stream of wounded and dead pouring into his beachside aid station attested to that.

Blank became angrier as time went on. To the corpsmen on Red-2, it was just a matter of patching the wounded as they arrived, playing God over who might live and who might not and making them as comfortable as possible as long as space and drugs held out. It had been bad at the start, and it was getting worse. As more and more wounded collected at the seaside aid station—a large steel sheet set against a wall—a Japanese sniper took notice. At length, he was zinging a round in every few seconds. And Harold Blank kept getting angrier and angrier. There were rifles lying loose all over the place, and Blank was about to grab one and go after the sniper, when the surgeon talked him out of it. The medical team had suffered its share of the 2nd Battalion, 2nd's losses and could not afford to lose Blank merely because he was bitched off at a sniper.

There was only one reserve landing team left, Maj Larry Hays's 1st Battalion, 8th. And it looked as though it would have to be landed in the early afternoon. The only other troops were gunners, pioneers, Seabees, communicators, tankers, MPs, clerks and technicians. But for Hays's battalion, there was no more infantry under Division control. MGen Holland

Smith would have to release the 6th Marines from Force Reserve to keep the specialists from going ashore as infantry. Unapprised of events at Makin, MGen Julian Smith decided to wait a while longer before asking for the 6th Marines.

Pvt Leland Ziegenhagen was getting frustrated. He had managed to stay with his company commander, 1stLt Jim Motley, of I Company, 8th, certain that Motley could wangle a ride ashore if anyone could. After transferring to a tractor from an LCM, the small group led by Motley had begun numerous runs to the beach but had been turned back time and again. The troops were bitching and feeling down until one of them reasoned aloud that they were being held from the battle to ease the burden of having to evacuate all the men who had already landed. No one knew whether or not he was kidding.

The supply situation was in total chaos, stemming largely from planning that had been based on two fallacious assumptions: sufficient water over the reef and a rapid victory.

Had there been enough water over the reef, a number of conditions that did exist would have been obviated, chiefly the enormous losses among assault and support units. There would not have been fewer Japanese alive on Betio, but the odds would have been far different if more men and supplies could have been landed by boat.

There was a very real fear that skimpy supplies of ammunition might be exhausted; holding back a reserve supply meant that troop leaders would have to be conservative in pushing attacks, where there was a choice to be made.

Fearing rapid and strong reprisals by Japanese fleet units based in the Marshalls and Marianas, particularly a sally by Japanese fleet carriers, the transport commanders were loath to hold anything that was volatile aboard their ships for a moment longer than was necessary. This was the chief lesson they had learned in the Solomons, and it was something they were doing their level best to master. At Betio, the fear was more real than the possibility, but the race to unload munitions was clogging the flow of supplies to the beach, not helping it.

The movement of supplies to the beach was the responsibility of Comdr John McGovern, who was aboard *Pursuit* at the Line of Departure. Once the supplies reached the beach, they were to become the responsibility of the Squadron Beachmaster, LCdr Lou Fabian, who had been hand picked for the job by the task force commander, RAdm Harry Hill. Initially, Fabian was to operate his own beach party and control smaller parties from six ships. Fabian's group was to act as liason between the Marines and the transports and regulate the flow of goods across the beaches to inland dumps, where they would pass to the responsibility of Marine pioneers from LtCol Chester Salazar's 2nd Battalion, 18th.

That's what it looked like on paper. The dodging tide, the unassailable Japanese defenses, and the rush to unload cargoes made for a very different set of problems than any that had been anticipated by the most negative planners.

LCdr Lou Fabian had been assigned to the fifth boat wave and specifically ordered to land only if a secure beachhead had been established. Nothing was more apparent as the fifth wave started for the island than the fact that a secure beachhead had *not* been established, so Fabian's coxswain was ordered by a control officer to pull out of the line of boats; no beachmaster was needed yet.

There was one thing Fabian *could* do. He was still Squadron Beachmaster, and the power he might have exercised on the beach was urgently needed to unsnarl the tangle of boats beyond the reef. And what a tangle! No one had really taken the dodging tide warnings seriously, and very few men in authority had been apprised of them as yet. Order was needed, and Lou Fabian was just the man to restore it.

Many people were working at serious cross purposes, even though their intentions were good. Ships kept loading boats with unnecessary gear. Then the boats would be ordered to stand clear, and no ship's captain was about to reload goods. Junior boat officers who took initiative often found their efforts stymied by more senior officers who did not yet realize the effects of their constantly changing directives. It was madness, and Lou Fabian was in the middle of it. His only advantage was that no one could countermand any of his directives, not even his superiors, for he was directly responsible to Admiral Hill.

But it was a losing fight, for more and more boats full of junk kept arriving. And more and more of them drifted helplessly onto the reef. In spite of his efforts, Lou Fabian was no more than a waterborne traffic cop at rush hour, with the traffic lights out.

• • •

After transferring a load of casualties to an outbound boat in the late afternoon, Lt Galen Brown, *Heywood's* boat group officer, received an urgent message from a Marine officer at the pierhead asking Brown to pick up a vital written message that could not be transmitted. The pierhead at that moment was under extremely heavy gunfire, so the approach was made with all hands except Brown and his coxswain sitting on the deck. The boat was hit by bullets from many guns but managed to come alongside a Japanese barge tied up at the eastern arm of the pierhead. The Marine officer, a haggard youth who was in the Japanese boat, gave Brown a gruesome rundown of the situation ashore. One of Brown's passengers, Lt(jg) Larry Crane, *Heywood's* beachmaster, asked the Marine if he should call in his beach party, which was embarked on another boat, and try to get something going at the pierhead. The Marine allowed as how that might be a waste of lives in view of the gunfire sweeping the platform. However, he did ask Crane to see about getting ammunition into the beaches, adding that all other types of gear would *not* be appreciated.

Brown's boat backed off and headed for a nearby destroyer with the situation report. The fire was so intense that Larry Crane, who was sitting on the deck again and could see nothing, actually yelled, "Hey, Brown! For Christ's sake, will you stop paralleling the shore and get out of here!"

The shocking, candid view of the fighting ashore was passed up to the destroyer and transmitted by blinker to *Maryland*.

As soon as Lieutenant Brown had passed along the message, he decided to do something about the ammunition. He assumed that it would be easy to locate cargoes of it aboard the boats milling about near the reef, but every boat Brown waylaid was found to have five or six different types of cargo aboard, ranging from the impractical to the foolish to the bizarre. At length, out of sheer frustration, he ordered the crew of one boat, which had *some* ammunition aboard, to jettison everything else and get it to the pierhead. In time, he sent every such boat to the pierhead. The crews willingly braved the fire. With the assistance of a scratch team of volunteers, mainly Marines, they transferred the precious supplies to the backs of men willing to wade to the beach.

• • •

Father Frank Kelly and the 2nd Regiment's surgeon, Dr. Don Nelson, had a problem with corpses already decomposing in the intense heat. When everyone still thought Betio would be a milk run, it had been decided to evacuate the dead to nearby Bairiki Island for burial. That was manifestly impossible; many of the *wounded* could not be evacuated!

With Colonel Shoup's concurrence, the padre and Rev. Norman Darling began interring the fallen in a small bit of level ground directly behind the Regimental CP. It was a job that had to be done, for reasons of morale as well as for health considerations. A cemetery was hurriedly laid out, and the chaplains and their clerks got to work. It was an enormous task.

Marines began bringing in their dead buddies as soon as the word got out. Amidst the flow of maimed and bloated dead was a weighted poncho slung between two grim-faced young riflemen. Father Kelly looked into the dead man's face and felt his entire being start. So! He would be administering a good "left-handed" burial for his friend, LtCol Herb Amey.

During his first hours ashore, Dave Shoup managed to assemble a picture of the situation on the beaches: He was getting virtually nowhere, and his communications were so incredibly poor that he could not begin to provide a detailed report to MGen Julian Smith. At 1230, it was decided to send a senior officer to *Maryland* to deliver a first hand verbal account to the Division Commander. Shoup chose LtCol Evans Carlson; the former Raider was an observer with no crucial job ashore, and he had the rank and personality to get the job done.

Shoup's message was strikingly clear: He was going to hold his beachhead no matter what happened. He need reinforcements badly. He needed supplies. He wanted the reinforcements to land on the eastern portion of Red-2.

Carlson readily agreed to the trip and asked Shoup to secure an amtrac for him. Shoup came through, but before Carlson made his journey to The Flag, he gathered several tractorloads of waiting, apathetic Marines from around the pierhead and shuttled them to the beach. Eventually, he transferred from the tractor to an outbound LCVP and made his way to *Pursuit*, then took another boat to *Zeilin* and a third boat to the battleship, where he was escorted directly into the Division CP. Within minutes of arriving, Carlson was speaking with Julian

Smith and his chief of staff, Col Merritt Edson, who had commanded a Raider battalion at the same time as Carlson.

Evans Carlson's verbal account galvanized Division into action it had not previously thought necessary. The clincher was Dave Shoup's determination to hold at any cost. Almost as soon as Carlson finished talking, General Smith radioed *Monrovia* and ordered his assistant division commander, BGen Leo Hermle, to immediately move his Division Forward CP to the beach.

Moments after Dutch Hermle was ordered to land, Julian Smith contacted his corps commander, MGen Holland Smith, and asked that the 6th Marines be released to 2nd Marine Division from Force Reserve. Holland Smith needed time to check more closely on the situation at Makin, which left the 2nd Division staff with tense minutes to kill. If Holland Smith said no, the special troops would be sent ashore as riflemen. That was at 1331.

In anticipation of an affirmative, The Flag contacted Col Elmer Hall of the 8th Marines at 1343. Hall, who was aboard *Sheridan*, was ordered to prepare his command group and the 1st Battalion, 8th, for a move to the Line of Departure, where he was to await final instructions from The Flag. The last remnant of 2nd Marine Division's authorized reserves would be going ashore, whether or not the 6th Marines was released.

Dutch Hermle radioed *Maryland* just as Colonel Hall was receiving his orders; Division Forward was in a boat and ready to go. Julian Smith ordered Hermle to sail for the pierhead, make an estimate of the situation and report findings to The Flag. A recent message from Col Dave Shoup indicated that Maj Tommy Tompkins, an assistant division operations officer already ashore, was on the way to meet Hermle at the pierhead.

Hermle next attempted to contact the beach to find out exactly where Dave Shoup had established his CP, in the event he missed his connection with Major Tompkins. However, there was no response from the beach.

Second Marine Division had its response from Corps by 1400: Holland Smith released the 6th Marines.

15

After spending nearly two hours at the reef under intermittent shellfire, 2ndLt Bill Howell, a platoon leader with C Company, 1st Battalion, 2nd, was ordered into one of eight LVTs his battalion commander, Maj Wood Kyle, waylaid in the lagoon.

The eight tractors set off slowly for Red-2 under the leadership of Capt Jim Clanahan, the C Company commander; the troops were to join with A and B Companies to begin a drive inland from the beach.

As Lieutenant Howell scanned the island with his binoculars, he spotted a tractor drifting on the far side of the reef. In it were two squads of A Company riflemen, some waving and shouting. Howell waved back, failing to comprehend that the A Company Marines were trying to warn him to expect a hot reception.

C Company moved westward, tractors abreast, to a point off the left half of Red-2 and executed a 90-degree turn to port. Seven tractors completed the maneuver and waddled southward in line. The eighth tractor had been damaged and could not turn left, so it made a 270-degree turn to the right and followed the others by several lengths.

Maj Wood Kyle, commander of the 1st Battalion, 2nd, waylaid another outbound tractor at about 1230, left D Company and most of his command group in the hands of his exec, and started for the beach. The only men with Kyle were his battalion intelligence officer, two radiomen, and two runners. If the battalion was to launch an attack, Kyle wanted to lead it.

Lt Bill Howell was frantically swiveling his tractor's .50-caliber machine gun in quest of a target, but all he could see were hundreds of Marines sprawled on the beach. The amtrac slowed 50 yards from the beach; its driver, who had been along the route before, was having serious doubts. One of Howell's line sergeants kicked the man squarely in the back of his helmet. The tractor picked up a little speed but grounded on the sandy bottom within moments.

Bill Howell leaped overboard as soon as the tractor stopped. As he cleared the side, he saw that he was coming right down on a dead Marine, so he wrenched away and clumsily splashed into the water beside the corpse. The next man over the side lunged to Howell's aid, certain the platoon leader had been shot. Howell clambered to the seawall as two squads of his riflemen expectantly deployed around him.

The remainder of C Company landed all around. The troops were hardly ashore before the tractors hauled clear of the beach.

Without waiting to be told what to do, Capt Jim Clanahan accosted the first officer he saw to get directions to the CP of the 2nd Battalion, 2nd; then he moved inland with most of C Company at his heels. Moments after Clanahan accepted orders from LtCol Irvine Jordan, he moved westward, contacted Capt Bill Bray's A Company, and went in on Bray's right.

Bill Howell did not see the rest of C Company take off, but he soon noticed that he was alone with his two squads. He reported to Capt Maxie Williams of B Company and asked for a mission. Williams told Howell that a covey of Japanese holed up in a nearby pillbox was tossing grenades across B Company's route of advance; the pillbox was Howell's, if he wanted it.

As soon as he got his bearings, Bill Howell ordered two men over the wall—directly into the detonations of several Japanese hand grenades. As the two slid back down behind the wall, Howell moved to help them, and found himself pushing one man's eye back into its socket. Fortunately, a corpsman took over before Howell really thought about what he was doing. The Marine would lose the eye.

The pillbox beckoned. Cpl Charles Rosales, a Guadalcanal veteran, volunteered to take it out. The assistant squad leader pulled the pins from two hand grenades and charged over the wall. A pair of explosions rocked the beach, and moments later a grinning Corporal Rosales reemerged.

* * *

Regiment began planning a drive as soon as C Company, 2nd, had landed. It was imperative to expand the holdings on Red-2 beyond the northwest taxiway, both for breathing room and for security in the event of a counterattack. Maj Tom Culhane, the regimental operations officer, began spreading the word among the active elements of the 1st Battalion, 2nd: Push inland as far as possible.

Orders are only orders. Although its widely separated elements had already seized some new ground, Kyle's battalion had been thoroughly shaken by the butchery it had already experienced. Most of the men decided to stay behind the seawall.

Then one man decided it was time to get going. His mind made up, 1stSgt Wilbur Burgess of A Company pulled himself to his feet, vaulted over the wall, and paced up and down in front of the cowering riflemen. Burgess read Marines off wherever he found them, whether he knew them or not. The bullets plowing in around him never got a rise out of the enraged top; he had 168 years of Marine Corps tradition behind his actions. His total disregard for the bullets aimed at him impressed many, but it did not get them moving. Finally, Burgess's chastisements ceased. He looked down his nose and slowly eyed the clumps of fearful men. Then the top's lips curled back in utter disdain, and he uttered the famous words of an earlier Marine Corps hero, Dan Dailey at Belleau Wood: "Whatsa matter? Ya wanna live forever?"

They moved because they were too beaten not to move. Singly and in pairs, they got up, gulped their throats clear, tightened sweaty grips on their rifles, and strode into the fire.

Men who had not heard Burgess's words saw what looked like an organized drive, or a breakthrough, and they took heart. There were not many at first, but there were more than there had been minutes earlier, and many more would follow.

Pfc Dick Clark found himself in the open, drawn forward by Top Burgess's words. Clark's group was taking fire from two sides, dropping off the dead, the wounded, the faint of heart. Before he realized it, Dick Clark was on the southern edge of the taxiway in an area littered with disabled Japanese trucks. There were a number of log aircraft revetments, but there appeared to be no Japanese—at least, none that Dick Clark could *see*. The gunfire forced Clark's group into one of the revetments. There, young Marines came face to face with their enemy. Several wounded Japanese were sprawled along the revetment's inner wall. One made his move, and Dick Clark sprayed all the bodies with his BAR.

Maj Wood Kyle reached the left half of Red-2 at about 1400 and dispatched one of his runners to find the Regimental CP while he tried to find his rifle companies. Kyle came upon Capt Maxie Williams's CP, where he gained radio contact with C Company's Capt Jim Clanahan. When Kyle realized that his battalion had been pretty well dismembered, he moved his tiny command group to the center of the beachhead and sought to regain control.

While elements of A and B Companies were gaining ground all along the front, elements of D Company, 2nd, began straggling in at about 1500 hours. The first D Company machine gun unit to land was 2ndLt John Terrell's 3rd Platoon, which had become disorganized in the water. The section under Terrell's platoon sergeant remained on the beach, where it eventually joined C Company, and Terrell's section advanced inland.

As Lieutenant Terrell led his men across the taxiway, the section was accosted by a larger Japanese group, and a hand-to-hand brawl broke out, every man for himself. Terrell and several gunners were cut down, as were some Japanese. The Marines gave ground. Later, after the Japanese had gone, the gunners moved to reclaim their dead and wounded. They found John Terrell's body mutilated almost beyond recognition.

WO Perry Hall's section of 81mm mortars crossed the seawall almost as soon as it landed. Hall, a Guadalcanal veteran, moved ahead of the group to find a suitable position for an observation post, but he soon took a round squarely in the gut and fell helplessly with arms and legs paralyzed; the bullet had passed completely through his body. As soon as Hall fell, several of his gunners moved to retrieve him. So did a group of Japanese. A brief firefight ensued and Hall was further wounded by American grenade fragments. His subordinates, however, won the fight and hauled the wounded gunner back to the beach for treatment. Perry Hall's ordeal was far from over, however.

After Hall's wounds were dressed, he was tagged for evacuation, inexpertly dumped on a litter, and carried to the stone jetty by the base of the main pier. A Japanese machine gun opened fire on the litter team as it neared its objective and sawed off one of the litter's wooden handles. No one was hit, but helpless, hapless Perry Hall was dropped onto the jagged rocks.

Lt Bill Howell was lucky to get two squads to the northern taxiway intact. He had lost only two men wounded since landing, and he felt good about his prospects. The understrength platoon made contact at the taxiway with two light machine gun squads, some intelligence people, and several B Company riflemen. There was also a lieutenant from the division staff and a Marine combat artist. These men agreed to form up under Howell's command.

As Howell searched for a way across the expanse of the main runway, he spotted a pair of Marine light tanks nearby. He was about to send a runner to enlist their aid, when the entire sector was blanketed by airborne machine gun fire. A flight of Navy F6F Hellcat fighters, clearly unapprised of the situation on land, was running opposition for the advance—more than they knew. Fortunately, Cpl Charles Rosales had a fluorescent yellow marker panel, which he calmly rolled into a tight little tube and sailed forward to the rifleman sitting in the hole closest to the edge of the open runway. The rifleman caught the panel and proceeded to lay it out, standing in the open and smoothing out the creases as if he were setting out an expensive linen tablecloth. The fire from above lifted before the Marine climbed back into his hole.

Nearby, Pfc Dick Clark watched amazed as the "friendly" fighters made their passes, strafing on the in run, bombing on the way out. It was impossible for the BAR-man to take his eyes from the winking yellow flashes on the leading edges of the fighters' wings.

Clark's group, which was under 2ndLt Bob Harvey, had had marker panels, but they had long since been scrapped. So the lieutenant ordered all hands to strip off their white skivvy teeshirts, with which he carefully marked the front. The strafing immediately stopped.

As soon as 2ndLt Bill Howell was safe from the friendly fighters, he decided to put the light tanks to work for him. One had been disabled by engine failure, but once the tank commander agreed to help clear Howell's front, the second tank was jockeyed up in front of Howell's small force.

Howell had just stretched out behind some logs to scan the front, when the Marine next to him uttered a soft, "Well, I'll be damned." Howell turned to see what the matter was. The Marine removed his helmet and showed the officer a hole dead center in the front. There was a similar hole in the back. The Marine shrugged and clapped the helmet back on his head, surely ready for anything.

With about 15 men trailing close behind, Bill Howell stood just in back of the light tank and guided the slowly moving hulk by means of the phone attached to the rear fender. Fire stitched the front of the tank and the ground on either side, but no man behind the vehicle was touched. Then the Marines started to panic; the tank was moving too slowly for them. Someone broke away and ran all out for a large mound near the center of the triangle formed by the taxiways and the main runway. The others followed. As Bill Howell took off, he saw the first man reach the mound and slam his body into the coral sand before rising to a kneeling position, the better to fervently cross himself and utter oblivious Hail Marys. Magically, upwards of 40 men appeared behind the mound, including Capt Maxie Williams, who took charge.

The force was small, little more than a platoon, and an uncohesive one at that. Captain Williams counted two rifle squads under Bill Howell, several more depleted squads from B Company, the survivors of a machine gun section, and a mixed bag of individuals. Several small knots of B Company Marines were scattered between the mound and the taxiway, now far to the rear.

To Williams's right, between 40 and 60 Marines from A Company, more or less under the control of Capt Bill Bray, occupied scattered positions between the center of the triangle and the northwest taxiway. Stragglers from G and F Companies and various support units were interspersed among the A Company groups. There were no Americans to Williams's left for a distance of about 100 yards. Beyond the gap were scattered mixed elements of the 2nd and 3rd Battalions, 8th, which had penetrated inland from Red-3. To Williams and Bray's rear were the bulk of Capt Jim Clanahan's C Company and scattered elements of the rest of the 1st Battalion, 2nd.

Farther back still was the main body of survivors of the 2nd Battalion, 2nd.

The danger lay not in the small number of Marines in the triangle but in the fact that reinforcement or relief could be stopped by a network of defenders thoroughly alerted to the dangers of allowing too great a build-up so close to their own secondary defenses. The Japanese had managed to cover the open ground with a large number of automatic weapons, no doubt stripped from emplacements along the southern beaches and placed in deep, well-hidden burrows.

When Captain Williams ordered Lieutenant Howell to string his men across the taxiway late that afternoon, Howell refused, on the grounds that his force had survived scathing fire getting across that open ground and would have no chance of doing so again. He did offer to make the move after nightfall, but Williams shook his head; anyone moving after dark would be assumed to be Japanese. Until reinforcements could get into the area, fewer than 150 Marines in the vicinity of the triangle were on their own, cut off from the rest of the invasion forces.

16

Several days after the fighting at Tarawa had ended, *Chicago Times* correspondent Keith Wheeler referred to the elements of the 3rd Battalion, 2nd, on Red-1 as "The Lost Battalion." In a literal sense, Wheeler, who was with the headquarters group, was correct: Maj Mike Ryan's mixed force on the western one-third of Red-1 was physically isolated from the remainder of 2nd Marine Division. But no unit on Betio made a better accounting for itself on D-Day. That those gains could not be adequately exploited was the fault of poor communications and dire emergencies elsewhere.

In the morning, shortly after Maj John Schoettel informed Col Dave Shoup that he was unable to land, the battalion command boat came upon six LCMs bearing the 1st Platoon of the IMAC Medium Tank Company. Major Schoettel ordered his boat alongside the command LCM, conferred briefly with 1stLt Ed Bale, the tank company commander, and ordered the armor to land as quickly as possible.

The tanks debouched onto the reef and followed a reconnaissance team sent ahead to guide them over hundreds of yards of unseen obstacles. The recon team worked diligently under heavy fire, guiding the tanks by means of signal flags. Many of the guides were shot, but other men always sprang to their places. None of the six tanks was lost on the way in.

As the six medium tanks approached the beach, it was found that the only break in the seawall was choked with injured Marines, many of whom could not be safely moved. The only option was for the tanks to drive through the surf and swing around the wall's left flank. Four tanks were abandoned in shellholes of varying depths during the move parallel to the beach. The survivors were *Chicago* and *China Gal*, the latter under the company commander, Lieutenant Bale.

115

That was at 1110. As soon as the two mediums arrived on dry land, they were accosted by several haggard riflemen. One was 1stLt Ott Schulte, who asked Lieutenant Bale to knock out several Japanese emplacements that were endangering the left flank of his isolated K Company platoon. The targets were in the beach boundary strongpoint, a heavily built-up area along the eastern arm of the Red-1 U. Many 75mm rounds were used to blot out one particularly dangerous bunker, then, after dropping off a pair of machine guns to bolster Schulte's defenses, Bale moved his tanks toward the main beachhead.

Pfc Dirk Offringa spent nearly three hours huddled behind the seawall with the survivors of his 81mm mortar squad before it was decided to set up the gun. The squad advanced a short distance inland and braced the weapon in the soft sand at the bottom of a deep shellhole. There was no fire control, but the crew decided to get off a few rounds to show the Japanese that there were heavy weapons on the beach. After the mortarmen fired several rounds indiscriminately beyond their position, they noticed a badly hurt Marine struggling back toward the northern beach. No word passed between the gunners and the wounded man, but everyone in the shellhole realized that their mortar might have inflicted the rifleman's wounds. If they had not hit him, they might have hit other Marines. The firing ceased.

Shortly after midday, at about the time Offringa's squad was firing, 2ndLt John Cannon's half-platoon came under direct, patternless mortar fire. One shell landed ten feet to the platoon leader's right. A large fragment nearly knocked Cannon's carbine from his hands while another steel sliver neatly sliced open the lieutenant's right boondocker, exposing his toes without inflicting injury. Cannon and his men dived for cover and remained immobile until the firing stopped minutes later.

When John Cannon reemerged from his cover, he could find only six of his men. It had been three hours since he had seen anything of the rest of I Company, 2nd, so he ordered his runner, Pvt Charles Hotchkiss, to go to the rear and report his position and get some ammunition and grenades. Hotchkiss returned within minutes to inform Cannon that the company commander had been killed, 1stLt Sam Turner had taken command, casualties had been heavy, and there was no ammunition to be spared. Cannon grimly nodded and ordered his tiny group to move out. They were already 300 yards inland, about 100 yards from the western beach, Beach Green, and they managed to move another 50 yards by zigzagging from tree stump to shellhole to low hummock to tree stump. As Cannon leaped into one hole, he felt a sharp tug on his pack. The next day he would find that a bullet had put 32 holes through his neatly folded poncho. The advance stopped there.

The heat of the day had wrung the energy from Pfc Jim Goldman and his buddy, Pfc Bob Mahaffey. The two had been sitting in a shell crater alone and untroubled by the Japanese for hours. When they finally used up all their water, Goldman spotted a canteen on the belt of a dead Marine nearby. Since there had been no shooting for a very long time, Goldman conned Mahaffey into fetching the water. As Goldman watched, horrified, a very patient Japanese sniper who had lain dormant for hours shot Mahaffey dead.

The 3rd Battalion, 2nd, was fortunate in having even two medium tanks covering its advance. Although there was only so much the two mediums could accomplish, they gave the riflemen an enormous boost in confidence when word got around that the tanks were helping to overcome some difficult situations. Luck, however, was something less than certain. After advancing nearly 400 yards from the seawall, *China Gal* struck up a duel with a smaller Japanese tank. Almost as soon as the first rounds were traded, the American medium's turret traverse mechanism was damaged. Its gun out of commission, *China Gal* raced forward and collided with the Japanese gun, which snapped off its precious 75mm gun. Lieutenant Ed Bale ordered his driver to make for the beach, leaving the fight to *Chicago*. To the sheer amazement of hundreds of onlookers, the plucky Japanese tank gunner set the second American tank afire with one round.

No one on Red-1 knew where Maj John Schoettel was. A few cryptic messages had been received from the battalion commander in the hour or two following H-Hour, but no one knew where he was. And, except for the times he gained contact, no one had time to worry.

A verbal radio message was received at Col Dave Shoup's

CP at 1458: "CP located on the back of Red Beach One. Situation as before. Have lost contact with assault elements."

Before Shoup could respond to Schoettel, *Maryland* cut in: "Direct you land at any cost, regain control of your battalion, and continue the attack." The message was signed "Smith."

First Lieutenant Ott Schulte had landed with about 30 men, and nearly 25 had already been wounded. A great deal of ammunition had been used to keep the Japanese at bay. By early afternoon, stocks within the tiny toehold were dangerously low.

Schulte would have liked to assault a pillbox-protected machine gun that had his troops pinned. He had thought it was out of action following the providential appearance of the two medium tanks earlier in the afternoon, but it had begun firing after more than an hour of silence. About the only thing the platoon leader could do was strengthen his lines and redistribute ammunition. He certainly could not mount an assault; he did not even have enough able bodies to haul the wounded toward the sound of heavy firing, far to the right.

Given no other option, the wounded officer asked GySgt Robert Van Buskirk to help redistribute the dwindling supply of bullets and redeploy a few of the men to better advantage. After visiting most of the men on the narrow shelf of beach, Schulte and Van Buskirk found themselves sprinting toward a small group of foxholes near a partially blown overwater latrine. Schulte, on the inland side, was gauging his leap for one of the holes, when a single shot rang out. Van Buskirk yelled and pitched himself into the nearest foxhole. He had been shot through the neck (but not seriously injured). Schulte dived head-first into another hole, landing on an effete-looking replacement who had troubled his mind since joining the platoon in New Zealand.

The lieutenant found that he still had his .45-caliber automatic pistol, but each time he lifted his head to get a sighting on the sniper, a bullet plowed into the foxhole's parapet. Schulte finally realized that the fire was coming from the latrine, ten yards to his rear.

As Schulte cast about for a safe way to turn and fire, he became aware that the Marine under him was facing the latrine and that he had a BAR. Schulte told the boy to fire three quick rounds into the lower half of the latrine structure—just three, for no more could be spared.

The Marine braced, then bolted to a sitting position and opened fire. Schulte counted three rounds and began to get to his knees for a better look. A full burst exploded an inch from the officer's ear. "What in the goddamned hell did you do that for?" The BAR-man shrugged and grinned, then explained in the most nerveless voice Schulte had ever heard, "Aw gee, Sir, that's the way Dick Tracy does it."

As Pfc Jim Goldman sat alone in his foxhole contemplating a bubble of blood ballooning from a hole in the chest of a lung-shot Japanese, his attention was diverted to an approaching Marine. The man looked disturbingly familiar and completely out of place. Then it registered. Goldman was face to face with a hometown buddy he had not known was in the battalion. The two childhood friends spoke for a few minutes, catching up on gossip about Louisiana town life. Then the friend got up to leave in search of his unit. Goldman's mind was filled with nostalgia until a shot rang out. The friend was on the ground. Goldman ran the 30 yards to his side, but the boy was dead.

Second Lieutenant Jim Fawcett did not know any longer whom he was commanding. And he really didn't care. He had lost many good men but had picked up others along the way, and he didn't care who they were as long as they filled a need. What mattered was whipping the *rigosentai* who held Red-1.

Fawcett's veteran platoon sergeant had been killed leading an attack across an open stretch of ground. The platoon's second-ranking sergeant, the right guide, had just been led to the rear, complaining of extreme nausea following his emergence from a particularly furious shell blast. (The sergeant, who had not one mark on him, died an agonizing death from massive internal hemorrhaging induced by the blast.)

Hours after reaching the edge of the cleared expanse across the center of the island, Fawcett's Marines fought their way into the first antitank ditch on the southern half of Betio. By that time, Fawcett's southwesterly heading had carried him to within 150 yards of Green Beach, the closest unit of Marines to the so-called Singapore Gun, the bunker housing a pair of Vickers 8-inch naval rifles guarding the southwestern tip of Betio. The huge multistory concrete bombproof, which had been wrecked in the pre-invasion bombardment, was Fawcett's objective by default.

After dodging extremely heavy fire from more than 50 Japanese, most of Fawcett's men took cover in the ditch. At best, there were 40 exposed Marines facing an entrenched enemy. Fawcett had no supporting arms at all, just rifles and grenades.

The gun was to the right front, about 160 yards away. Midway between Fawcett and the battery was another antitank ditch, which sealed off that corner of the island. Another 100 feet on was a Y-shaped trench. Its open end faced Fawcett, and the stem of the Y led downward right behind the concrete-encased steel turrets. There were at least four medium fieldpieces around the battery and a profusion of pillboxes and one- and two-man rifle pits.

Fawcett's scratch platoon fired its rifles and BARs and took off, only to be stopped after light gains by increasing fire from the defenders. Fawcett elected to try again. The men took off. They made slightly better gains this time but were driven to cover once again. Jim Fawcett hoped that his Marines still had some fight left in them when he ordered another sally. The platoon charged forward with a final burst of energy and got nearly as far as the first intervening antitank ditch. Two riflemen and a BAR-man got to the ditch itself.

Fawcett started to send a flamethrower team to the ditch, but he realized that it would still be a hundred feet from the guns, out of range. Grenades were of no use. The three men in the ditch had cleaned out several nearby emplacements, but they seemed to be cut off from the platoon's main body by heavy Japanese fire.

As Fawcett sat trying to find a solution to the puzzle, he was joined by K Company's commander, Capt Jim Crain, who ordered him to take part in a general withdrawal to a more defensible line to the north. Before Fawcett would consider such a move, he had to try to extricate the three men from the ditch ahead. He sent a volunteer to explain the plan and lead the way, then ordered the fiercest fire his group could manage to cover the men. Three of the four Marines bolted to the rear, but only two made it. Then the BAR-man, who had elected to cover the others, made his bid. He was pitched into the dirt only yards from safety. A half-dozen men moved to recover him, wounded but alive. The injured BAR-man rode piggyback on another Marine as Fawcett's group managed a slow withdrawal to the northwest.

Groups of Marines were buttoning up all over Red-3. Lt John Cannon had been stopped cold in a copse about 350 yards south of the beach. Artillery, mortar and rifle fire had him and his half-dozen Marines pulled in tight. They had not heard from anyone in hours. As darkness approached, Cannon decided that he required instructions. Once again, Pvt Charles Hotchkiss was sent to the rear for help, but he returned with news that no reinforcements were available. Cannon shrugged off his dismay and ordered his men to keep still, for a small knot of figures was approaching from the left rear, walking upright. The group included Maj Mike Ryan, the beach commander.

Mike Ryan's battalion—and it was *his* battalion—was badly chopped up. Even if it had been able to secure the southern beach, it was doubtful that it would have been able to hold it. Most of Ryan's 600 or so Marines were holding an area 600 yards long on a north-south axis and about 150 yards wide. That was spreading limited resources to the breaking point.

Major Ryan gathered Lieutenant Cannon's team and odd stragglers and led them northward about 100 yards, then ordered Cannon to dig in along a line already alive with the activity of dozens upon dozens of other Marines. Lt Ed Bale's *China Gal* was on Cannon's left. Its only weapon was its .30-caliber bow machine gun.

When John Cannon asked for a machine gun of his own, Mike Ryan bluntly told him that he had none to spare and that Cannon's BAR would have to suffice. However, Private Hotchkiss, the runner, said he knew where a gun and crew had been an hour earlier. Ryan wheeled and asked the runner to go find it. The gun was 200 yards to the south and its crew eagerly pulled back at Hotchkiss's suggestion to join Cannon's platoon.

Other members of Cannon's dispersed platoon were buddying up and digging in all over the beachhead. Pfc Jim Goldman, who was still grieving over the loss of his boyhood friend, went to ground with Pfc Johnny Byots. Neither of them had any notion as to where the rest of the platoon was, so they shared the dreadful thought that they were its only survivors.

Another group from Cannon's platoon was looking for good positions for the night, when a stranger came by and told them that an I Company Marine had been shot nearby. Pfc Dale Young, a BAR-man, collared the platoon corpsman, PhM3 Harold "Tex" Lingofelter, and went off to find the man, who turned out to be a member of Young's squad. Doc Lingofelter bore most of the wounded man's weight so Dale Young could cover them, and the three rushed back over 50 yards of open ground. The injured private, who had been shot through the shoulder early in the day, kept repeating that a Japanese tank had passed right over him. He was placed on an old door and hauled back to the beach by four of his buddies, apologizing the whole way for being a burden.

Maj Mike Ryan's troops were hot, thirsty, hungry, bleeding, aching, and dying. There had been no news of relief or reinforcements. There was little contact of any sort with the outside world. The nearest help on Betio was over 600 yards to the east, across the toughest defensive strongpoint on the island. There was no telling whether friendly forces might decide to shell occupied ground in the hope of assisting Ryan.

The only thing anyone could count on was a night attack by the Japanese. The only way to resist such an encounter was to establish a strong, integrated defensive position. So, at the expense of a bit of indefensible, tenuously held ground, the remnants of the 3rd Battaion, 2nd, pulled back and prepared for anything.

17

First Lieutenant Robert Rogers, commanding E Company, 8th, on Red-3, had his orders; Maj Jim Crowe had told him to get across the seawall. Rogers had nearly 30 Marines to do the job, including several riflemen from G Company, a few stragglers, and a .30-caliber machine gun squad.

After working out a route of advance following a careful survey of the front, Rogers gave the signal and led the way. Not one of his 30 men showed the slightest hesitation. Opposition was surprisingly light through the largely unfortified axis of their advance, and there were other small groups of Marines covering the first 50 yards.

The initial advance carried the group to the main taxi apron at the angle of the taxiways. There had been no casualties. To the front was a vast open expanse, at least 100 yards square. Fire from light automatic weapons to the left made the position very hard to hold. But Rogers had no intention of holding; his orders read "Advance!" Large craters pocked the open area, so it was duck and bob and weave and dive all the way across. First one man took off, zigzagged, and dived for a hole. Then a second, by a slightly different route. Then the first again, and a third, until dozens of random patterns had been played out to confuse the enemy. Gains were measured in feet, more feet, yards, and tens of yards. Sometimes left, other times right. Once in a while, it was prudent to move a few yards back to gain a safer route. A few men were hit, and others lost nerve. Finally, the group, now numbering 20, reached a large trench and building. The Japanese holding them were killed in a brief fight. Lieutenant Rogers decided that he had gained the best possible position, so he stopped and deployed his men.

In the 75 minutes between 1100 and 1215, the Marines assaulting due east toward the huge covered bunker were held to extremely small gains. Three mixed platoons suffered crippling casualties to intense fire from the main objective and outlying buildings. The Japanese were moving dozens of fresh defenders through the rubble that covered the area, and the fire was building in intensity with each passing minute. The Marines managed to set fire to a number of the log outbuildings, but the Japanese simply moved outdoors to prepared trenchworks or sniped from the ruins. In the end, the American assault gave way to the spirited defense, and the survivors moved back to regroup and await further orders.

Jim Crowe contacted Division at 1229: "Resistance stiffening. Request strafing."

The resistance was indeed stiffening. The Japanese had had four hours to work in reinforcements from the east, a relatively easy task. Many *rigosentai* simply followed the southern beach, staying low behind the seawall, and then moved northward by way of a maze of fire and communications trenches. Others moved westward through trenches stretching across the center of the island. Unassailed by Marines to their rear, Japanese throughout Maj Jim Crowe's sector were free to shift about to escape from Marine attacks to positions from which the same attacks could be blunted.

A new threat appeared by 1234, when an urgent message from Crowe reached Division: "We have tanks to our front."

Fortunately for Crowe, four 37mm antitank guns were on the beach. As soon as word of the arrival of two tanks was passed to the antitank platoon leader, the guns were rushed to the seawall. The crews were momentarily stymied, for there was no passage through the wall. The tanks were still coming forward, although neither had fired. At length, as the tanks closed with the frantic gunners, Sgt John Hruska uttered the simplest of solutions, "Lift 'em over." There were more than enough free, eager hands to get two of the 900-pound guns over the wall and forward to the southeast flank. A few well-aimed rounds stopped one of the tanks, and the other turned tail.

Slowly, inexorably, the tide turned as 1,500 Marines sought to increase their holdings. On the right flank, Maj Jim Crowe paraded the beach, challenging and browbeating young riflemen into crossing the seawall and getting on with the fight.

On the left, Maj Bill Chamberlin, Crowe's exec, tirelessly bounded in all directions to get the troops moving.

Sgt Elmo Ferretti's assault engineer squad scrambled eastward to link up with the rifle platoon to which it had been attached for a drive on the Japanese headquarters bunker. The squad was so intent upon its work that it passed through the easternmost line of F Company, 8th, and actually reached the Burns-Philp wharf, where it went to ground in a large shellhole surrounded by three burned and twisted amtracs. Several Marines were already in the hole, and they warned the exhausted engineers to keep their heads down lest they be hit by the fire that crisscrossed the area.

Disdaining the advice, the engineers darted forward to another hole beyond the wharf. There, they came upon five stranded Marines, who told them that they were as far east on Red-3 as any other Americans.

As the engineers spoke with one of the riflemen, three others ran into the water and ducked behind a pair of beached Japanese landing barges, from which they sniped at several pillboxes just off the beach. The Japanese returned the fire. Suddenly, one of the snipers was engulfed in smoke and flame. He was dragged to the beach by his two fellow snipers and complained of serious injury. It was found that all the bullets in his web belt had been cooked off when one round had been hit by a Japanese bullet. Except for painful bruises about his waist, the man was fine.

The engineers wanted to head back, but they assented to a request by the aggressive riflemen to destroy a particularly bothersome machine gun.

As three Marine riflemen near the Japanese barges provided steady covering fire, Cpl Harry Niehoff worked forward. The TNT charges he carried were in frightful condition; their fuses were frayed, and the electrician's tape that bound them was coming unglued. But it was all he had. Niehoff ignited the fuse of the first charge with his cigarette, rose, and threw it. It was a dud, as was the second charge. The third charge blew the dugout, freeing the engineers to backtrack in the hope of joining the rest of their platoon.

Time correspondent Bob Sherrod got ashore following a long, death-filled walk from the reef. Sherrod had been scared wordless by the isolated struggles for survival he had seen every step of the way. He had found that getting to the beach was simply a matter of getting one foot out in front of the other through the *sput-sputting* geysers of machine gun bullets that had dogged his trail.

He had passed three Marines who were tinkering with a bulldozer stalled in the surf; it was needed ashore to bury pillboxes full of Japanese. And he had seen thousands of dead fish bobbing gently against the pier in the tidal swell.

Sherrod moved to the seawall, ducked low, and sprinted to a canted tractor, LVT-23, about 100 yards to the left. He saw his first dead Marine there, a young boy awash in a great sticky pool of blood on the tractor's bow. As Sherrod stared at the body, a big, loud redheaded Marine sauntered up and asked for the name of the dead man. A nearby rifleman told him, adding that the boy had just married a New Zealand girl. The redhead identified himself to Sherrod as "Crowe," and then answered the writer's first question: As far as he knew, Sherrod was the only living reporter covering the battle.

Lt Robert Rogers was right in the midst of it. The E Company commander estimated that his position was half or a third of the way across Betio, and there were Japanese all around. He had no communications with Battalion, and he was taking light-to-medium fire from the left. His 20-odd Marines were well entrenched and had sustained no casualties since going to ground. Somewhere to the rear, a young rifleman pressed into service as a runner was on his way to get help, or to die.

As Rogers passed the time taking quick peeks over the edge of the trench, he saw a large mass of brush about 50 yards to the south begin to move. It had to be a tank. Rogers kept watching, fascinated and oblivious to the danger he courted by keeping his head up. The tank ran to the west, parallel to the trench, behind a line of palms and brush. The officer cautioned his men, who were totally defenseless against the tank, to remain motionless. The tank surged past, and the tension, by then palpable, lifted somewhat.

Lieutenant Rogers consulted his watch. The runner had had more than enough time to get to the beach, give his report, and return with reinforcements. A second man was sent while the rest of the Marines waited and wondered what was to become of them.

Maj Jim Crowe had a reasonably organized line by 1300, by which time he knew that most of the six rifle and two weapons companies on Red-3 were fairly intact and viable. On the right, by the main pier, E Company held a continuous line about midway between the seawall and the northeast taxiway, with a few increments along the taxiway. Command of the company had fallen to 1stLt Aubrey Edmonds since 1stLt Robert Rogers was among the missing. Elements of G and H Companies and the 3rd Battalion, 8th, were mixed with Edmonds's troops.

On Edmonds's left, the headquarters and one platoon of Capt Steve Munson's G Company and a few stragglers from other units were holding an intermediate position.

Farther along the inland line was a mixed team of engineers, pioneers, and straggling riflemen under 1stLt Orlando Palopoli, the F Company exec.

On Palopoli's left, beyond a wide gap, were elements of K Company, two platoons of G Company, and a platoon of F Company. Most of these troops were facing east, with the K Company group's southern flank bent back a bit to the west.

Nearer the beach were the remaining elements of Capt Martin Barrett's F Company. The 1st Platoon held a line facing east between the water's edge and the seawall. Facing south were 2nd Platoon and elements of the company weapons platoon. Barrett was supported by his own 60mm mortars, a 37mm antitank gun, and a halftrack with a 75mm gun and a broken axle.

Portions of all three rifle companies of the 3rd Battalion, 8th, were strewn all over Red-3, mostly on the beach. I Company's command group was still afloat, and L Company's was operating independently near the beach. One platoon of K Company, plus assorted stragglers, was near the beach boundary. Those portions of M Company, the battalion weapons company, that had landed were parcelled out wherever needed.

Elements of two 37mm platoons of Weapons Company, 8th, had landed intact; their guns were spotted around the beachhead. Both halftracks of the 75mm platoon were immobilized. One section and platoon headquarters of the Scout-and-Sniper Platoon, 8th Marines, were guarding Maj Jim Crowe's CP. The 2nd Platoon, C Company, 18th, which had been badly mauled, was operating in roving teams throughout the beachhead. Two platoons of F Company, 18th, had been more or less disbanded to provide fillers. Some of the pioneers were with Lieutenant Palopoli, and others had been pressed into service as stretcher bearers. One group under the command of 1stLt Sandy Bonnyman had scrounged all sorts of explosives and a flamethrower and had worked its way to the front to act as assault engineers.

Elements of the 3rd Battalion, 8th, command group were ashore, but the battalion commander, Maj Robert Ruud, had been unable to land, so he had spent most of the day aboard *Pursuit* with Col Elmer Hall, commander of the 8th Marines. Ruud's exec, Maj Stanley Larsen, was at work in the water by the pier, trying to get supplies to the beach.

There was no line on Red-3, merely small mixed groups in shellholes, often 10 to 30 yards from the nearest support. The orientation of these positions was defensive.

Maj Jim Crowe began a careful redeployment of his troops at about 1300 hours. Until then, virtually all deployments had been accidental. Crowe believed that a secure toehold on the beach could be exploited to become the base for some real groundtaking.

The first part of Crowe's plan entailed a withdrawal by elements of E Company from the area between the seawall and the taxiway. The company was severely disorganized, and its sector was constantly endangered by small groups of Japanese manning bypassed emplacements. Crowe wanted the area heavily bombarded, then reoccupied in a more orderly fashion.

Mixed units on E Company's left were allowed to maintain their positions under the command of G Company's commander, Capt Steve Munson.

Groups of about 30 men from I Company and 35 from K Company were hastily thrown together under a stray company officer and pushed into a gap on the extreme right, near the base of the pier. This force was to mop up in the area and gain firm physical contact with the forces on Red-2. The most important aspect of this move was the security the group would provide for the troops who were beginning to shuttle supplies from the pierhead.

The main elements of K Company and Lieutenant Palopoli's mixed group were to remain in positions along the east and southeast flanks.

F Company's 2nd Platoon was pulled off the line to reorganize, and 1st Platoon, badly mangled in repeated bids to secure the Burns-Philp wharf, was pulled back to a secure line 30 yards from the objective.

Following these and other shifts, Crowe's beachhead was as secure as it could have been. To facilitate command, Crowe gave his exec, Maj Bill Chamberlin, full authority on the left.

With the better part of two battalions crammed into so small an area, Crowe could rely on succeeding defensive lines to blunt and turn back just about any counterattack the Japanese could muster. Many of the officers would have welcomed such an attack, for they and their troops were eager to *see* the elusive enemy and have an opportunity to whittle down the odds in a forthright manner.

While Major Crowe was reorganizing his meager holdings, men caught in areas beyond his control were frantically struggling to pull back or permanently secure their positions.

First Lieutenant Robert Rogers glanced anxiously at his watch. It was getting late, and neither of the two runners he had sent to the rear had returned. Repeated glances over the trench's parapet failed to reveal signs of any Americans nearby. Japanese fire had been coming in from the left for hours. Rogers decided that it was time to see for himself what was going on. He told 1stLt Louis Curry, a machine gun officer, to take charge and hold the trench. At the next lull in the firing, Rogers boosted himself out of the trench and took off.

Diving, ducking, bobbing, and weaving, Robert Rogers moved northward. At length, he hit a good, deep hole. The fire intensified, and Rogers decided to sit tight.

After many long minutes the fire shifted elsewhere, so Rogers sprang to his feet and zigzagged, curiously untroubled by the bullets dogging his footsteps. He was making an all-or-nothing gamble. Just as more machine guns were brought to bear against him, he spotted a deep-looking hole and made a last-gasp leap, falling ten feet to the bottom of a 16-inch shell crater. As Rogers looked up, he first saw the wide-grinning face of his colleague, Capt Steve Munson, the G Company commander. Munson's face was beaming as he gleefully described his colleague's undignified entrance. Rogers sheepishly smiled and filled Munson in on the condition and location of the men he had left with Lieutenant Curry. Then he hurried off to find Jim Crowe.

Action behind the lines was stiff, and many men were hit in "secure" areas. Sgt Ernie Butner and a half-dozen fellow radiomen had been trapped in a log pillbox almost since they had landed. Although they had gotten into the emplacement without difficulty, the Japanese eventually took notice of them and fired every time someone stuck his head out the door for a look around or breath of fresh air.

Down the beach, *Time*'s Bob Sherrod was getting loads of material for his dispatches. As he sat with his back against the seawall, trying desperately to dry out the pages of his notebook, the newsman spotted a Marine walking upright along the beach. A single shot rang out above the din of battle, and the Marine wrenched sideways. Then he was up, holding his helmet aloft for all to see. The top of the cover had two holes in it, one on either side, but the man's only injury was a scratch across the bridge of his nose, the result of impact when the helmet had been wrenched from his head.

Less than 15 minutes later, the sniper lowered his aim a bit and put a round through the temple of another Marine, dropping the man where he stood.

Despite these incidents and dozens like them—and over the objections of Jim Crowe and most officers—the troops continued to walk upright, infected by a curious fatalism common to men in battle. Some were lucky, others were not.

Bob Sherrod made special note of the name of E Company's exec, 1stLt Aubrey Edmonds, because Edmonds was particularly disdainful of the snipers. The lieutenant took a round in the back toward dusk.

When Jim Crowe saw that he was being slowly bled white by the snipers, he ordered the troops around his CP to get one particularly effective marksman. Pfc George Fox of K Company and Cpl Hank Mast, a flamegunner, teamed up for the kill. Fox vaulted the seawall carrying a pair of fused TNT charges while nearby riflemen fired at the aperture of a nearby pillbox. Just as Fox was closing in, Mast nervously cut loose with a burst of flame, nearly burning Fox in the bargain. George Fox kept going and stuffed his charges into the pillbox. As he went to ground, a khaki-clad figure emerged and lit out for open ground. Hank Mast coolly snaked a stream of flaming diesel after the bluejacket, shriveling the sniper like so much wastepaper. The ammunition about the man's waist cooked off for several minutes, after which George Fox hobbled back to the seawall to thank Hank Mast for the hotfoot.

Near LVT-23, the canted tractor hulk which served as a combination CP and aid station, the line of stretchers kept growing longer. The doctors and corpsmen dodged from man to man to dispense morphine, plasma, sulfa, evacuation tags, and words of encouragement. And blankets to cover the faces of the dead.

"Major, send somebody out to help me. The sonovabitch got me." Two corpsmen took off in search of the plaintiff and returned a short time later supporting Pfc Nick Lavrentiev. The husky, blond rifleman had taken a bullet through the thighbone, inches above his knee. He was in extreme pain, groaning and near tears which would not come. Through his pain, Lavrentiev described where the sniper who had shot him could be found.

A Marine named Wilson showed Bob Sherrod his leg wound. A round had gone completely through the calf muscle, which wasn't even bleeding.

A small group of bug-eyed, grimy riflemen told Sherrod of their friends: of a boy named Jones, who had had the tip of his thumb shot off while he was walking upright; of T. C. Martin, who had had a leg blown off; of the 50-odd casualties their company had sustained.

Attention shifted down the beach, where an 81mm mortar squad was trying to fire on a target. One of the three gunners kneeling to adjust the sights tumbled over with a bullet through the neck. One of his companions jumped to lend a hand and took a bullet through the heart.

George Fox and Hank Mast rushed in and began working over a pillbox near the mortar position. Fox heaved a large bundle of TNT and blew the guts out of the pillbox. With the sand covering dislodged, Mast cut loose, spurting liquidous flame between the uneven logs. Later, four charred Japanese would be hauled from the emplacement. For the moment, however, Mast and Fox ducked to avoid being hit by small arms ammunition cooking off through the firing port and the cracks between the logs.

• • •

A rumor was making the rounds on Red-3 in the late afternoon: Another battalion was to be landed behind the 2nd and 3rd Battalions, 8th. That would have to be the regiment's 1st Battalion. If the landing was made on the unoccupied beaches east of the Burns-Philp wharf, the bulk of the Japanese facing Crowe would be outflanked and cut off from their supports. In that event, Crowe could concentrate his dwindling reserves on an attack to the south.

The men on the east flank under Maj Bill Chamberlin had already spent most of the day trying to anchor the flank to form a line of departure for further attacks to the east. In anticipation of the arrival of the 1st Battalion, 8th—for the rumor was true enough—Bill Chamberlin formed an assault force to take the covered bombproof immediately below the Burns-Philp wharf and due east of his lines. He had two 37mm guns in the vicinity of the log revetment at the corner of his position and a 60mm mortar and machine guns nearby. F Company, largely behind the seawall to the rear, could lend support with a second 60mm mortar and several of its machine guns.

The task of assaulting the covered bunker went to 2ndLt George Bussa's 2nd Platoon, F Company, 8th, which was understrength but available. If Bussa succeeded, other Marines could be thrown in to consolidate the gains. Bussa was going to make for the northern entrance to the bombproof, which faced east at the northeast corner of the structure. Japanese machine guns atop the bombproof had an unobstructed field of fire and could easily hit Bussa's platoon as it moved into the open. However, the Japanese gunners could be kept down by mortar fire.

The bombproof was filled with Japanese, as many as 200 armed men who had been driven inside during the course of the day.

Bussa's two-squad platoon jumped off from behind other F Company units and immediately got hit hard. The platoon had to move the full length of the northern side of the mound, and it was subjected to intense fire from within. Several men actually reached the entrance, but it was even more strongly defended than the route to it. The survivors recoiled in the face of mounting opposition and pulled back to their starting point, leaving George Bussa and half his Marines dead in the beaten zone.

A second assault was mounted against the southeast entrance

by a mixed pioneer-infantry group under 1stLt Sandy Bonny-man, who had been leading successful hit-and-run forays for most of the afternoon. Bonnyman was facing slightly better odds than had Bussa; he had less ground to cover, two 37mm guns could fire direct support, and his force was larger, perhaps 40 men in all.

Bonnyman's group made a good start while partially covered by smoke from burning buildings in the area. The Japanese fire was no less intense than what Bussa's platoon had faced, but Bonnyman's group initially made swifter progress. The Japanese threw in more troops and appreciably slowed the assault. Several men reached the southeast entrance, but casualties were by then prohibitive, and a withdrawal was ordered.

It was by then too late for Bill Chamberlin to organize another assault—even if he had had the troops. The Japanese had held, and enough was enough, at least until dawn.

18

Most of the advances that were to be made on D-Day had been made by late afternoon. Betio had been expected to fall within hours of the initial landings, but it was far from occupied. For many Marines, the initial fear and shock that had motivated them to move off the beach had worn off, and the energy that had carried the assault inland in the morning had long since dissipated. The men were tired. Their quest for revenge had dissolved. The inspired warriors of the morning were weary, rational men by sunset.

During the hours after 1400, the almost total disorganization that characterized the invasion was transformed to a nominal, informal organization. Wherever two or five or twenty men gathered, one took charge. Often, rank was the deciding factor; often, ability or a willingness to accept responsibility. Individuals saw what had to be done and they got others to help them do it. Many formal units managed to gravitate together after being dispersed over 50 or 100 yards of beach. Thousands of questions had been asked of hundreds of men, and the chance responses had helped to reunite hundreds of comrades. All of the formal units were smaller than they had been at sunrise. Most groupings were impromptu.

There was not a Marine on Betio who expected to get through the night without having to face the dreaded *banzai*. Enough was known of Japanese tactical doctrine to warrant such dread. Indeed, enough was known of the American situation to warrant that dread. Few if any Marines slept through that night. Of those who did, few would feel rested in the morning.

From the Japanese standpoint, however, a night attack would have been disastrous. First they would have had to mass troops. On an island as small as Betio, with few safe rallying points, discovery would have been certain, and reprisal, swift.

A "banzai", as Americans preferred to call it, was a harbinger of defeat, and 3rd Special Konkyochitai was a long way from losing.

There was another good reason for not mounting a counterattack that night. The defenders were almost totally reliant upon wire communications because of the small size of the area to be defended and the static nature of the defenses. Runners could not have been of much use because of the exposure inherent in their work. Unfortunately for the defenders, little wire had been buried within the incomplete defensive sectors and nearly all the wire that had been strung above the ground had been cut to pieces by shell fire. Thus, the defenses were pretty much compartmentalized, and massing troops from throughout the island was out of the question. In fact, units not under the immediate supervision of the island commander, Admiral Shibasaki, were on their own.

Lt Jim Fawcett's mixed platoon, holding the center of Maj Mike Ryan's line south of Red-1, was tied in with elements of I Company, 2nd, on the right and L Company on the left. Fawcett collected and redistributed all the ammunition his men could find; there wasn't much, but it would have to do. Water was also in short supply. The heat of the day had resulted in heavy consumption, and nearly everyone's canteen was dry. Fawcett's men were a bit more fortunate than most; they had found a barrel full of water just before dark, and each man had been allowed to fill one canteen, provided he treated it with halazone tablets. All the good water the troops had carried ashore was pooled and redistributed equally in each Marine's second canteen.

Few men ate that night; most had grounded their packs upon landing.

As was true elsewhere on Red-1, Fawcett's defenses consisted of pillboxes, buildings, shellholes, and foxholes. The men teamed up in twos and threes in hopes of sharing the watch and getting some sleep, but the line was spread too thin, and most had to maintain night-long vigils.

Closer to the beach, several members of Fawcett's original platoon anxiously prepared a position for the night near the place they had landed that morning. A Nambu light machine gun discovered by Pfc Bernard Zerr while he was rooting through a destroyed pillbox was incorporated into the defenses, providing the leaderless Marines with needed confidence.

Throughout Red-1, whether or not they were incorporated into Major Ryan's formal defenses, small groups of Marines were preparing to make the stand they assumed they would have to make that night as payment for their failure to win Betio early.

Pvt Joe Murray of L Company dug in for the night a bit behind the main line. He and his foxhole buddy had arranged to sleep in shifts, but both men were kept awake by intermittent fire, which sounded more like slow-firing American machine guns than Japanese weapons. Since Murray could see and hear no Japanese attack, he assumed the shooting to be completely one-sided. But that was far from being the case.

Pfc Jim Goldman and his foxhole buddy, Pfc Johnny Byots, got no sleep that night. During the night they continually heard voices calling "Come help me," or "Help, I'm wounded." Neither of the I Company Marines moved, fearing that the pleas for help might be Japanese ruses to pick off lone Marines. It was difficult to ignore the calls, but very few men were willing to take the risk. Marines had been taught to stay still at night and to assume that anyone moving after dark was the enemy. Besides, there were plenty of trigger-happy Americans to contend with, even if the calls were authentic.

Like everyone else on Betio, 1stLt Ott Schulte expected to be attacked. Unlike most of the others, Schulte had almost no prospects for survival if he was attacked. He commanded a very small, totally isolated pocket of men. Schulte's platoon had been getting ready for a counterattack for most of the day, collecting and redistributing ammunition and water from dead men who had fallen near the tiny platoon enclave.

There were a great many machine guns in the hands of Schulte's 25-plus Marines, but that was about the only advantage they had. In addition to the guns they had carried ashore, Schulte had begged two air-cooled .50s from the medium tanks and had captured several Nambus. And two .50s and two .30s had been salvaged along with a great deal of ammunition from a pair of disabled amtracs 50 yards down the beach.

Schulte's line was set by 2300. All the wounded still capable of putting up a fight were ordered to man the machine guns. All the litter cases and every bit of gear not in use were placed under a tractor that had been canted on end in a hole at the water's edge.

The Japanese hit at midnight. The fight was short and furious. Schulte's men held.

As soon as the firing subsided, the wounded platoon leader made his rounds. A whisper in the dark reached his ears, "Lieutenant, I got a prisoner." This was contrary to orders. "Shoot him!" The reply came after a moment's thought, "But I don't think he's a Jap." Schulte moved to check it out and found what appeared to be a Korean laborer, whom he was unwilling to have shot. The prisoner was stripped, bound, and gagged and placed in the custody of his captor.

A Japanese twin-engine Betty medium bomber appeared over Betio at 2100, flying lazy circles, dropping small bombs here and there, more of a pest than a weapon. The sole intent of the effort was to keep the Marines tense and on edge from lack of sleep. It did the same to the defenders.

WO Perry Hall, the luckless mortar section leader, was leaving Red-2. He had been paralyzed by a gunshot wound, injured by grenade fragments, and dumped on a rock jetty. As Hall's outbound tractor left the beach, it was swamped by one of the Betty's bombs. As the luckless gunner was going down for the third time, he *knew* that the battle had been designed specifically to get him. But a pair of hands reached out from the darkness and pulled him up to the air. He was loaded aboard another tractor and carried to the nearest ship for treatment.

Gilbert Bundy, a civilian artist in the pay of King Features Syndicate, came ashore in the dark following a most harrowing day, to say the least. His trip to the beach had begun before dawn aboard Col Dave Shoup's command boat. However, to be closer to the assault troops, Bundy had transferred to another boat scheduled to go in earlier than Shoup's. He was standing at the rear of the troop compartment when he was knocked flat. When he had an opportunity to look around, he found that the boat had taken a direct hit and that 22 Marines aboard had been killed. Three of the dead Marines had fallen over Bundy, securely pinning him to the deck. Unable to move, the civilian spotted a wounded man nearby, the only other living soul on the boat. Bundy treated the injured Marine's wounds with one hand because the other hand was pinned. The boat drifted through the day, during which Bundy managed to extricate himself. Late in the afternoon, the boat had drifted near a tractor manned by Capt Henry Lawrence, who had taken over the tractor battalion following the death of its commander. Lawrence nearly shot Bundy for a sniper but finally took him and his wounded companion aboard his tractor. The civilian artist transferred to another amtrac and, undaunted, finished his journey to Betio.

Acting on the express orders of Colonel Shoup, Maj John Schoettel landed with the command group of the 3rd Battalion, 2nd on Red-2, at which point the harried regimental commander ordered Schoettel to mount an attack westward to join his battalion on Red 1. Schoettel's small force of staff officers, clerks and heavily laden communicators were getting set to execute the order when Shoup relented and told the battalion commander to dig in.

When PlSgt Art Maher, of F Company, 2nd, was ordered to fall back to the line only 20 feet from the seawall—from a line twice that distance away—he realized that he had wasted the entire day waiting for orders to evacuate Betio. When the order to pull back arrived at dusk, Maher's professional pride overwhelmed his daylong apathy. He had enlisted in the Marine Corps to be among winners. When Maher realized that, for him, evacuation and defeat were beyond possibility, he turned his mind and spirit to preparing for the full day of fighting that lay ahead.

Far to the front of the 2nd Battalion, 2nd, in the southernmost Marine positions on Betio, Capt Bill Bray and Capt Maxie Williams of the 1st Battalion, 2nd, were braced and ready to stand against anything the Japanese might hurl their way. Early in the evening, when it looked as though a scarcity of water and ammunition might force the company commanders to withdraw, an eleventh-hour resupply had been undertaken by the regimental operations officer, the tireless Maj Tom Culhane. The new supplies gave Williams and Bray hope that they had a better-than-even chance of holding or

defeating a nocturnal assault. Their line was well positioned
and strongly held by mixing groups of Marines from the 1st
and 2nd Battalions, 2nd, emplaced in a string of Z-shaped fire
trenches captured from the enemy. It was relatively quiet,
too—far quieter than it had been during the day. But there was
an incessant, maddening chatter from behind Williams's line
that kept the troops on edge. The next morning, 18 Korean
laborers would be found huddling in a large shellhole by the
taxiway.

Life on Red-3 was miserable. No beachhead was as
overcrowded, as small, or as close to more Japanese manning
more unassailable positions. By dusk, in fact, Maj Jim Crowe's
toehold measured no more than 200 feet in average depth and
350 yards at its widest east to west measurement. The east
flank rested 30 yards shy of the built-up area south of the
Burns-Philp wharf.

A 37mm gun on the east flank opened fire at about dusk. Its
target was between 100 and 200 Japanese moving from the
south beyond the flank. The canister rounds accounted for
many casualties among the reinforcements.

At about 1600, E Company withdrew to the seawall to give
Navy guns room to adequately soften the Japanese-held area
farther south. When the shelling ceased at 1700, E Company
drove southward. It easily reclaimed the ground it had given up
an hour earlier and took some new ground. By dusk, both of
the company's flanks were tied in with nearby units. At the
same time, elements of I and L Companies extended to the
west, consolidating most of the ground within the triangle.

At dusk, a nine-man raiding party from F Company hit the
Burns-Philp wharf to keep the Japanese from consolidating
there. Eight Japanese were killed, and all nine Marines
returned safely at dawn.

Pvt Leland Ziegenhagen of I Company, 8th, never did get
ashore that night, at least not permanently. By dusk, Ziegenhagen and the men with him, including 1stLt Jim Motley, had
grown accustomed to transferring from one amtrac to another,
to another, to another. None of them expected to reach the
beach at all.

Finally, after dark, Motley's small group encountered an

inbound tractor. A voice called in the dark, "Okay, you can go in now if you go about 800 yards down the beach to the left."

The troops were thrilled, not so much at the prospect of battle as of regaining the feel of solid ground underfoot. The tractor turned hard to port and made for the beach, as directed. It was hit by heavy fire from dead ahead, and the driver and his assistant were both shot. Lieutenant Motley vaulted the gunwale, followed by a line sergeant. Leland Ziegenhagen was right behind. The sergeant, a big man, was shot dead; he fell back on Ziegenhagen and pinned him to the deck.

While Ziegenhagen struggled to move the dead man, Motley searched in vain for fellow Marines. Then it hit home! In his eagerness to land, the I Company commander had neglected to interpret the "left" of the outbound tractor as his own right; Motley's tractor had traveled hundreds of yards toward the eastern tip of Betio, which was enemy country. Although the assistant driver was grievously wounded, he clanged his gears into reverse and pulled away from the beach. Jim Motley made it back aboard with a running, flying leap.

After changing tractors and getting the assistant driver to safety, Motley's group circled and circled and circled offshore.

Pvt Vince Michalski, of H Company, 8th, was paired off with his gun corporal in a two-man foxhole; they were to sleep in four-hour shifts. Michalski drew first watch and kept his eyes peeled and ears keened. Then he woke the corporal and dozed off. After what seemed like only a few minutes, the corporal woke the ammunition carrier and told him it was his watch again. Michalski realized in time that he had been duped. The corporal had been a nervous wreck all day and was obviously cheating. But Vince Michalski had long since stopped caring about anything, so he let the cheater sleep through the night. He felt safer watching out for himself and spent the night staring at the darkness.

19

MGen Julian Smith realized that the Japanese were probably expecting additional landings along the northern beaches, but he knew that such additional landings were necessary if 2nd Marine Division was to attain victory on Betio. So he began taking steps to land Maj Lawrence Hays's 1st Battalion, 8th, during the night, when resistance would certainly be less effective than it would be before sunset and after sunrise.

Maryland attempted to query Col Dave Shoup at 1445 as to the advisability of landing Hays on Beach Green or on Red-2 or Red-3. As it happened, Shoup's lone communicator, Pfc John Gross, was having difficulties with his small radio, and the inquiry was never received.

Forced to act on secondhand information, Julian Smith decided to send Hays, with the 8th Regiment's headquarters, against the tapering eastern tail of Betio. He set H-Hour for 1745 and ordered details radioed to *Monrovia* for Col Elmer Hall. The transport acknowledged receipt. *But not delivery.*

Hall was not aboard *Monrovia*. He had shipped out with the 1st Battalion, 8th, and was awaiting orders near *Pursuit*; he thought the Flag knew of his whereabouts. He never received the message.

There was, withal, one safeguard. Spotter aircraft from *Maryland* had been asked to monitor Hays's progress.

Throughout the afternoon, LtCol Presley Rixey, commander of the 1st Battalion, 10th, the 12-gun 75mm pack howitzer battalion assigned to the 2nd Marines, had been at Colonel Shoup's CP trying to learn where he might land his guns. Red-1 had the best ground, but there was not enough known of conditions there to warrant a commitment. So, the boats carrying the pack howitzers had circled beyond the Line of Departure all afternoon. Late in the day, Rixey decided to get his battalion to Red-2 and ordered A and B Batteries to transfer their disassembled guns to tractors near the pierhead for an immediate landing.

Rixey did not know that there were only enough tractors on hand to carry a section each of the two batteries, but the battery commanders ordered all their boats across the Line of Departure, and C Battery's boats followed in the confusion.

That was at 1548. At that moment, LtCol Jesse Cook, a senior division staffer, was taking his turn aloft to monitor the battle. Cook's spotter plane flew over the Line of Departure just as the boats bearing the artillery were crossing below; he took them to be Hays's battalion—a natural error in the confusion of battle—and reported that Hays was soon to be on Red-2. Division updated its situation map and waited for further news. The fact that the 1st Battalion, 8th, was still standing by near *Pursuit* would not be discovered for hours.

A section each from A and B Batteries—two pack howitzers—landed on Red-2, while three C Battery guns went into the pierhead, where the gunners dismantled them and carried and floated them to the beach. By dawn, a five-gun composite battery was emplaced on a north-south line several dozen yards west of the base of the pier.

Maryland received a message at 1740 from BGen Dutch Hermle, the first news from him since he had started for the beach after noon. He was at the pierhead, under fire, and had contacted Col Dave Shoup's guide, Maj Tommy Tompkins.

Seventeen minutes later, Hermle was back on the air to say that his Division Forward command group was under intense fire at the pierhead, but they had contacted disorganized remnants of the 3rd Battalion, 8th. The message did not get through, and, as it went unacknowledged, Hermle dispatched a messenger to the nearest ship to send it again.

The elements of Ruud's battalion that Hermle found consisted of parts of the battalion headquarters and two rifle companies under Maj Stanley Larsen, Ruud's exec. Larsen told Hermle that Ruud had proceeded to the beach in the hope of finding Shoup's CP but had been out of contact for hours.

The assistant division commander decided to use his own communications team to collect as much information as he could before he would act. In the course of intermittent conversations with Shoup's CP and Crowe's CP, Hermle's radiomen learned that water and ammunition were vitally needed.

At 1930, after nearly two hours of contacts with Shoup's CP, Hermle was suddenly cut off. He also lost contact with Maj Jim Crowe. As he had done all he could at the pierhead anyway, he ordered Major Tompkins and Capt Tom Dutton, a supply officer, to find Dave Shoup and learn which beach was most suitable for landing the 6th Marines after dawn.

Many of the wounded who had taken refuge under the pier were routed out by the Division Surgeon, Dr. French Moore, who pressed every able-bodied man he could find into rescuing them. They flagged down landing craft shuttling supplies and evacuated all the wounded Marines and sailors.

In the meantime, Major Larsen was ordered to organize whatever troops he could find to begin getting supplies into the beach. These Marines had not been able to make even a one-way trip during the day, but they were going to haul supplies into the beach through the night, each time braving a particularly dangerous 50-yard stretch of fireswept water near the beach.

After 2000, a series of incidents touched off by faulty communications began an all-night comedy of errors, which in retrospect, shows how absolutely divorced Division was from the nightmare happening ashore.

The play began at 1755 with a message from Division to Hermle asking him to proceed to Shoup's CP and assume command ashore. This decision was made by Julian Smith because of Hermle's access to the beach and because the nearly two regiments that had landed would severely strain Shoup's experience and limited facilities. The brigadier general had the requisite rank for the job, and the necessary equipment and staff. Division, which thought the 8th Marines' command group had landed, knew that Colonel Hall outranked Colonel Shoup.

The message was not received by Hermle, or, for that matter, any unit ashore.

Following this, LtCol Cliff Atkinson, a senior division staffer, became concerned because all messages from the beach continued to emanate from Shoup, not General Hermle, who was not even acknowledging messages to him.

Shoup's repeated and urgent requests for supplies of water, medical equipment, and ammunition were all filled by Division, but receipt of the goods was never acknowledged. In order to find out where Hermle was and to trace the supply consignments, Division dispatched Capt Ben Weatherwax to the beach. He left *Monrovia* at 2100 and, after stopping briefly near *Pursuit,* made for the pierhead and landed on its eastern arm. He did not know that Hermle was a few years away, on the seaplane ramp. Unable to find the general, Weatherwax began making his way to the beach in the hope of finding Colonel Shoup.

During the time it took Weatherwax to get ashore, Maj Tommy Tompkins and Capt Tom Dutton had spoken with Dave Shoup and were on their way back to report to Dutch Hermle. It is likely that they passed Captain Weatherwax in the dark. It was way past 0300 before Tompkins and Dutton rejoined Hermle. Although they probably knew as much about the situation ashore as anyone else, at that point Hermle's radio failed them. Tompkins and Dutton talked Hermle into accompanying them to *Ringgold* to use her radio. They all arrived at 0345.

Captain Weatherwax reboarded *Monrovia* a short time later and informed Division that he had found Dave Shoup, whose radio batteries had faded, but that he had been unable to find Hermle.

Hermle suggested at 0445 that Hays's battalion—which Division had learned was still afloat at about midnight—be landed before sunrise on Red-2, close to the pier. This message was not received, precipitating a brutal tragedy.

Hermle radioed Dave Shoup at 0510 to say that he had received no response to his suggestion regarding Hays's battalion and therefore assumed that Division had not received it. Minutes later, Hermle was ordered to remain aboard *Ringgold,* which would carry him to *Maryland.* Dave Shoup would remain in command on Betio on the second day.

All the frantic efforts and risks undertaken by members of the division staff that night had come to nothing. In fact, because of several inadvertent omissions, the effort would bring on a tragedy before the new day was out.

These men were every bit as brave and every bit as competent as commanders on the beaches, perhaps more so.

But unlike the men on the beaches, they depended a great deal on secondhand information. Since they were not completely informed up to the minute, they could not make accurate assessments. If the men on the beaches were playing it by the seats of their pants, there is no way to describe how the division staff was playing it.

As so often happens in the chaos of bloodletting, the commanders and the commanded were fighting two entirely different battles.

The assault waves head for burning Betio on D-Day morning.

Amtracs stalled on Red-2. Note dead Marines in bottom right half of this photograph.

OFFICIAL *USMC* PHOTO

Marines, living and dead, behind the fireswept seawall.

OFFICIAL *USMC* PHOTO

A Marine BAR-man killed in the detonation of a medium-caliber shell.

Marines wade through low water beside the main pier. *Niminoa* can be seen at top center of photo.

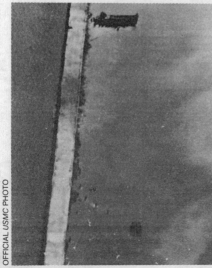

Aerial view of same area as above photo taken by a Navy air observer on D-Day between 1300 and 1500 hours. (This is the first time this and other aerial photos are being used in a book about Tarawa.)

Marines move up on a Japanese strongpoint under heavy fire.

A Marine .30-caliber light machine gun returns Japanese fire.

Red-2 from the air. LtCol Herb Amey was killed trying to pass through barbed-wire barrier in the center of the photo. The concrete tetrahedrons in the center of the photo stopped 2ndLt Ray Marion's amtrac.

Some Marines sit and wait while others prepare to advance over the seawall.

A Marine plays hardball with the Japanese while his comrade takes time out for a drink of water.

Red-1 from the air. Pfc Andrew Polmaskitch was killed on the sandbar at left bottom. 1stLt Ott Schulte's enclave is marked by "X".

A beachside aid station.

Wounded Marines being evacuated from Betio by rubber boat.

Large-caliber shells detonate on Betio's tail while landing craft mill around off the reef.

A view of burning Betio from near the pierhead.

Col Dave Shoup

1stLt William Deane Hawkins

MRS. C. JANE HAWKINS

MAJ JAMES L. FAWCETT

The Officers of K Company, 2nd Marines: (top, l. to r.) 1stLt Ott Schulte (wounded), 2ndLt Tom Becker (killed), 2ndLt Jim Fawcett; (sitting, l. to r.) 1stLt Mike Hofmann (killed), Capt Jim Crain, 1stLt Clint Dunahoe (killed).

Black-2 looking north toward Red-2 and the main pier. This photo gives an excellent idea of the many open areas that had to be crossed by the 1st and 2nd Battalions, 2nd Marines.

Beach Red-3. The main pier is just out of view to the right and the Burns-Philp wharf is just out of view to the left. Trees to the left obscure the large covered bunker. The beached amtrac just right of center is LVT-23, which shielded Maj Jim Crowe's command post.

Colorado, the only surviving medium tank on Red-3, fires on the Japanese steel pillbox holding up the advance of F Company, 8th, on D + 2.

1stLt Sandy Bonnyman and the first of his mixed assault group break through to the top of the large covered bunker south of Red-3 while reinforcements work along the L-shaped fence.

TSgt Norm Hatch (in center, with movie camera) calmly films Bonnyman's breakthrough moments before the Japanese counterattack.

Smoke pours from RAdm Shibasaki's command post moments after Pfc Johnny Borich sprayed the inside with his flamethrower.

Marines search for Japanese holdouts in a rabbit's warren of pillboxes backing the seawall.

Many cornered Japanese killed themselves rather than surrender.

Victims of *Banzai.*

Aerial view of the beach boundary strongpoint between Red-1 and Red-2. Aircraft revetments can be plainly seen at left center.

Removing the dead from the battlefield. (Note, in lower left, Marine occupying former Japanese one-man spider hole.)

Father Frank Kelly and his clerk recite a Mass for the dead they have helped to bury behind Col Dave Shoup's CP on Red-2.

Part III
THE SECOND DAY

20

MGen Julian Smith had problems, lots of problems. The commanding general of the embattled 2nd Marine Division had spent all of November 20 getting in too deep to back out. His division had already paid a terrible price and had gained little. There was reason to believe that the division had already lost more than it would ever recoup. As soon as the sun came up, the price of battle was going to become more expensive. Smith could be certain of that.

The general had a choice. He could cut his losses and pick up his marbles, or he could reinforce his embattled battalions and hope that they could still gain a victory.

Julian Smith had been a Marine since 1909. He held the Navy Cross for three years' duty in Nicaragua in the 1930s. He was not the sort of man to pick up his marbles. All he could do, short of quitting, was send in more troops after dawn of the second day, for it was clear that Betio would not fall to the Marines already arrayed on the island.

At 0430 on the morning of Sunday, November 21, 1943, Smith sent a radio message to Col Elmer Hall of the 8th Marines: Hall was to round up Maj Larry Hays's 1st Battalion, 8th, which was then afloat, and land it near the extreme eastern end of Betio's northern shore beginning at 0900.

As Hall was briefing Hays and getting a control vessel to mark a line of departure east of Red-3, BGen Dutch Hermle, aboard *Ringgold*, was talking with Maj Tommy Tompkins and Capt Tom Dutton. As a result of the conversation, Hermle told Smith, "Shoup desires One-Eight to land on Beach Red-2."

Division moved at 0515, two minutes after receiving Hermle's message. Colonel Hall was to send Hays's battalion into Red-2, where it would reform and attack in the direction of Red-1, through the beach boundary strongpoint.

All the riflemen on the beaches, and most of their officers, were unaware of Division's plans. Few had given Division much thought, although many were wondering what the senior staff was going to do on their behalf.

After repeated transfers between tractors over a 20-hour period, after nearly being killed out of sheer stupidity, after losing an entire night's sleep (and half of another night's, and the full day between), after getting used to the bilious taste of seasickness, after complete apathy had set in, Pvt Leland Ziegenhagen and a dozen other I Company, 8th, victims were cleared to land on Red-3. This was one of many indications that morning that The Flag intended to fight it out ashore.

Bleary eyed and hungry, 2ndLt Jim Fawcett watched intently as a lone Marine worked his way toward the front-line shellhole the platoon leader had chosen for his CP. Fawcett correctly figured that the man was bringing orders from his company commander, Capt Jim Crain: Fawcett was to join Crain at his company CP, which was located in a Japanese bombproof to the rear. Fawcett was Crain's surviving officer. They both knew that at least three K Company officers were dead, and they assumed the same for the missing 1stLt Ott Schulte, who had not been seen for over 22 hours. Crain wanted to quickly reorganize K Company to get set for renewed attacks to the south.

PhM3 Harold Blank was tired and ornery. He had been working nonstop through the night to save as many lives as he could. Sometimes, he was surprised by his life-saving powers. The dark hours had abated the flow of bleeding and broken bodies from the vicinity of Red-2, but this was a new day, and more men would be killed or maimed. Doc Blank knew that he would have no rest on the second day.

First Lieutenant Lou Largey and the crew of *Colorado*, the last remaining tank on Red-3, were about ready for action. The crew had spent the night guiding *Colorado* to the reef to collect fuel, ammunition, and replacement parts from another medium that had gotten hung up there the day before. Then they guided the tank back to the beach and reported to Jim Crowe.

• • •

Supply units and shore parties began rallying on the pier shortly after sunrise. Lt(jg) Larry Crane, *Heywood's* beach-master, made it to the pierhead following three unsuccessful approaches in the dark. After a brief pause, he and his navymen went to work unloading landing craft at the edge of the seaplane ramp. The pierhead was high and dry and the target of many Japanese guns. The first cases of nonlethal supplies had to be manhandled up the incline by men on their bellies, who sought to build a protective wall of wooden crates filled with food, medical supplies, and a weird assortment of other gear.

Capt Joe Clerou, commander of F Company, 2nd Battalion, 18th, also made it to the pierhead after being driven off by intense fire during the night. His small company headquarters group pitched right in to help with the supplies.

LtCol Chester Salazar, Clerou's battalion commander, arrived to take charge of over 100 Marines who had materialized from under the pier. He organized carrying parties and waylaid noncombatants on the way to the beach. Within an hour of sunrise, a crude but effective supply service was sending in all the gear Col Dave Shoup would need to keep the fight going.

Beyond the reef, the Navy was pitching in to care for the wounded. Shortly after dawn, a New Zealand pilot succeeded in conning transport *Doyen* into the lagoon. Her medical staff had been beefed up to handle priority cases. The less seriously injured would be sent to ships farther out.

Seamen aboard *Ringgold* were glad to see *Doyen* arrive. D-Day had been gruesome for the officers and men of the spunky destroyer. Throughout November 20, *Ringgold* had been the ship nearest the fighting. Since she had a surgeon aboard, she had accepted dozens upon dozens of badly wounded Marines. Why she had taken the wounded is not altogether clear for, compassion aside, one of the shells that had hit *Ringgold* on her D-Day passage through the reef had destroyed nearly all her medical supplies. Another shell had left her with a 26-degree list, and repeated calls for shelling from the beach had stripped her magazines of 5-inch shells. *Ringgold* should have been ordered clear of the lagoon, but she had stayed, probably because of the wounded.

Radarman Jack O'Brien had helped with the wounded, carrying them from the rail to the wardroom, feeding them and nursing them, watching their guts spill out, listening to them cry, watching them die or begin recovering. On D-Day afternoon, *Ringgold's* whaleboat had been sent to get more medical supplies and had returned loaded to the gunwales. Those supplies had been used up, and the stream of seriously injured men had continued unabated.

A line of canvas-covered corpses continued to stretch across *Ringgold's* fantail.

Jack O'Brien was glad to see *Doyen* enter the lagoon. He was still too close to the Marine lieutenant who had been brought aboard alive with both legs and part of his abdomen gone. And he was still too close to the Marine whose basket litter had been accidentally tilted, dumping a long ribbon of the boy's entrails into the lagoon. He was too close to the feeling of death, and now it was the turn of *Doyen's* crew.

In a little plot of ground behind Col Dave Shoup's CP on Red-2, Chaplains Frank Kelly and Norman Darling continued to bury the dead.

21

Most of the men of the 1st Battalion, 8th, expected an easy landing. No one had told them otherwise. Although they had seen signs aplenty in their 20 hours afloat to indicate that there was resistance ashore, no one dreamed that they would be sent into Betio without ample warning if there was substantial danger.

A full day in a moving boat and a night filled with scuttlebutt had left Pvt Clarence Shanks happy to get The Word. Shanks, who was green, had had a day more than the green men of the 2nd Marines to come to terms with himself. But he still did not realize the extreme danger he was about to face.

Shortly after sunrise, Shanks's boat came alongside *Pursuit* and the minesweeper's crew passed coffee over the side. Word was that the battalion was going ashore on a Marine-held beach, so the troops were ordered to keep their weapons unloaded as a precaution against mishap. A Japanese shell splashed into the water near Shanks's boat almost as soon as the order was given. The roar of the water-muffled blast was followed by the rattling of eight-round clips being thumbed home into untested M1 Garand rifles. Pvt Clarence Shanks finally felt resigned to whatever the Fates had ordained for him.

A Company, 8th, hit the reef at 0615, just about sunrise. The Japanese took little notice of the four LCVPs in the boat-filled lagoon. Few shots met the slightly stupefied Marines, even after the boats collided with the coral and dropped their ramps.

By the time B Company approached the reef, however, the Japanese had seen their predicament; they would be over-whelmed unless they could disperse the landing troops.

First Lieutenant Dean Ladd, a mustang veteran of the Guadalcanal fighting, took to the water and found it to be between shoulder and waist deep, and surprisingly warm. He immediately became acutely aware of arcs of bullets from traversing machine guns that approached from one side or the other and passed by him.

Others were less fortunate. Three of Ladd's B Company riflemen were shot dead in an instant.

The men of all the landing units had been expressly forbidden to stop for the wounded. The only way to beat the fire was to wade nonstop to the beach. Much against his better instincts, Dean Ladd was looking to catch men acting in defiance of the brutal but necessary edict. He never expected to press the issue, but he felt he had to make the effort for the record. And, just for the record, Lieutenant Ladd yelled, "Let's go!" as he held his M2 carbine at high port and led his men through the fireswept waters. Just as Ladd turned back to face the beach, he felt a strange, sickening *splat* an inch below his navel, somewhat like an inner tube being swatted against his bare belly. Stunned, he yelled, "I'm hit!" And then he ordered his men to keep moving. He chucked his pack, a small radio, carbine, and helmet, but he was too weak to maintain his balance and kept staggering beneath the surface.

A hand caught the lieutenant, and a calm voice asked him how he felt. Pfc T. F. Sullivan, one of Ladd's riflemen, had come to the rescue. Ladd said he was fine, although obviously he was not, and he ordered Sullivan to keep moving. Ladd was certain that he was beyond help. He was unwilling to have another man die in his behalf. He felt regret for the sorrow his parents would face and resigned himself to death.

Sullivan refused to obey. He dragged the wounded officer back to the reef, then went to rescue several other Marines, whom he gathered below the open maw of an LCVP. Ladd ordered that one of the wounded, a well-built young man who appeared to have lost an eye, to be taken aboard first. All hands turned to and boosted the Marine into the boat. Then, to Ladd's astonishment, the man turned and lifted him aboard, one-handed.

Closer to the beach, A and B Companies, 8th, were getting mauled. In addition to taking terrific fire from the front, the troops were subjected to crossfires from the hulk of *Niminoa*, aboard which several Japanese machine guns were still firing.

Second Lieutenant Bob Munkirs, commanding B Company's Weapons Platoon, started for the beach in a low crouch, his chin touching the water. That lasted only a few moments. What Munkirs needed was speed, so, swallowing hard on the grapefruit-sized lump in his throat, he rose to his full height and started moving. In minutes, Munkirs came upon a young Marine standing with his back to the beach, holding a wounded comrade out of the water. The man opened his mouth to speak to the shaken platoon leader but issued only a bloody upheaval and slipped beneath the surface.

Bob Munkirs was shot in the leg only 50 yards from the beach; he never did get to Betio.

C Company reached the reef right behind B Company, and Pvt Clarence Shanks hit the water right next to his squad leader. Just as the sergeant yelled "Spread out!" he slipped below a bubbling pool of pink. Shanks moved to help but was warned clear by his buddies, for he was about to move into a clearly defined firelane, as had the dying sergeant.

The water was about four feet deep, warm, and vaguely refreshing. There was not a cloud in the sky. The beach was over 500 yards away. The air had a *snap* and *crack* to it; bullets passed close by a thousand ears, churning the water in some places into a ferocious froth. Gunfire seemed to be arriving from all directions, but many Marines discerned patterns as the Japanese gunners corrected aim or simply traversed their weapons back and forth. For those who noticed the patterns, survival became easier: stop here, wait, move a bit faster, zigzag.

Col Dave Shoup helplessly watched the ordeal of the 1st Battalion, 8th. As the word passed along Red-2, hundreds of Marines turned to watch the spectacle in the lagoon. Shoup grabbed his radio and called for air support and naval gunfire. He wanted *Niminoa* blown apart. At the same time, two 75mm pack howitzers on Red-2 were turned 180 degrees to bear on the two largest bunkers in the beach boundary strongpoint. They fired delayed-action rounds in hopes of penetrating the thick concrete, but the guns could do little to stop the slaughter in the lagoon.

The infantry battalion's mobile shore fire control party was pinned securely to the reef aboard a disabled LCM to the left of *Niminoa*. One of the boat's crewmembers was steadily firing one of the LCVP's .30-caliber machine guns at the hulk as the rest of the complement attempted to get a tow. Then the gunner was hit. Pfc Ted Jachiemowicz leaped to the gun. As he did, another member of the team boarded the jeep they were to bring ashore and frantically radioed for ships' fire. He had no such luck, but an airstrike was sent in.

From the beach, from the ships in the lagoon, and most particularly from the lines of wading riflemen, Marines and seamen cheered the naval aviators as they dived on the bristling hulk. The aircraft bombed her, strafed her, tore her to pieces. And still *Niminoa's* Japanese crew kept firing.

C Company Marines watched intently as a dive-bomber dived right at them. When it released its bomb, which seemed to hurtle right at them, they waded faster and cursed from between fear-clenched teeth. As the bomb angled directly into the hulk, the wading men turned their attention back to the beach.

The wading lines grew thinner and thinner. Bloody, dazed Marines began turning back. The water turned a sour red as blood mingled with blood.

Two hundred yards out, Pfc Stan Kazmierski heard a disembodied voice ask, "Do you want to live or die?" And Kazmierski heard himself mouth words in favor of life. The voice told him to move his head to the right, and he did. An instant later, a bullet plowed into his bayonet handle, in direct line with where his head would have been. Stan Kazmierski rejoiced, certain that that had been *the* round with his name on it. He felt that he might become maimed beyond use, but he was certain he would not die at Betio.

Elements of D Company and the battalion headquarters ran the gauntlet behind C Company. They were better off than the groups preceding them because the bombing and shelling was beginning to tell on the Japanese.

Pvt Clarence Shanks could think only of survival. As soon as his squad leader was hit, he hunkered down in the water, leaving only his head exposed. The going was slow, and Shanks had plenty of time to think more on the subject. He decided that there were better places to be hit than in the head, so he stood up. On reaching the inshore side of the reef, he decided to rest behind a big coral rock and sat down there to watch the show. He spotted *Ninimoa* for the first time, saw that gunners there had a clear shot if they wanted to get him, and got to his feet and moved once again toward the protection of the pier, where dead Marines and Japanese bobbed against the log pilings amidst thousands of dead silver-colored fish.

Lt Galen Brown was on his way into the pierhead with another load of supplies when an LCVP raced by, flat out. Brown turned to see that three of his cocky young *Heywood* boatcrewmen were going after *Niminoa*. The LCVP's two fixed .30-caliber guns were manned and firing at the hulk and, balanced precariously on the inclined bow ramp, a third bluejacket was having the time of his life, firing a third .30-caliber gun barehanded.

Shortly after the 1st Battalion, 8th, hit the reef, Lt John Fletcher and Lt(jg) Edward Albert Heimberger, respectively *Sheridan's* boat group and salvage officer, discovered that as many as 150 wounded Marines were under fire on the reef. Fletcher and Heimberger independently began picking these men off the coral and taking them to LCMs farther out for transport to hospital ships.

Heimberger's boat ran afoul of the reef after three or four such trips and suffered propellor damage. The boat limped back into the lagoon, where Heimberger commandeered another LCVP and headed back to pick up more wounded Marines. The situation was becoming increasingly desperate, as the tide was on the way in and the Japanese were beginning to fire on the wounded and their rescuers. As Heimberger's boat took fire for the first time, he realized that his one-boat runs were barely making a dent in the crowd of wounded, so he rounded up several other LCVPs on his next trip out. Heimberger then ordered his coxswain to continue to rescue the wounded, and he transferred to a third boat and ordered it to the reef. The boat was fired on from the beach boundary strongpoint while still 2,000 yards from the beach. When the coxswain slowed the LCVP to throw off the aim of the gunners, Heimberger discovered that he was also being fired on by *Niminoa*. Return fire from the boats, all of which were armed with air-cooled .30-caliber machine guns, silenced the hulk-bound Japanese for a brief interval, but it was clear that the gathering boats were drawing too much fire on the waiting wounded. Heimberger signalled the other boats to wait 200 yards back of the reef, then moved toward the reef alone.

As the lone LCVP worked its way toward the reef, it began

drawing fire from a Japanese sniper who was hiding aboard a wrecked LCVP 40 yards away. Heimberger's .30s dueled the sniper to his death, but the danger was extreme, for the American boat was carrying eight drums of high octane gasoline.

When their LCVP finally arrived at the reef, Heimberger's crewmen took 13 Marines aboard, leaving 35 in the water. The 35 were all uninjured, and they refused to come aboard, asking instead that Heimberger collect enough weapons to replace the ones they had lost in the water. Heimberger said that he would try, wished them luck, and ordered his coxswain to back off. In the meantime, the remainder of the crew and several injured Marines had been stamping out Japanese incendiary bullets, which littered the deck of the floating fuel dump.

Heimberger next encountered Col Elmer Hall, who was on his way in to the beach. As the Navy lieutenant told the regimental commander about the men on the reef and the snipers aboard *Niminoa*, Hall ordered his surgeon aboard Heimberger's boat.

Heimberger, who made continual runs through the day, was something of a celebrity in civilian life. A rising young actor and sometime writer, Heimberger worked professionally under his first and middle names, Eddie Albert.

Pfc Stan Kazmierski joined three other Marines about 150 yards from the beach and turned toward the main pier to get away from the gunfire. There were few men left in the water nearby. One of the group, who appeared to be in a complete state of shock, kept stumbling below the surface. He was shot dead only 75 yards from dry ground.

Stan Kazmierski dashed the last 50 yards to the pier and turned for the beach, which was still 30 yards away. Kazmierski stepped over and around Marines who could not or would not move and made his way to the shore, where he was told that C Company was reforming down the beach.

It had taken 75 minutes for half of Hays's battalion to reach the beach, following the collision of the A Company boats with the coral reef. When Maj Larry Hays reported to Col Dave Shoup at 0800, he told the haggard colonel that his battalion had lost all its demolitions and flamethrowers, its jeeps, and much of the heavy equipment it had started with. Hays had no idea how many rifles his men had brought ashore, but there seemed to be more men than weapons. Shoup, by then resigned to relying on improvisation and individual initiative, ordered Hays to salvage what he could from along the beach and reform what was left of the 1st Battalion, 8th, on the western flank. As soon as the battalion was in line and had caught its collective breath, it was to execute limited assaults in the direction of Red-1, clearing the stubborn beach boundary defenses in order to link up with Maj Mike Ryan's command.

22

First Lieutenant Deane Hawkins's Scout-and-Sniper Platoon had been extremely fortunate to get through the first day intact. Despite coming under heavy fire while landing in the middle of D-Day afternoon, the platoon had lost only one man killed. Later on D-Day, it had emerged without injury from a number of tough pillbox-busting missions south of the taxiway. The only injury anyone suffered was a cut on Lieutenant Hawkins's hand from a mortar fragment. Later in the day, Hawkins was ordered to secure Col Dave Shoup's CP against snipers. It was no easy task.

At dawn, one scout-and-sniper section was sent south of the seawall to assist the 1st Battalion, 2nd, while Lieutenant Hawkins led the remainder of his Marines westward along the beach to destroy a three-pillbox complex that seemed impervious to the attentions of the five-gun 75mm howitzer battery.

The scouts moved 75 yards along the water's edge to the pillboxes, where Deane Hawkins vaulted to the exposed foredeck of a stalled amtrac and fired his carbine down into the first open emplacement. The Japanese returned fire, but they were all quickly eliminated by the platoon leader. The remaining scouts poured over the other two emplacements and destroyed them with TNT.

When the scouts returned to the regimental CP, several noticed that their platoon leader was bleeding from a wound in one shoulder. They talked him into visiting an aid station. When Hawkins was told that the bullet would have to stay in his shoulder because surgical instruments had not been landed, he smiled at the doctor and said, "Forget it."

While under the temporary command of GySgt Jared Hooped, the platoon was ordered south at 0830 to spot for Marine mortars. Shortly after the group moved into the open, several scouts dropped for cover, but Pfc Basil Gillis kept moving and was shot well to the front of the others. Instinctively, Pfc William Matteson ran into the open and dragged Gillis to safety. The effort drew considerable fire, but Matteson finished the job without being hit. Gillis, however, had been mortally wounded in the attempt. The chastened scouts completed the spotting mission and returned to the beach, where Deane Hawkins was waiting with new orders.

The entire platoon was to drive westward along the beach to take out a five-pillbox complex several dozen yards beyond the three pillboxes that had been reduced earlier. As the platoon reached the first emplacement, Hawkins motioned that he would take it. The nerveless platoon leader crawled toward the live machine guns emplaced in the first pillbox while his men put out suppressive fire. Hawkins took a slug in the chest while only yards from his objective. Momentarily dazed, the thrice-wounded lieutenant pressed his attack. He dropped a grenade through the pillbox embrasure, and it killed all the Japanese.

Although the scouts protested, Hawkins refused aid or relief. The latest wound had been stunning but not incapacitating.

One of the four remaining pillboxes could be approached only by crossing a small open area guarded by a waist-high wall. Pfc Jerry Grummel led the way. One of the older hands, Grummel had had long months of training in just the sort of tactics required for the job. He moved fast and low, hit the wall almost parallel to the ground and immediately rolled down and away, unhurt.

The next man into the pillbox was Pfc Marcel Krzys, who was a newcomer to the platoon and not as skilled as Jerry Grummel. He crossed the wall fast, but he was not low enough, and he was shot dead from a nearby pillbox before he hit the ground. Ironically, Krzys died for nothing. By the time Krzys moved, Jerry Grummel had found that the occupants of the pillbox were dead; their rifle barrels were pressed up to their gory chins, their big toes were in the trigger guards, and their brains were spread over a wide arc.

Two more pillboxes fell in quick succession.

Deane Hawkins insisted on leading the fifth and last assault. He seemed not to notice his latest wound as he moved to within a few yards of the pillbox's firing embrasure. He flexed and carefully timed his leap. Just as Hawkins rose for the kill, a 13mm explosive bullet caught him on his uninjured shoulder and severed an artery. He dropped as his scouts overran the gun.

Too dazed and weak to protest, Lieutenant Hawkins allowed three of his men to carry him to the nearest aid station. Before his scouts left, Deane Hawkins uttered a weak good-bye. "Boys, I sure hate leaving you like this."

Hawkins, who would be awarded the Medal of Honor he had been sure he would win, succumbed to shock before he could be evacuated from Betio.

23

Well before the 1st Battalion, 8th, began landing on Red-2, the main body of the 3rd Battalion, 2nd, began flexing for a drive to the south shore.

Capt Jim Crain hit upon a simple method for softening the way along Beach Green, the battalion's right flank. Transmitting over an improvised radio link, Crain asked for a naval gunfire liaison officer, a specially trained naval artilleryman who could coordinate ships' fire from the viewpoint of the infantry; none had been assigned to the 3rd Battalion, 2nd, and none, in fact, was available. In response to Crain's request, 2ndLt Tom Greene, a forward observer from C Battery, 1st Battalion, 10th, was sent to fill in.

Lieutenant Greene's initial worry was the southwest tip of the island. In addition to the Singapore Gun, the area contained five antiboat guns, many pillboxes, a number of protective bunkers, an extensive network of fighting trenches, and dozens of rifle pits. Although several of the antiboat guns and the 8-inch Vickers guns had been knocked out in prelanding bombardments, the rubble thrown up by the naval gunfire had resulted in a jumble almost too extensive for infantry to tackle. It was Greene's hope that he could suitably rearrange the heavily defended rubble.

A single destroyer materialized off Beach Green, and, with Lieutenant Greene calling the shots, the target area was blanketed with 5-inch shells and strafed by 20mm and 40mm rapid-fire guns.

As soon as the bombardment began, Capt Jim Crain and 2ndLt Jim Fawcett raced to the front to get K Company saddled up. Other officers were doing the same throughout the occupied areas of Red-1.

Pfc Bernard Zerr and four buddies had decided at dawn that they could not spend another day sitting on the beach as they had on D-Day, so they made their way to the front. Shortly after the five stragglers crossed the seawall, they spotted Lieutenant Fawcett, who said he had heard that several of them had been killed in the landings. But there was little time for talk. The group was quickly incorporated into the attack force.

First Lieutenant Ed Bale, the medium tank company commander, decided to make an attempt at reinforcing his impotent one-tank armored force. He moved his scarred medium, *China Gal*, to the beach and passed a towline to *Cecilia*, which had bogged down the previous morning, and reeled her in for a quick refurbishing.

Pfc Jim Goldman and Pfc Johnny Byots, of 2ndLt John Cannon's I Company platoon, had been looking for trouble since sunrise. Neither had seen their outfit since landing, so, with neither orders nor leadership, they began mopping up pillboxes on their own initiative. All they found, however, were dead Japanese. Much to their amazement, many of the corpses seemed to be suicides. As Goldman and Byots moved, they attracted other stragglers. No one asked who was in charge. By tacit agreement, they performed as a group, following the best suggestion of the moment.

The main body of the 3rd Platoon, I Company, 2nd, was together and leaderless. It was pinned down by the destroyer fire raking the ground around its impromptu hedgehog defense.

Pfc Ruel Lefebvre, one of the I Company men, decided that he would not be able to wait for the shelling to stop before he would have to relieve himself. Through a misguided sense of cleanliness, Lefebvre told his foxhole buddy, Pfc Dale Young, that he was leaving their foxhole for a moment. Young said that he didn't care about a mess, but Lefebvre moved into the open. A moment later, a fist-sized lump of steel landed in the small hole, tearing up the sand where Lefebvre had been sitting until he departed. The fastidious Marine returned within minutes, totally unaware that he had been spared death.

As the shelling dwindled, Maj Mike Ryan appeared in the platoon's area to organize the leaderless riflemen for an assault. Since Pfc Dale Young was still carrying his BAR, he was singled out to lead the attack. There were too few troops available for conventional tactics, so Major Ryan was sending his automatic weapons in first instead of using them to establish a static base of fire. Ryan was counting on the shock value of keeping his firepower mobile. There would be no back-up once the riflemen were committed.

Second Lieutenant John Cannon got The Word from 1stLt Sam Turner, the I Company commander. Cannon was to gather as many men as he could find and get them under cover. When the naval gunfire ceased—there were destroyers, cruisers and battleships lined up for this round—a salvo of smoke shells would be fired to signal and mask the attack. All able-bodied Marines were to fight their way as far forward as they could get.

Pfc Minor McLaughlin, an 18-year-old 60mm mortar gunner, was in his first battle and had already learned to accept the bizarre and improbable. But he could not quite accept a tableau of the grotesque that occurred that second morning. As McLaughlin's squad was setting up its mortar to support the drive, one of the men, a shellshock victim, wandered over to a table in an open area and sat down in a chair beside it. As the squad looked on, the Marine took out a C-ration can and his eating utensils. He opened the can with excessive care and carefully wiped his spoon clean. In the midst of the most violent fight of the war thus far, the fastidious diner ate his cold breakfast.

Lt Ed Bale was ready with *China Gal* and *Cecilia* by 1110. The command tank's 75mm gun had been disabled on D-Day, and the turret .50-caliber machine gun had been given to 1stLt Ott Schulte. But the tank itself was mobile, and its .30-caliber bow gun was operational. *Cecilia* was 100 percent intact. In fact, her turret gun was the *only* artillery on the beachhead but for one 81mm mortar and several 60mm mortars.

The shelling went on for some time, beginning with one destroyer and ending with a significant portion of the task force. For the most part, it went over the heads of the troops tucked into the northwest corner of the island. For most of those men, it was an unforgettable experience.

Second Lieutenant John Cannon was surprised to hear a low-pitched sound of yelling intermingled with the deep rumbles of the bombardment. Marines all over Red-1 were cheering on the naval gunners. But the cheers were short lived, for the guns pulled the range down to within 50 yards of Mike Ryan's massed Marines. The ground shook crazily. Men were bounced against the sides of their crumbling entrenchments. Some eardrums were blown out, and nearly everyone had a headache.

Then the air was still, quiet. But just for one beat. Suddenly, rebel yells and the yammering of automatic weapons filled the air. The Marines were moving.

Fire-and-move was the only tactic to be used on the way to the southern beaches. Ryan's Marines worked in small groups, isolating and destroying anything or anyone that looked hostile. Every satchel charge or hand grenade the Marines could unearth was moved to the front and put in the hands of any willing sapper. Under heavy, close fire, lone Marines sought out firing embrasures through which they might thrust an explosive charge. Muffled explosions and piteous shrieks of pain or surprise echoed back and forth across the breadth of Betio as Ryan's Marines filtered forward.

Pfc Dirk Offringa, a mortarman, was sent forward with a carbine to help guard the life of a flamegunner. Every man was a rifleman.

In the main, I Company attacked nearest Beach Green, while K Company moved on its left, inland. Elements of L and M Companies, with specialists, headquarters people, stragglers, and others, were interspersed throughout or given mopping-up chores.

China Gal advanced on the left with K Company, while *Cecilia's* 75mm gun was used against emplacements along Beach Green. *Cecilia* benefitted immensely from using a narrow truck road about 25 yards inland.

Lt John Cannon had started his day with a half-dozen members of his I Company platoon and an attached machine gun squad. As the attack progressed, however, more and more of Cannon's own riflemen returned to his command. There were not many of them left, but he was glad to be leading them as a team for the first time since losing track of most of them on the beach.

At length, I Company stood aside and allowed *Cecilia* to lead the way. The tank moved to within 20 yards of the nearest Japanese emplacement and fired its bow machine gun, which was followed by the flat *crack* of its 75mm main gun. The way was cleared. As several men broke off to mop up, the medium lumbered on, repeating the basic tactic until it was stopped momentarily some distance along the beach. The smoke from the bombardment had completely obscured the route of advance for the tankers buttoned up inside *Cecilia*, and the 75mm gun could not be accurately aimed.

First Lieutenant Sam Turner, who had been following *Cecilia*, reached for the telephone on the tank's back fender, but it had been shot away. The company commander then wheeled toward the I Company men behind him and yelled for a volunteer. Pfc Dale Young was sure that Turner was looking right at him, and he began to move. But he was beaten out by a fellow BAR-man, Pfc Jim Goldman.

Goldman slung his weapon and nimbly made his way to the tank's rear deck, just behind the turret. A quick rap of his fist on the turret hatch brought the tank commander into view, and he gladly allowed Goldman to call the shots.

Jim Goldman motioned the riflemen to lead the smoke-blinded behemoth. Each time the men on the ground came upon a target, they passed word to Goldman, who relayed coordinates to the gunner using clock-direction signals. Goldman had never before seen a tank in action and he was surprised by the accuracy of the 75mm gun.

Emplacement after emplacement was reduced to rubble.

John Cannon was a short distance from *Cecilia* during most of the advance. He was thoroughly relieved when the inertia of the assault carried him through a tangled, wooded area to the last stretch of open ground near the southwest corner of the island. The open area had been badly churned up by heavy shell fire and was being swept by the automatic weapons guarding the Singapore Gun, but the attackers could at least see where the fire was coming from, as could *Cecilia's* gunner.

Cannon finally reached the tank trap, the final barrier before the gun complex. There, John Cannon made a running, flying leap in an attempt to cross the wide, deep barrier. He missed, and the wind was knocked out of him as he tumbled to the bottom of the ditch.

Marines poured into the ditch and reformed. Then they went over the top in parade-ground style: two men boosted several others, one at a time. The attack on the far side of the trench was made against limited opposition. When John Cannon spotted three Japanese in the open, running madly for the protection of the gun complex, he knew that he had won.

Inland, Capt Jim Crain's K Company, with attached units, made a startlingly rapid advance against light opposition. The open area that was the western end of the main runway, an impenetrable domain on D-Day, was easily overrun. Very few Japanese had returned to occupy their entrenchments and emplacements following the bombardment, and Crain's force sustained few casualties.

By 1205, Pfc Jim Goldman, Lts John Cannon and Sam Turner, and the survivors of I Company, 2nd, were standing at or near the base of the Singapore Gun. Two hundred yards to the east, Capt Jim Crain and 2ndLt Jim Fawcett and the survivors of K Company were standing atop the seawall overlooking the southern beach.

At 1205, Maj Mike Ryan calmly informed Dave Shoup that he was holding all of Beach Green behind a 200-yard-deep perimeter.

A few Japanese could be seen scuttling hither and fro beyond the Marine lines on Beach Black-1, the southern beach opposite Red-1. It was evident that a head-on eastward drive from Ryan's unconsolidated position would be heavily contested. Ryan did not have the manpower to manage it alone and asked if the 1st and 2nd Battalions, 2nd, could help.

Far from it.

24

The situation on Red-2 was, at best, confusing. The sudden, rapid advances undertaken by elements of the 1st Battalion, 2nd, late on D-Day, together with the inability of the 2nd Battalion, 2nd, to follow, had created two relatively distinct Marine perimeters in the northern half of the central beachhead. Between the two occupied areas were Marines from both battalions, but not many. An unfillable gap existed across the northwestern taxiway, which was tabletop flat, hardtopped, and impervious to entrenching tools, although not to shellfire.

The lack of exploitation of the rapid advance by portions of Kyle's battalion meant that considerable numbers of Japanese were still operating throughout the occupied areas. They would oppose all attempts to advance by Jordan's battalion. The area in front of the 1st Battalion, 2nd, was also strongly defended. To take all the ground to Beach Black-2, the southern beach opposite Red-2, would entail two separate assaults. And, because there were small groups of Marines intermingled with larger groups of Japanese, the ground between the battalions could not be prepped by naval gunfire.

The negligible gains near the beach resulted in a number of trying circumstances, not the least of which was the fact that two of five 75mm howitzers on Red-2 were not, strictly speaking, within Marine lines—a circumstance made even stranger by the fact that the five guns were deployed hub-to-hub!

Jordan's 2nd Battalion, 2nd, was making efforts to close the gap with Kyle's 1st Battalion, 2nd.

Second Lieutenant Joe Barr and PlSgt Art Maher had about 50 men under their control, only half from their own F Company, 2nd. Maher had spent most of D-Day near the beach because he expected to get orders to evacuate. When, by nightfall, those orders had not come, he had decided to get in on the killing. Maher's ear, damaged in the obliteration of the torpedo warhead storage dump on D-Day, hurt badly, but Maher took his platoon leader's calm courage as an example. Joe Barr had been severely wounded in the left arm, but he steadfastly refused to see a doctor, despite the obviously severe pain he was experiencing; the officer could barely wield his light M2 carbine.

In fact, all the F Company officers but one had been injured. Farther inland than Art Maher but still shy of the taxiway, Capt Lefty Morris, the company commander, and 2ndLt George Cooper, a platoon leader, gathered a group of about 15 Marines and started them in the direction of the taxiway to mop up. Morris was wounded; Cooper was not.

Almost as soon as the 2nd Battalion, 2nd, began advancing from the seawall, PhM3 Harold Blank was ordered to move southward to establish an advanced aid station. Artillery fire that had plagued Blank's healing efforts near dawn had mysteriously ended. Although the front was only yards away, the beach seemed more like a rear area. The doctors manning the station, however, preferred a very literal translation of "forward" aid station, and they decided to move behind the troops.

The advances eventually brought all five guns of the 75mm composite battery well within friendly lines.

At the most, 175 Marines were actually within the western portion of the triangle formed by the main runway and the two taxiways. These were mainly members of A and B Companies, 2nd, neither of which was in any way homogeneous. The only thing to differentiate one unit from the other was the identity of the unit leaders; Capt Bill Bray was the commander of A Company, so anyone under his control was in A Company for the time being; on Bray's left, Capt Maxie Williams commanded the mixed unit called B Company. Behind Williams and Bray, north of the taxiway, was Capt Jim Clanahan's C Company, a bit more homogeneous than its sister companies, but still a very mixed bag.

When Clanahan's Marines organized their perimeter the night before, they had been in tenuous contact with Williams. By first light, the Japanese had worked in several light machine guns to cover the lightly held and fully exposed gap. There was no longer any contact between C and B Companies.

As soon as Maj Wood Kyle learned of the loss of contact with his forwardmost units, he ordered one of his .30-caliber machine gun platoons to set its guns facing westward, toward the new Japanese line. Concentrated machine gun fire, augmented by rifle fire, forced the infiltrators back. As soon as it was demonstrated that the taxiway was safe, Clanahan sent a platoon to fill the gap. He followed shortly thereafter with an effort to push all of C Company south of the taxiway.

Captain Clanahan pushed ahead with nearly every rifleman in his sector. Opposition on the front was meager, and the advance southward, on a southwestward axis, moved along rapidly. Strong Japanese emplacements on the right, however, poured a heavy flanking fire into the advancing elements. After Clanahan's troops had moved nearly 100 yards, the C Company commander was forced to call the whole thing off. There were no Marines to spare to cover the right, so the entire company was in danger of being chewed to bits.

C Company's drive, as far as it went, was so steady that there had been no time to effectively reduce a large number of emplacements on the western side of the taxiway. Small security details had been dropped along the way to keep an eye on these positions. Long after the drive halted, these Marines remained under intermittent sniper fire.

The phone to Capt Bill Bray's CP went dead at about noon. Wire teams rushed to splice the link, and, as soon as the work was completed, Major Kyle ordered Captains Williams and Bray to drive nonstop to the south shore. The two company commanders readied their mixed units and pushed every able-bodied Marine southward.

Second Lieutenant Bill Howell, operating with Bray, led his C Company Marines straight ahead in a staggered line. Howell's men, along with other leading groups, managed to force their way across the wide, open main runway against very light opposition. They got to a wide, deep trench within a dozen yards of the beach, where Howell reformed all the Marines he could find and turned westward at a dead run to intercept defenders trying to scramble to safety. A flurry of fire erupted, but the Japanese escaped in the confusion of unexpected direct contact. Too small to maneuver outside the trench, Howell's group stopped and deployed in a tight, protective knot.

Second Lieutenant Bob Harvey's A Company platoon, operating with Capt Bill Bray, succeeded in crossing the triangle without untoward incident. Since it had started well behind the front, it had had the bulk of A Company running opposition for it. On reaching the main runway on the heels of the leading files, however, Harvey ran into increased fire. The platoon took off in single file, zigzagging for a large shellhole in the center of the runway. The Japanese hit it then with three machine guns, two to the right and one to the left. The effect was devastating. Many of Harvey's men were mowed down in the open.

The survivors, numbering about 12, dived into a five-foot-deep shellhole and kept down until the shock wore off. One after another, four Marines peered curiously over the lip of the hole. Each was shot through the head. Despairing of ever reaching safety, one boy flexed and took off for the trenches to the south. He just about made it, but only feet from his goal he was felled next to a dead Japanese. The seven survivors decided to await the destruction of the machine guns.

The force of the drive got the leading elements of A and B Companies to within a dozen yards of Black-2. Too weak to muster a renewed drive, the troops consolidated along a 200-yard-long line running parallel to Black-2.

But the advance had opened the gates. Small units trailing behind Williams and Bray from the northeast and opposite C Company, in the northwest, began working through the triangle. Holed up in a large shellpit midway across the triangle, Capt Lefty Morris and his 15 F Company Marines were looking for the best moment to make their bid to cross the main runway. Morris was readying his men for the move, when a straggler ambled in and gave the captain a box of cigars. All hands stood down until the cigars were passed around and kindled. Then the group took off, slowly at first but gaining appreciable speed as it made its way into the open. The group crossed the main runway at a dead run and, just beyond, sought cover in an open trench about eight feet deep and 30 yards long. There had been no casualties so far.

Lefty Morris ordered his Marines to attack eastward to clear the area. One man was killed and four were wounded, including Morris for the second time and 2ndLt George Cooper, the last of the uninjured F Company officers.

While Morris's group was expanding its holdings, additional F Company Marines landed in the trench amidst the bursting rounds of a friendly artillery barrage that hit them in the open.

One of the new arrivals was PlSgt Art Maher, who was told that many earlier casualties had been inflicted by friendly artillery. The slim, redheaded noncom glanced northward and saw Marine 75mm pack howitzers firing point blank at the Marine-occupied trench. He lunged to his feet, pulled off his helmet, and removed the liner. Then, standing atop a shattered stump, he wigwagged semaphore signals to the gunners with the helmet and liner. The firing stopped.

As soon as A and B Companies had started their drives, Major Kyle ordered C Company and all available elements of D Company to follow, bearing westward to come in on the right of the leading units. Capt Jim Clanahan placed all his machine guns in a base of fire, then withdrew his riflemen to the east side of the taxiway to occupy the positions recently vacated by Williams and Bray. From there, he drove south-westward again, crossed the main runway, and placed his troops in the trenches on the right. The supporting .30-caliber machine gun platoon, with covering riflemen, then followed the same route.

While C Company was making its final drive on the main runway, a large force of Japanese counterattacked Capt Maxie Williams's line on the east flank. The attack was easily repulsed, but the Marines manning the unconsolidated positions suffered many casualties.

For all practical purposes, the southern beach, Black-2, was taken—24 hours behind schedule and at a cost far in excess of the direst predictions of the planners.

25

Maj Jim Crowe's two-battalion force remained hard pressed through the second day, partly because it had lost its momentum on D-Day, partly because of the casualties it had sustained, and partly because it was holding a position with an open flank.

Most of the trouble came from the terrain to which Crowe was confined and from the Japanese defenses on the ground he still had to take. The area held by the Marines, and most of the area to the south, was no more extensively defended than similar areas near Red-1 and Red-2. However, to the east were two exceptionally large multistory bunkers. As Betio's defensive keypoints, they were heavily protected by outlying strongpoints. And, aside from the physical defenses, the Japanese were able to employ the large manpower pool that had been charged with defending the untouched eastern portion of the island. That supply of fresh *rigosentai* seemed inexhaustible.

As 1stLt Lou Largey's medium tank *Colorado* was preparing to move inland about an hour after sunrise, a Japanese bluejacket—no doubt an infiltrator from the east—appeared as if from nowhere and attempted to stuff a hand grenade into the tank's wheel assembly. Fortunately, the Japanese was gunned down before he could cause any damage. But there were plenty more where he came from.

Pvt Leland Ziegenhagen and a dozen other late arrivals from I Company, 8th, eagerly scampered over the seawall as soon as they were deposited on Red-3. As the small group penetrated to the northeast taxiway, it noticed that a Japanese machine gun at the apex of the triangle had the area zeroed in. There was, however, one bit of cover in the cleared area: an unexploded 16-inch shell in the center of the clearing.

One by one, the new arrivals braced and moved out,

machine gun bullets following at their heels. On reaching the mammoth shell, nearly every man flopped down behind it, did a slow take to the right to check the Japanese gun, then legged southward to the next haven. The gun hit no one.

The next way station was a well-populated bomb crater 200 yards beyond the taxiway, and a second hole was just to the south of that. As soon as Ziegenhagen completed his dive into the second hole, he struck up a conversation with its occupants, who said they were pinned by a Japanese sniper who had shot every man trying to advance farther. It was clearly time for a breather.

After a time, even though the other men in the hole assured him he would die, Ziegenhagen got the itch to advance and talked a Private Lepansky into joining him. The two took a good running start and rushed south to the burned-out hulk of Marine medium tank *Charlie*. They hit the ground beside the hulk and found a very well-hidden group of Marines already there. Ziegenhagen entered the hulk through the driver's escape hatch in the floor and passed out the .30-caliber bow machine gun and the crew's four .45-caliber Thompson submachine guns. But Ziegenhagen stayed inside; as far as he was concerned, *Charlie* was an armor-plated foxhole. Private Lepansky agreed and joined him. The two probed the wreckage, found a pinochle deck, and knocked off for a quick two-handed game.

A day and a night in the lagoon were enough for 2ndLt Bill Fenerin of Weapons Company, 8th. He had to get a 37mm gun and a radio jeep to Red-3. Though his boat crew had been injured trying to unload him at the reef on D-Day, Fenerin decided to gamble his life on a run right down the pier. The boat arrived at the pierhead in good shape and the men unloaded the gun and jeep. When Fenerin told men already on the pierhead of his plan, he was told that he was crazy and his plan was suicidal. Fenerin bowed to superior wisdom and told his men to leave the gun and jeep and wade in.

Shortly after Fenerin reached the beach, he met Jim Crowe, who had commanded Weapons Company, 8th, at Guadalcanal. On hearing Fenerin's tale, Crowe ordered the 37mm gun retrieved and driven to the beach. Bill Fenerin never gave a thought to *not* obeying Crowe; he returned to the pierhead and, following a hair-raising drive down the pier, delivered the gun and himself to Major Crowe's beachhead.

Unlike most units on Red-3, F Company, 8th, was fairly well organized, although considerably understrength. Its job was relatively simple: hold the beach flank of the eastern sector and, without actually occupying it, deny use of the Burns-Philp wharf to the Japanese. The company had considerable support; elements of G, K, I, and L Companies were covering the area to the south of the east-facing line, and there were several 60mm mortars and 37mm guns in the sector.

F Company got hit shortly after dawn. Isolated groups of Japanese just south of the Burns-Philp wharf struck with sheets of rifle and machine gun fire, inflicting heavy casualties upon the thin platoons. The company's position became untenable within moments. It had to withdraw 30 yards and abandon the area between the water and the seawall, which was fully exposed.

Colorado was brought up behind F Company, and 1stLt Lou Largey used its 75mm gun to suppress much of the fire, then fired on the wharf for good measure.

At the same time, Capt Martin Barrett managed to gain direct radio contact with a pair of destroyers standing just beyond the reef. The ships' 5-inch guns pounded the area until the opposition had been all but completely destroyed.

While F Company's front was being cleared by friendly guns, Jim Crowe dispatched all elements of G Company that remained in the western sector to rejoin the main body of the company in the east. These groups were immediately worked into the line adjacent to F Company. A short time later, Crowe dispatched a 37mm gun to be incorporated directly into F Company's line. The result of these moves was that Maj Bill Chamberlin, Crowe's exec, actually had direct control over about two-thirds of Crowe's battalion. In all, he commanded all there was of G and F Companies, portions of H Company, most of K Company, and elements of I, L, and M Companies. Of the four majors on Red-3—Crowe, Chamberlin, Ruud, and Larsen—Chamberlin was the junior.

The shift of weight to the left was based on several possible sets of contingencies.

The first possible use of so many troops was an all-out attack to the east, aimed at securing the headquarters bunker of the

3rd Special Konkyochitai. There were large Japanese forces in the area, and it would take large Marine forces to scatter or destroy them.

At the same time, because the Japanese could mount a serious assault as easily as Crowe could, the left had to be bolstered against a breakthrough.

A third alternative was landing to the east by one or more battalions of the 6th Marines and an attack by Crowe's force to keep the Japanese occupied while the 6th waded ashore and deployed to deliver its own attack.

For the moment, all of these possibilities seemed equally viable, and Crowe was keeping his options open. In the end, a fourth plan would take precedence.

Early on D + 1, FM1 John Lane and a small group of Marines succeeded in advancing about 100 yards to a 40-foot-long trench in the triangle. After spending close to two hours in the trench, which was already occupied by several dozen other Marines, Lane was ordered to help wrest a bit more ground from the Japanese.

The green 17-year-old moved out under fire with several other Marines, following a young lieutenant who had just arrived and taken charge. The group worked to the left and stopped in a shallow depression between two palm trees, as the fire became too intense for further progress. Sensing, at length, that his group was too dangerously exposed, the lieutenant ordered it to return to the trench from which it started. As John Lane rose, he saw the man next to him fall and heard him emit a sound like he had been hit by a pumpkin. Before Lane could act, a corpsman kneeled beside the fallen Marine and motioned Lane away. Under heavy fire, the doc began treating the man, who had been hit in the head. Although grey matter was in evidence, the corpsman decided that there was enough life left to warrant heroic measures. He grabbed a roll of adhesive tape from his pouch and pieced the shattered skull back together. Then he hoisted the critically wounded Marine to his shoulder and stumbled back to the trench, uninjured.

Shortly after returning to the trench, the Marines were harrassed by a Japanese mortar. Forward movement was out of question, and there was no point in holding, so the lieutenant ordered his men to pack up and move back north.

Although FM1 John Lane was more than willing to abide by

the completely reasonable order, he had other things to contend with, like relieving his bowels for the first time in 36 hours. While Lane's fellow Marines pulled out, he remained to finish the job he had begun. Doing so probably saved his life, for the cluster of Marines was ripped apart by the mortar fire as soon as it got into the open. Lane helped two other Marines who had stayed behind man a .30-caliber machine gun they had salvaged from the debris. None of them knew the first thing about machine guns, but they managed to feed in a belt of ammunition before sitting back to nervously await the next horror in a day filled with a lifetime of horrors.

Shortly before dusk, just as Red-3 was buttoning up for the night, Maj Bill Chamberlin returned to the F Company CP, where he had spent the previous night. As soon as Chamberlin arrived, Capt Martin Barrett requested permission to send a combat patrol to intercept Japanese bent on reoccupying the Burns-Philp wharf. Mindful of the yeoman service done by a similar group the night before, Chamberlin readily assented. To improve chances of success, however, 15 men were sent (there had been nine the night before), and they took along two machine guns. The Japanese moved on the wharf after midnight. In the brief firefight, two Marines were wounded and 15 Japanese were killed.

Although the 2nd and 3rd Battalions, 8th, had taken far less new ground on D + 1 than units on Red-1 and Red-2, they had made quite a good accounting for themselves for the second day in a row. Sufficient inroads had been made against the Japanese defenders to warrant an optimistic attitude about Crowe's chances on the third day of battle.

26

Second Lieutenant Al Tidwell of A Company, 1st Battalion, 8th, counted only 21 of the 42 men he had led out of their LCVP. He had already lost his platoon sergeant, right guide, one squad leader, three assistant squad leaders, and 15 riflemen. Tidwell's platoon was by no means unique. The 1st Battalion, 8th, was disorganized and bleeding. More than 100—ten percent of the battalion—were dead or missing, and over 200 had been wounded, although many of the injured had joined the battalion and refused medical treatment.

Momentarily out of contact with his company, Al Tidwell led his men down the beach until he came upon LtCol Presley Rixey, commander of the 1st Battalion, 10th, who commandeered the demiplatoon for stevedore service. The artillery battalion was so shorthanded and so overworked that two newly-landed 75mm pack howitzers were sitting idle at the water's edge. Within minutes, Tidwell's tired survivors were gasping and fuming as they hauled the heavy guns into the artillery line.

Col Dave Shoup happened upon the platoon just as it finished moving the guns. After listening to Al Tidwell's story, Shoup tacked the platoon onto a nearby rifle company, which had itself been torn apart the day before. After spending all of 20 minutes with the strangers, however, Tidwell was off again in search of the rest of A Company, 8th, which had been located farther down the beach by runners sent out earlier.

Pfc Stan Kazmierski of C Company, 8th, arrived on the beach less than 20 yards from the main pier, where he found a dozen C Company Marines hugging the seawall. They told Kazmierski that the company commander had survived the journey to Betio and was trying to reform his unit. Other Marines from C Company arrived within minutes and crouched behind the seawall with those already there. The whole group, 30 badly shaken and leaderless men, was further stunned by a loud explosion nearby. One man timidly peered over the log wall and reassured his companions that a 75mm pack howitzer was firing from less than three yards away.

Pvt Manuel Souza, an ammunition carrier with D Company, 8th, was amazed to learn that he and a boy named Ryan were the only uninjured members of their seven-man .30-caliber machine gun squad; three of the others had been wounded and two had been killed getting ashore. Almost before Souza had an opportunity to collect his wits, he was accosted by a wild-eyed stranger from the 2nd Marines, who dropped to the beach from the seawall and called for volunteers to help haul stretchers from the front. Since he had lost his weapon and could find no one he knew, Manuel Souza shrugged and followed along with a small group of similarly disoriented stragglers.

Even in the most brutal moments of collective dismay and nearly total disintegration, there always seemed to be at least one man who, by his example, was able to instill confidence again where it had been lost. Lt Wyeth Willard, the 8th Marines Protestant chaplain, a veteran of six months of duty on Guadalcanal with the 2nd Marines, paraded the beach in full view of all who cared to see, Japanese or American, and chanted, "I'm Chaplain Willard and you can't shoot me!" He was right, too.

Shortly after finding the remnants of A Company, 2ndLt Al Tidwell was placed in command of the company's only platoon, a composite unit of 60 riflemen. On orders from Dave Shoup, transmitted through Maj Larry Hays, the battalion's rifle companies, such as they were, had to form a skirmish line and advance westward along the beach against the Japanese defending the beach boundary strongpoint.

Scouts were dispatched from A and C Companies to check out the pillbox network destroyed earlier by 1stLt Deane Hawkins's Scout-and-Sniper Platoon; when they returned with favorable news, the battalion moved out.

Al Tidwell's large platoon slowly expanded southward about 30 yards against moderate opposition, then wheeled to the right to form a continuous westward-facing line. They were tied in with elements of the 2nd Battalion, 2nd, at the seawall and with B Company, 8th, inland. Farther to the left, inland, C Company was wandering forward, disorganized and confused.

Pvt Clarence Shanks had not the vaguest idea where C Company was headed. He was not even certain it was adhering to a plan, but he was content to be swept along and do whatever fighting he must. Most of Shanks's buddies seemed to share his attitude.

The steady advance was punctuated by moments of notable bravery and common terror as apathetic men braved real fire or fearful men fired in panic at the slightest movement.

Under the firm leadership of GySgt Jared Hooper, the remnants of the 2nd Regiment's Scout-and-Sniper Platoon ranged along Hays's front, blasting and killing. As the fight intensified, several newly landed M3 light tanks were called up and placed in Hooper's hands for direction until the scouts were pulled back by Regiment for another job.

After the scouts left, direction of the tanks were left to 1stLt Jim Westerman of A Company, a mustang with combat experience at Guadalcanal. Moments after Westerman climbed aboard one tank, the small vehicle was blown out from beneath his feet. Undaunted, he scampered aboard a second tank and directed an attack on a large pillbox, which was left smoking.

Second Lieutenant Mark Tomlinson, another A Company officer, boarded another light tank and helped it destroy the nearest emplacement with its small but potent 37mm gun. As Tomlinson stood in the tank's open hatchway, he spotted Al Tidwell and directed the tank to a position beside his fellow platoon leader. Tomlinson removed his helmet to mop his brow and opened his mouth to speak, but before he could utter a sound, he flopped over dead, stitched from behind by an unseen machine gun.

Pfc Dodson Smith, one of Maj John Schoettel's communicators, was routed out from behind the seawall by a strange major who was organizing an assault in the direction of Red-1. The assault was momentarily stymied by fire from a large pillbox nearest the beach. Smith was sent to help open the way.

The group of Marines forming around Dodson Smith timed the lulls in the fire from the pillbox and took off one at a time for a log barricade that would serve as a stepping-off place for the final assault. Smith's turn came up quickly. He charged across the short stretch of open ground and arrived safely at the barricade. The next man panicked halfway and dropped into a shellhole to regain his courage. As soon as he lifted his head for a look, he was shot dead. The next man made it at a dead run, profusely commenting on his good luck. Everyone around him was laughing, for water was pouring from his bullet-riddled canteen.

The large group quickly gathered, but nothing more happened; no one was sure what to do next. A dazed Japanese bluejacket suddenly staggered into the open. One of Dodson Smith's fellow communicators quietly raised his carbine and drilled the man. Then the group got down to working out a plan. All agreed that a head-on assault would be disastrous, but no one could see an alternative. At length, a medium tank arrived and fired at the sand-covered emplacement, but without effect. The riflemen debated the possibility of advancing up the beach behind the tank. The idea was discarded, as no one really wanted to leave the security of the log wall.

In time, the tank ran low of 75mm ammunition, and the commander asked the indecisive riflemen to go back and get some more. Several Marines, including Pfc Dodson Smith, braved the fire across the beaten zone and in time returned with heavy cloverleaf containers of three 75mm rounds each.

Despite the activity of snipers throughout the area, the ammunition bearers were obliged to walk upright to keep the heavy containers in balance on their shoulders. When Dodson Smith arrived at the rear of the tank after a heart-stopping trot across the open ground, his third crossing that day, he was amazed to see that Japanese machine gun bullets had worn all the paint off one side of the medium tank's turret.

Marine mortars were placing rounds dangerously close to friendly troops and had to be told to secure. The duel between the tank and the pillbox continued until one lucky shot nosed through a weak spot and cooked off the ammunition in the Japanese emplacement. All the Marines waiting in the area swarmed over the pillbox and on down the beach.

Despite a severe shoulder wound he had received just shy of the beach, 2ndLt Augustine Jauregui, a B Company mustang, refused evacuation and opted to carry out demolitions assaults against Japanese pillboxes in the beach boundary defense complex. He was shot dead during one such assault.

Another officer responsible for demolishing pillboxes in the path of the 1st Battalion, 8th, was 1stLt Gordon Leslie, the engineer officer who had been the first man to assault the pierhead on D-Day. Leslie had lost track of his platoon, which had been virtually destroyed, but he had been able to outfit himself and one enlisted engineer with a flamethrower and explosives. The supply of fuel and TNT, however, was limited, and Leslie was eventually forced to call it a day.

Despite its often valiant struggle to take ground, the 1st Battalion, 8th, had been too grievously hurt in landing to keep up a sustained advance. The men were beat, and the Japanese were too well entrenched. After hours of fruitless fighting in which gains were measured in mere feet, the time to call a halt arrived. The battalion had at least successfully penetrated the beach boundary strongpoint, which provided cover for the hunters as well as the hunted.

The cover was good, but the danger was not over.

Late in the afternoon, Pvt Clarence Shanks's C Company group was ordered to cross the main runway and did so, taking fire from two directions as it pounded across the coral topping. Shanks and the others immediately went to ground to await orders but were told within minutes to return to their original position. The Marines once again pounded across the runway to safety. No one ever told them why they had had to cross in the first place.

Second Lieutenant Al Tidwell was conferring with his runner ten paces behind the front line when a Japanese bluejacket emerged from the debris of a small building and lit out for safety. Tidwell had his back to the enemy and first learned there was a live target on the loose when his runner screamed, "Shoot him! Shoot him!" Tidwell wheeled, carbine at the ready, and watched the Japanese disappear. Stupefied, the officer asked the runner why he had yelled and not fired. The laconic reply: "I didn't think of it."

The 1st Battalion, 8th, settled in for the night. Few of the troops had slept in the 36 hours since leaving *Sheridan*. Few would find rest this night.

27

The entire 1st Battalion, 2nd, was ashore by noon on D + 1. The last unit to arrive was 2ndLt Walt Yoder's 1st Platoon, D Company, 2nd, a machine gun unit. Yoder had been a member of the platoon since it was formed in San Diego in 1941 and had been upgraded from warrant officer at Guadalcanal. He had spent all of D-Day and the entire first night aboard his LCVP. In all, he had managed to get one gun ashore on D-Day.

Shortly after dawn, Yoder ordered his coxswain to make for the pierhead. As the LCVP passed *Niminoa*, Yoder watched several Navy TBF Avenger torpedo-bombers circle in from the southwest with their bomb-bays open. The first airplane planted its four 500-lb bombs directly in the boat's path. The tiny vessel barely escaped destruction as the coxswain heeled it over hard and roared out to the deepest part of the lagoon.

With eyes peeled for the menacing aircraft, Yoder's coxswain tried again, making for the small boat channel down the side of the pier. The boat made it halfway before getting caught in a machine gun crossfire, at which point the coxswain jammed it into reverse and guided it clear.

Yoder and the coxswain next adopted a ready-or-not attitude and planned their third approach. The boat was guided in at right angles to the pierhead, its ramp lowered on the run. As the vessel came to within yards of the log structure and bobbed in the swell, each gunner charged the full length of the deck, climbed the ramp, and leaped as high and as far as he could. All hands emerged unscathed and dry and hurriedly reformed.

Lieutenant Yoder led the way to Betio as soon as he spotted a clear-looking route directly down the pier. A hail of gunfire quickly showed him the folly of his intentions, and the gunners took to the water. After pushing on beside the pier and passing rubber rafts filled with wounded Marines, the platoon landed intact; the gunners even got a loaded ammunition cart ashore.

The sobered gunners moved west behind the seawall, where they passed aid stations and long lines of litters before coming upon Maj Wood Kyle's CP. Kyle commandeered the ammunition cart and told Yoder to stand by for orders. When Kyle returned, he asked Yoder to follow him. The two officers worked their way inland about 100 yards and sought refuge behind a large lumber pile. A heavy fire fight was going on to the left, and Yoder could see some of the action on Red-3. The lumber was hit every few moments by a spray of machine gun fire, which sent splinters in all directions. Yoder felt a bit excited but noted that his battalion commander was not disturbed one whit. Kyle pointed to a line of fuel drums on the south shore, and Yoder drew out his fieldglasses for a better look. The major stayed his hand and explained that fieldglasses had a way of drawing immediate, deadly fire, as the Japanese made every effort to kill troop leaders. Yoder chucked the glasses and his map case, another dead giveaway that he was an officer.

After a short briefing, Kyle ordered Yoder to move his gun platoon south to join Capt Maxie Williams on Black Beach. He said, "Good luck," and moved on, leaving the platoon leader to fend for himself.

Yoder returned to his waiting platoon and ordered the men to move out. Then, holding his platoon sergeant back, Yoder explained the dangers of keeping fieldglasses and map cases. However, GySgt Henry Gregerson was an old-time Marine, and he had too much respect for the value of Marine Corps property to be talked into throwing any of it away.

The gunners moved off in single file as far as the lumber pile. Then, with Lieutenant Yoder leading, they moved from hole to hole to hole under heavy fire to the edge of the northwest taxiway. There seemed to be only one way to cross the wide open space. Walt Yoder sprang to his feet alone and dashed into the open, leaving the others to follow or not, as they wished. As the platoon leader gained speed, he realized that he would soon have to find cover. Finally, he saw a mammoth shellhole directly in his path. He took the usual flying leap and, as he landed in the bottom, heard a quiet voice say, "Watch it, Mac, there's water." Yoder was by then sopping wet to the waist. He moved to the dry rim of the tiny lake and heard the same voice say over and over, "Watch it, Mac, there's water." Each warning was accompanied by a splash as another gunner hurtled into the hole. A quick nose-count revealed that no one had yet been hit.

The platoon reformed into a double column and moved out toward the oil drum landmark at a walk, Yoder again leading. As the tension mounted, the lieutenant steadily quickened the pace, almost to a dead run. Fortunately, the gunners happened to have chosen a lull for their acts of bravado, and all hands reassembled in the occupied trench just to the left of the oil drums, where Walt Yoder reported to Capt Maxie Williams.

Williams was overjoyed to get the guns and quickly led Yoder to the east end of the trench to set in the platoon. Along the way, the platoon leader saw four dead officers lying in a row at the bottom of the trench. Each still had on his map case and fieldglasses.

Fifty yards beyond the end of the ditch was a row of Japanese-held pillboxes which Yoder was to hold in check. Luckily, the firing embrasures were all pointed out to sea and there was no way for the Japanese machine gunners to fire into the Marine-occupied trench.

Yoder's machine guns were carefully deployed.

At about 1300, long after the 1st Battalion, 2nd, began its drive to the southern beach, and shortly after the leading elements gained the trenches just shy of the beach, LtCol Irvine Jordan informed Col Dave Shoup that he was no longer in contact with Marine units south of the northwest taxiway and that none of the runners he had dispatched had yet returned. Coincidentally, Shoup had just received word about the successes of the Marines holding the trenches to the south. Pfc Charles Stevens of F Company had just returned to Red-2 on orders from his company commander, Capt Lefty Morris.

Stevens's primary mission was to secure some water and rations. His inquiries led him to the regimental CP and, on finding Colonel Shoup, Stevens had stated his needs. Shoup was not at that moment certain that he had troops so far south, so he closely questioned Stevens. After getting all that Stevens knew, the colonel asked the rifleman when he had last had something to drink. Stevens allowed that it had been five or six hours.

Without saying another word, the regimental commander handed the rifleman his canteen and told him to drink up.

Stevens obligingly tilted his head back, poured, and came up sputtering and coughing. The colonel's canteen was filled with bourbon.

Shoup's first order was for Stevens to round up whatever he needed and find a way to transport it southward. The second order was for LtCol Irvine Jordan: The bulk of the 2nd Battalion, 2nd, was to immediately begin moving south, and Jordan was to establish a CP as far south as he could manage.

At about that time, LCdr Robert MacPherson, *Maryland's* senior air spotter, took his light plane over Betio's southern beaches, where he noticed a large number of unidentified troops in the vicinity of Black-2. Uncertain as to their nationality, the aviator was happy to see that they all dropped what they were doing to wave at him.

Second Lieutenant Larry Vlach ordered his 2nd Battalion machine gunners to move from the vicinity of the seawall. The platoon jogged southward with the general flow until it reached a trench full of Japanese and became embroiled in a fire fight. Within moments, the Japanese facing Vlach's gunners, many of whom had been wounded on D-Day, received heavy fire support from the right. Many of the gunners, including Vlach, were put out of commission, and the remainder had to disengage.

The gunners returned to Red-2 in pairs and trios, each man supporting at least one other who supported him in return. On regaining the beach, the wounded were lined up for treatment, and the uninjured were moved back to reacquire the guns and continue the journey to Black-2. For all practical purposes, however, Larry Vlach's platoon had ceased to exist.

Shortly after 2ndLt Walt Yoder set in three of his machine guns at the eastern end of Capt Maxie Williams's trench, he moved to the western end to report to the company commander. By that time, a group of A Company riflemen had arrived after taking a dreadful beating in the open. Williams and Yoder surmised that Yoder's platoon had been allowed to pass by the Japanese, who apparently hoped to draw larger units into the killing ground by making the route seem safe. The ruse had worked quite well.

A lone D Company .30-caliber gun that arrived with the A Company Marines was turned over to Walt Yoder to replace the gun he had sent ashore the day before but had been unable to relocate since his own arrival on Betio.

Slowly, almost imperceptibly, the line along the southern beach was strengthened to withstand counterattack and to serve as a base for the final drive to the water's edge.

Within an hour of gaining the southern trench, Pfc Dick Clark of A Company noticed a lull in the fighting and took some time out to shoot the breeze with his platoon leader, 2ndLt Bob Harvey. Harvey and Clark had been raised in the same town near Kalamazoo, Michigan, and Harvey was married to one of Clark's sister's closest friends. The two set aside their ranks and talked at great length.

After a while, Harvey became curious about the lull and rose to peer over the edge of the trench. He stayed up with his head exposed for a few moments, then slowly returned to the bottom of the cut, profusely bleeding from a hole in his forehead. Without uttering a sound, Bob Harvey died in a few moments.

At about 1600 hours, four hours after receiving his traveling orders, LtCol Irvine Jordan arrived in the southern trench accompanied by his command team and some straggling riflemen. On receiving reports from the senior officers, the ad hoc battalion commander estimated his force as being 70 Marines from A Company, 60 from B Company, 75 from C Company, 15 from E Company, 10 from F Company, two organized gun platoons from D Company, and assorted gunners and guns from H Company. In all, the forward positions were manned by about 200 Marines and supported by as many as 150 others just to the north. The small toehold was boxed in on three sides, either flank and the front. Many Japanese, including machine gunners, were operating throughout the sparsely held regions just to the north.

Within a quarter-hour of Jordan's arrival, the Japanese struck from the east for the second time that day.

Pfc Dick Clark and his companions, who were 50 yards from the end of the trench, spotted a number of the enemy taking cover behind a log wall at the narrow eastern end of the trench. Clark's BAR was inoperable, so he hauled a sack of hand grenades to the sound of the firing. With the help of three other Marines, Clark hurled the grenades as quickly as he could pull the pins. Cries of pain rose from behind the log barricade, and the attackers scuttled for cover under intense fire.

Immediately after the attack, Irvine Jordan contacted Dave Shoup via a phone that had just been run forward; he was ordered to get into physical contact with the 3rd Battalion, 2nd, to the left. Jordan called Captains Maxie Williams and Bill Bray for a council of war, at which the company commanders advised against an attack because the force was understrength and badly fatigued and there was little ammunition left on hand. Jordan concurred and phoned Shoup, who postponed the attack until the morning.

Pfc Charles Stevens returned to the trenches at about 1700, guiding an amtrac filled with 5-gallon water cans, cases of C-rations, and boxes of medical supplies. Dozens of hungry, thirsty Marines swarmed over the tractor and hauled out the cache of food. In place of the supplies, 30 wounded Marines were crowded aboard the tractor and sent northward.

Stevens grabbed a can of water and rushed to find his buddies. He sloshed the precious fluid into a shiny new C-ration can and passed the container around. But someone had goofed. As Marines all over Betio had been learning through the day, the water was fouled. Either the 5-gallon cans had not been properly cleaned before they were filled with the water in New Zealand, or the lead-based paint used as a liner was decomposing. Many thirsty Marines refused more than a first tentative gulp.

Pfc Dick Clark and three buddies were joined by a fourth Marine, who was dragging a full case of C-rations from the western end of the trench. The man asked if the A Company Marines had eaten and, when they told him they had not, left a few cans of food and moved on. Moments later, another Marine arrived to tell Clark and his companions that they should pull back to make way for a mortar barrage, which they did with alacrity. They sat down in a quiet place to watch the mortars hit the Japanese beyond the trench and began eating.

Clark turned for a moment to set his ration can down so that he could fumble through his pockets for his can opener. The only spot he could find for the can was on the chest of a dead Japanese. He was just reaching into a pocket when the first mortar shell hit 30 yards away. Immediately, the second round plowed in only 15 yards away, and Clark felt a dull thud and sharp pain in his right knee and across his back. He felt as though he had been lifted from the ground. Dazed, the BAR-man's thoughts turned to his companions and to wondering why they had not come to succor him. Shrugging mentally, he fumbled for his first aid pouch, from which he fingered a pair of sulfathiazole tablets. After popping the sulfa into his mouth, he began looking for his buddies.

One of them happened to be sitting directly across the trench, looking right at Clark. It took the dazed BAR-man a moment to realize that the man had a hole the size of a billiard ball in his forehead. The others were also dead.

Maj Wood Kyle arrived at LtCol Irvine Jordan's CP at about 1800 hours, releasing Jordan to journey back to Red-2. As the command was being transferred, contact with Red-2 was lost, so Jordan immediately moved out with a wire team to reestablish the vital link. The new phone line was in by 1825.

After dark, 2ndLt Bill Howell of C Company heard a violent stream of chatter emanating from a line of bunkers to the front. Howell's men had already cleared the trees and scrub in the area, but the platoon leader wanted to be certain he would not be attacked during the night. From his position in a small depression just outside the main trench, he ordered a rifleman, a former semipro pitcher with a mean left-hand fastball, to hurl some grenades at the bunkers.

Only a few grenades were thrown before Howell heard from his superiors: The 6th Marines was due to land on Beach Green and should be approaching the Marine enclave off Black-2 at any time. Howell acknowledged the message and stopped the grenade throwing. After further reflection, however, he decided to meet any unidentified activity with grenades, despite the alert that friendly troops *might* transit the area.

The decision was a prudent one. Some faint rustling near the trench in the dead of night was treated with a grenade volley. First light would reveal the mangled corpse of a Japanese bluejacket who had not been in evidence at dusk. The man had reached the lip of the trench with a large explosive charge strapped about his waist.

28

Beaches Red-1 and Green were secure.

Casualties sustained by the 3rd Battalion, 2nd, had been exorbitant. Of the 37 Marine officers and two Navy surgeons with the battalion on the eve of the battle, one of the surgeons and eight Marine officers were dead, and nine Marine officers were wounded. The enlisted ranks, with higher casualties, made out a little better on the percentages. But it wasn't over yet.

The perimeter established across the breadth of Betio about 170 yards east of Beach Green was lightly held by unbelievably tired men, many of whom were wounded or the victims of battle fatigue. Barring an overwhelming assault, however, the line could be held. Rear areas would have to be mopped up and patrolled, and it was inevitable that Marines would be killed or maimed doing those chores.

Second Lieutenant John Cannon's life had been in danger for over 29 hours, but he got a lift when he heard that the heavy fighting was over. All he had to do was probe through several apparently abandoned Japanese emplacements along Black-1, about 100 yards east of the Singapore Gun.

Cannon's small platoon started midway along Beach Green and made rapid progress around the point to begin the last leg of its short hike. Six riflemen were in the lead, and the remainder of the squad-sized unit was trailing by a few yards. Suddenly, a land mine exploded in the midst of the leading element. This was the first indication that any of the beaches was mined. Cannon and many in the trailing increment were knocked down.

As the lieutenant scrambled to his feet, he saw that all six of the men in the lead were down, dead or unconscious. His first impulse was to rush to their aid, but the likelihood of detonating another mine rooted him to his place.

One of the wounded Marines was Cannon's runner, Pvt Charles Hotchkiss. He had blood running from one ear and was trying to regain his feet. Cannon and the others yelled for the runner to watch for more mines, and the stunned youngster seemed to understand. Next, Cannon told the runner to wade into water and walk around the mined area. Hotchkiss started, but stopped when he heard another of the injured beg for help. The other man was rolling around, trying to find a way to get to his feet. Hotchkiss followed his footsteps back into the danger zone and dragged the other man to safety, then went back for a third man. The others were dead.

John Cannon reported the presence of the mines, then started getting his wounded back to Red-1. Hotchkiss, still dazed, was up and around on his own feet with a shattered eardrum, but he was well enough to remain with the platoon. The second survivor, propped up by a corpsman, hobbled back for treatment. The third man had suffered extensive wounds in his left leg and side, so he was placed on an impromptu stretcher made of shirts and ponchos and carried the short distance to the seawall overlooking Beach Green. Cannon's dog-tired men were too far gone to carry him farther.

At this juncture, while awaiting relief stretcher bearers, Cannon sat beside the wounded man just as he came around. The youth recognized his platoon leader and said, "Lieutenant, I never did make corporal, did I?" Cannon took one look at the mutilated rifleman and said, "Son, I'm proud of what you've done, and I'm appointing you corporal right now." The injured Marine sort of grinned, then lapsed back into unconsciousness.

As the wounded man rested beneath an impromptu shelter that his buddies fashioned from a few poles and a sheet of corrugated metal, PhM3 Tex Lingofelter returned to tell Cannon that no stretchers or bearers were available and only one doctor was on the beach. Cannon sent Lingofelter back to get a litter team, no matter what. It took another thirty minutes.

The troops were exhausted. Private Hotchkiss was staggering around in a daze, the side of his head bloody from the ruptured eardrum. It was a real horror show, and Cannon finally ordered Hotchkiss to get to the beach for treatment. By then, Doc Lingofelter had returned with a litter but no bearers. Hotchkiss trailed behind while Cannon, Pfc Dale Young, and another Marine carried the wounded man. The unremitting sun and the soft sand completely sapped the strength of the exhausted bearers. After frequent stops, they finally staggered into the aid station. They had carried their burden over 400 yards.

The litter was set down on the beach, which was crowded with wounded men. Bullets were still zinging in from the east, and Dr. Glenn Warrick was working behind a wrecked amtrac like a man possessed. He rushed from man to man in a crouch to avoid incoming bullets, treating some, checking others. For many, losing the surgeon to a Japanese bullet would have meant certain death.

John Cannon grabbed Warrick's arm and forced him to stop his rounds. The lesson Cannon was about to learn is basic to warfare.

Warrick bent over the grievously wounded boy and made a cursory examination. If nothing else, the overworked, over-tired doctor had learned how to diagnose injuries in a matter of seconds. He tiredly rose to his feet. His eyes did not meet John Cannon's as he shook his head and hurried away.

Cannon looked from the retreating back of the doctor to the wounded man and saw a slight movement at the jaw. There was still hope. The platoon leader, who had never heard the term "triage" nor seen the concept put to use, sprang to his own tired feet and ran to intercept the surgeon, telling Warrick that he had seen the wounded boy move and that something should be done. Glenn Warrick looked at the young officer and said in a tired, plaintive voice, "John, he has no chance. I've got to work with those who have a chance."

By the time Cannon regained his senses, he was sitting hunched up with his back to the seawall, ravenously spooning the contents of a C-ration can into his mouth. He was sobbing uncontrollably, shedding big tears down his grimy cheeks.

A voice from behind said, "John, are you hit?"

Cannon, who was just getting himself back under control, saw that he was being addressed by his company commander, 1stLt Sam Turner. Through his shame at losing control of his emotions, Cannon muttered, "Naw, I'm okay. Just brought a man in. I'll be with you in a minute."

Turner ignored the tearstains. He was probably as embarrassed over the encounter as Cannon. "Hurry up, then, John. Get me all the men you have and come on."

• • •

First Lieutenant Ott Schulte stared incredulously as a pair of dark human figures darted out of the distance and made their way eastward along the fringe of Red-1. The two heavily burdened men appeared to be carrying a machine gun. Farther back, a few more dark figures emerged. Schulte stared at the strangers, trying to determine whether they were Japanese coming to wipe out his forgotten little toehold on the otherwise unoccupied beach or Americans coming to his rescue.

Neither. The gunners dropped into a shellhole twenty yards from the westernmost foxhole of Schulte's enclave and set up the gun.

Ott Schulte had long since decided that an effort of one sort or another was being made by Marines to the west. He had heard gunfire and artillery most of the day. Now it was midafternoon, and the wounded platoon leader was convinced that the 3rd Battalion, 2nd, had successfully secured a major portion of its objective. He had watched the 1st Battalion, 8th, get butchered in the morning and reasoned that Division would not land troops at such risk if it did not intend to win Betio.

Schulte cut his reflections short when he noticed that the newcomers' .30-caliber machine gun was pointed right at his own small perimeter. Almost before he thought, Schulte heard himself yell, in his best platoon-leader's voice, "Hey! What are you doing over there?"

The startled gunners looked up, divined the source of the query (for Schulte's 30-odd men were buttoned up really tight), agreed among themselves that it was a friendly sort of question, and answered that they had been told to anchor the "left flank."

"Well," replied Schulte, "I've got a platoon of Marines down here and we're in your field of fire." He marked the line before it dawned on him that he might be able to get to the main body of the battalion. When that inspiration struck, the haggard, injured officer crouched low behind the seawall and ran to the gun pit. There, he explained his predicament to the squad leader, who gave him directions to the battalion CP. Schulte left his Marines in the care of GySgt Robert Van Buskirk, who had been shot through the neck on D-Day and could not speak, and jogged westward to find help for his wounded.

• • •

The machine gun squad that found Ott Schulte was but one small part of a major effort by Maj Mike Ryan to consolidate his gains along Beaches Red-1, Green, and Black-1 against expected Japanese counterattacks from the unoccupied territory to the east. Ryan's main headache was the small size of his battalion. He had been losing men all day, and he still had no artillery or support except 1stLt Ed Bales's two medium tanks, *Cecilia* and *China Gal*. There was still only one operable 81mm mortar and a few 60mm mortars in Ryan's enclave. Thankfully, Ryan was in firm radio contact with the 1st Battalion, 10th's fire direction center, and there was usually at least one American destroyer standing by off Beach Green.

Ryan had no desire to take more ground; he could barely cover the ground he had taken. In fact, prudence dictated that he relinquish certain of his holdings in the interest of a balanced defense. He had the beaches, and that was what counted.

Ryan relied heavily on the flat nature of the terrain, on which he had had his subordinates establish a general line of defensive emplacements manned by small groups of riflemen and machine gunners. By taking care to plot interconnecting fields of fire, his troops could cover a maximum of ground with a minimum of manpower. Mobile supports would be provided by the two medium tanks and by the warships offshore. With luck, Division would be able to spare troops to bolster or, better, to relieve the remnants of Ryan's battalion.

Following a tiring but uneventful journey along the beach, 1stLt Ott Schulte arrived at the battalion CP and reported to Capt Jim Crain, who happened to be conferring with Mike Ryan. After Schulte described the condition and position of his platoon, he asked Crain how the remainder of K Company had fared. He was shocked to learn that three of its six officers were dead and that scores of enlisted Marines were dead, wounded, or missing.

Crain ordered Schulte to report to the aid station, where Dr. Warrick treated his wrist and shoulder wounds. Warrick ordered him to catch the first outbound tractor to get needed inoculations aboard ship; Warrick had no antitetanus serum and Schulte's last booster had long since worn off. But Schulte was adamant. He had only left his platoon to find help for men in worse condition than he, and he refused to think of evacuation, tetanus or not, until they had been brought to safety.

Fortunately, 2ndLt Joe Roach of L Company happened to be at the aid station helping the doctor. He had not been able to locate his platoon since landing and was chafing to be of some use, so he volunteered to accompany Ott Schulte back down the beach to assume command of the lost platoon.

The two officers reached the platoon perimeter without mishap, and Schulte immediately ordered the walking wounded to form ranks on the beach. About 20 men reported. Six or eight others could not move under their own power, and another half-dozen were in so-so condition. Leaving Joe Roach in charge of those who would be staying to man the position, Schulte ordered one of the uninjured riflemen to take the point. GySgt Robert Van Buskirk, who was fine except for the loss of his voice, was given a rifle and told to protect the rear.

The ragged line of weary, wounded Marines set off down the beach.

29

When Maj Mike Ryan informed Division at 1235 that his force had secured the entire length of Beach Green, *Maryland* replied that the 1st Battalion, 6th Marines, would land at 1515. In the meantime, Ryan was to strengthen his position and continue mopping up.

Planning for the advent of 6th Marines units on Betio had been going on since 0900, when MGen Julian Smith had ordered Col Maurice Holmes and the staff of the 6th Marines to board *Maryland* to confer with the division staff.

As the conference progressed, it was decided to land Maj Willie Jones's 1st Battalion, 6th, by rubber boats in column of companies on Beach Green. Jones's battalion would reform behind Ryan's, then attack eastward as far as it could go by nightfall. LtCol Ray Murray's 2nd Battalion, 6th, would embark behind Jones in LCVPs and LCMs and would land if needed. LtCol Kenneth McLeod's 3rd Battalion, 6th, was to stand by aboard ship, as it was the last rifle battalion that *could* be made available at Tarawa.

Division queried Col Dave Shoup at 1022 to ask if he felt there were enough troops ashore to win Betio. Shoup replied that the situation ashore, while improving, was still tenuous. The news was passed to Colonel Holmes, who then left *Maryland* to brief his battalion commanders.

Division received a message at 1303 from an unidentified source indicating that a number of Japanese had been seen wading from the eastern tip of Betio to neighboring Bairiki. A message from Dave Shoup within the half-hour confirmed the report.

Division contacted Colonel Holmes within minutes of Shoup's confirmatory message and directed that he send Murray's 2nd Battalion into Bairiki. That island could not, under any circumstances, be allowed to fall into the hands of large Japanese forces. Besides, an occupation of Bairiki by a strong blocking force would restrict the Betio defenders to Betio.

Murray, whose battalion was in boats near its transport along with elements of the 2nd Battalion, 10th, could not respond to the new order by his own radio, so he asked his weapons company commander to query Division for additional details. The officer learned that only organic units were to be landed, not the artillery. After acknowledging the message, Lieutenant Colonel Murray ordered his battalion to start for Bairiki. He and his Marines faced a two-hour journey, at least.

Almost as soon as Murray's new orders were cut, Division directed LtCol Kenneth McLeod's 3rd Battalion to take to its boats and prepare to back Jones's 1st Battalion on Beach Green. At the same time, the light tanks of B Company, 2nd Tank Battalion, were ordered to land immediately behind Jones to support his assault through Maj Mike Ryan's lines and on down the long axis of the island. As Ryan had warned of obstacles on the southern half of Beach Green, the armor was ordered into what was to be called Green-North.

Problems immediately arose. The light tanks were divided between three transports—one platoon per battalion of the 6th Marines—and all were at the bottoms of the holds to which they had been consigned. Since the 6th Marines had not been committed until the last minute, very little of the gear stored above the tanks had been removed. It would take hours to get at the armor and offload it into LCMs. In the meantime, the transport division commander ordered all available LCMs to secure from all previous missions and stand by; that would at least save some precious time at the back end of the frustrating operation.

Colonel Shoup first learned that Jones's 1st Battalion was to be sent to Green-North at 1345. At 1347, Shoup managed to gain direct contact with Jones, whose entire battalion was still aboard transport *Feland*. One of the colonel's first requests was for Jones to bring as many flamethrowers as he could find.

At 1420, Major Jones informed his regimental commander, Colonel Holmes, that his Marines were moving over *Feland's* sides. There was no way Jones's battalion was going to be in a position to land by 1500. Still, since *Feland* was as close to Green-North as was safe, there was some hope that the 1st Battalion, 6th, could be landed by 1530.

Then the biggest snag of the day hit. Senior naval officers, oblivious to the conduct of the battle, decided that *Feland* was too close to the reef, and they ordered her to deeper water. The move forced Jones to secure with less than half his battalion disembarked.

When Dave Shoup asked Division at 1525 when he could expect Jones to begin landing, Colonel Holmes broke in to inform his colleague that the 1st Battalion, 6th, might be ashore by 1700. Shoup was stupefied by the news.

Aboard landing craft bound for Bairiki, LtCol Ray Murray's Marines were both elated and ill. They were elated because the 2nd Battalion, 6th, was considered a crack battalion and they were getting a chance to prove their worth. They were sick because the last meal aboard ship had been unusually greasy. In the boat carrying E Company's 3rd Platoon, Cpl Carl Hanson, a Guadalcanal veteran, wondered how his squad was ever going to fight. The combination of the greasy food and the pitch of the boat had left Hanson with a dozen extremely queasy riflemen.

Just before Murray's battalion landed on Bairiki, a flight of Navy fighters and dive-bombers worked the island over. One tracer round hit some gasoline the Japanese had stored in the center of the island, and the dump blew. Minutes later, at 1655, Murray's troops hit the beach.

Although the lead wave took a bit of fire just prior to landing, the airstrike had apparently cleansed the island. There was barely a shot fired by nervous Marines, and not one round in response. The battalion completely scoured Bairiki, but all the 1,000 ready-to-fight Marines could find was a small pillbox housing 15 charred corpses; the small force of defenders had foolishly barricaded itself in the fuel dump.

As no other Japanese could be found, Murray's troops lounged on the beach.

At 1706, Dave Shoup provided Division with a situation report as of 1600 hours. After discoursing on the deployment and progress of his troops, the colonel closed with: "Casualties many; percentage dead not known; combat efficiency: We are winning!"

Shoup contacted Division again at 1748 to learn whether Jones had landed. Then he asked Division to tell Major Jones not to advance through Ryan's battalion until sunrise. Division passed the advice to Colonel Holmes, who relayed it to Major Jones with further news that he was well senior to Major Ryan. Neither major received the message.

Jones's leading elements arrived at the reef off Beach Green at 1845 and transferred to seven- and eleven-man rubber rafts. A Company, in the lead, drew light fire from an unknown source as it furiously paddled through the surf, but no casualties resulted, and the fire ceased within minutes.

The only casualties sustained during the entire landing of the 1st Battalion, 6th, resulted from a collision between a supply-laden amtrac and a Japanese mine. Only one crew member survived the blast.

Willie Jones found his way to Mike Ryan's CP as soon as he landed and asked Ryan to provide a guide to show him the 3rd Battalion, 2nd's lines. Since neither Jones nor Ryan had received the message forbidding Jones's planned 2000-hours passage of the lines, the two coordinated their plans and helped one another deploy their troops to the best advantage to support and undertake the assault. Fortunately, Division got through to Jones within the hour and told him to delay the assault until sunrise. Jones immediately deployed his battalion on a line about 50 yards behind the 3rd Battalion, 2nd, and continued to prepare for the dawn attack, which would be delivered along the south shore.

After contending for most of the day with the Navy's views on combat loading, the 3rd Platoon, B Company, 2nd Tank Battalion, was further frustrated by unfavorable conditions at the reef off Beach Green. The platoon spent a great deal of time trying to find a way to get to the beach, but only two light tanks actually landed. When it became too dark to risk more vehicles in the water, the company commander decided to land the remainder of the company elsewhere. Division ordered the balance of the company to Red-2 via the west side of the main pier, where the armor was further delayed.

The landing of Jones's battalion was the most favorable boon granted 2nd Marine Division to that time. It was the first of seven rifle battalions to arrive ashore intact and at full strength. The troops were fresh and, as late arrivals, perhaps a bit more willing than most to prove their worth. It was the only battalion on Betio that night that was neither in direct contact with the Japanese nor at full alert.

The battalion staff was able to select a route of attack that would initially bypass strong defensive areas in favor of swiftly advancing through lightly held sectors in order to stitch the separate elements of 2nd Marine Division into a cohesive whole; the bypassed strongpoints would be left to the battalions already ashore. Also, the west-to-east axis of the assault would bring the battalion at right angles to most of the Japanese defensive lines, which would be automatically outflanked. The battalion's potential for achieving gains was enormous.

30

The tide had turned.

Whereas in the morning there had been sufficient reason to doubt the ability of the committed battalions to hold their meager gains, by dusk there was no doubt that those same battalions and those reinforcing them would win the battle for Betio.

Attitudes had markedly changed by sunset of D + 1. As tired and beaten as most early arrivals were, they had the look of victory about them. They were still taking risks, which is the sign of winners, and they openly expressed their optimism.

All three battalions of the 2nd Marines had seized their D-Day objectives. They were a day late and their positions were not secure, but they could prevail if the fresh 6th Marines could knit them together in the morning. The three battalions of the 8th Marines were well short of their goals, but each had developed exploitable holdings, and each was in decent shape to advance in the morning.

While the line battalions were ekeing out gains against the stubborn defenders, supporting arms and the supply services gained strength throughout the day.

Although it was supposed to have landed in its entirety on D-Day, not one gun of the 1st Battalion, 10th, was ashore by the first sunset, and only five of 12 guns were landed by dawn of D + 1. It is remarkable that those five guns were fired without the aid of the precise and arcane tools of the battalion's fire direction center. The gunners had to act on the basis of educated guesses with the help of an improvised communications net, often including untrained volunteer forward observers. Even more to the credit of the gunners is the fact that the battery fired all its initial missions while it was being peppered by small arms fire, something artillerymen fear and loathe.

Shortly after the 1st Battalion, 8th, landed, a 15-man headquarters increment of the 1st Battalion, 10th, arrived off the pier. It included several battalion officers, enlisted communicators and fire direction center specialists under the command of the battalion operations officer. After the protesting coxswain of the group's LCVP was forced to drop the ramp under fire, the artillerymen crouched behind several gasoline drums to await orders. The group briefly attempted to reach the beach by way of the pier, but it was forced into the water.

Pfc Clarence Frost, a computerman, went into water quite a bit over his head and had to pull himself hand over hand toward the beach along a hawser that had been stretched the length of the pier. Frost had never before seen a wounded man—much less a dead Marine, of which many were still bobbing in the swell beside the pier—and he was shocked by the merriment exhibited by the wounded on the way out. One grinning Marine said to another that he had "the prettiest hole in my arm you ever did see."

Much of the group's delicate equipment was ruined on the way to the beach by immersion in seawater, a factor that would require much additional time in getting missions fired by older, less reliable methods. The only thing the gunners had in their favor was the short distances over which they would have to fire; they usually could see the results of their salvos and could correct on that basis. By dusk of D + 1, all of the 1st Battalion, 10th's 12 guns were ashore and in battery, and that made a great difference in the outcome of the battle.

The supply situation took a turn for the better by noon. The progress was virtually imperceptible.

Small groups of riflemen, pioneers, and support personnel ran the gauntlet of fire to move a trickle of critically needed goods from the pierhead. Some men were ordered to help while others volunteered or simply fell into it.

The only radio at the pierhead was in the hands of Lt(jg) Larry Crane, *Heywood's* beachmaster, who had landed in the middle of the morning of D + 1. As soon as Crane realized that most of the urgent calls from the beach were being ignored by senior commanders aboard safe transports, he decided to serve as a direct link between the Marines and the transports. Crane was swamped with calls as soon as he went on the air. Priority calls from the beaches were channeled directly to the transports, circumventing senior naval officers and their staffs.

LCdr Lou Fabian, the squadron beachmaster, received orders at 0918 to report to Comdr John McGovern aboard *Pursuit*. Fabian, who had spent the night trying to keep order among the milling supply craft beyond the reef, was eager to get to the beach. He ordered his coxswain to the control boat, from where he was certain the commodore would send him ashore.

McGovern was thoroughly disgusted with Fabian. He had been all through the boat area searching among hundreds of landing craft trying to find the squadron beachmaster, and he had failed. McGovern's tone was sharp. Fabian was to organize the boats into landing waves and get essential supplies to the Marines, no matter what.

Fabian picked up a new radio set sent over from *Zeilin* and moved with alacrity to organize the hodgepodge of boats. As he was getting set to send them to the pierhead, his own LCVP was approached by an unseaworthy craft bearing LtCol Dixon Goen, Dave Shoup's regimental exec. Goen transferred from the sinking boat to Fabian's and asked the beachmaster what was going on. Fabian told him that, under direct orders from Commodore McGovern, food and medical supplies were being organized for transfer to the beach. Goen was astounded. He had just talked with Dave Shoup, who had clearly indicated that troops and ammunition were needed more than anything else.

Lou Fabian pounced on the news. He had been given extraordinary powers in his capacity as Squadron Beachmaster. Although McGovern was his nominal superior, he had the backing of the task force commander, RAdm Harry Hill. The 40-year-old Reserve officer had long since learned in business that extraordinary powers are worthless if they are not used. He immediately countermanded McGovern's directive and gathered all the Marines he could find and sent them to the pierhead with several boatloads of critically needed supplies and equipment. Then LCdr Lou Fabian followed, determined to get ashore to undertake his very special job.

It took until noon for Fabian and Goen to reach the pierhead. From there, the beachmaster's party and Goen's headquarters increment took a by-then typically exciting trip to the beach.

• • •

The high command was talking things over.

BGen Dutch Hermle, aboard *Ringgold*, sent the following to Division at 1158: "Supply summary about as follows: Captain McGovern has been on the *Pursuit* all morning making every effort to forward ammunition, water, rations to Beaches Red-1 and [Red]-2. These supplies boated and are in lagoon area. Division quartermaster sent in with working party to gather supplies from various boats in the lagoon and deliver to Red-1 and [Red]-2. Three LVTs dispatched 1145 with 75mm gun ammunition for Beach Red-2. Division quartermaster and McGovern are working together to land all working parties and supplies now in lagoon area."

At 1245, in response to repeated queries from Division, Dave Shoup radioed, "Situation ashore uncertain. Colonel Carlson en route to Division with pictures of the situation."

For the second time in 24 hours, LtCol Evans Carlson had been asked to brave the rigors of an outbound trip to *Maryland*. And, for the second time, the ex-Raider was to have a tremendous effect upon the supply situation.

At about the time Dave Shoup was sending his message to The Flag, Carlson reached the pierhead and looked for a free amphibian tractor. As he searched, he was approached by the pioneer battalion commander, LtCol Chester Salazar, who had evolved a new plan to iron out the numerous snags encountered in shuttling supplies to the beach.

The tractor shuttle begun by Dutch Hermle the preceding afternoon was working so well getting supplies from the reef to the pierhead that the small work party was swamped. At the same time, it was getting too crowded to stow the wounded who were awaiting evacuation from the beach, and Navy boat crews were growing increasingly hostile over the dangerous long waits at stationary pick-up points along the reef. It was decided by Carlson and Salazar that the only effective solution lay in allowing the tractors to work between the beach and the pierhead as well as between the pierhead and the reef. Casualties could be moved directly from the beach aboard the armored tractors, and that would undoubtedly save lives; they would be transferred directly to speedier LCVPs at the seaplane ramp. It was further agreed that Dave Shoup or his senior staffers would determine priorities based on real needs. Heretofore, naval officers far removed from the sound of the guns were making supply decisions based on what they had the most of.

Carlson resumed his journey to *Maryland*, but, before he could go to the flagship, he was obliged to round up additional tractors for Salazar to use. He ran into Commodore McGovern, who offered to find the required amtracs; in fact, he marshalled 18, which was an incredible accomplishment at the time.

On reaching the base of the pier, LCdr Lou Fabian and LtCol Dixon Goen got directions to the regimental CP. The first 100 yards were traversed with undue difficulty, but, as Fabian rose to walk the rest of the way upright, Dave Shoup screamed, "Oh, my God, run! This place is alive with Japs!"

A brief conversation with Shoup revealed that the only useful place for a beachmaster was at the pierhead, so Fabian backtracked through the water. Once there, he was gratified to learn that junior Navy and Marine officers were working together to circumvent higher authority and get supplies moved. The men handling the gear were exhibiting unbelievable devotion to duty. But there was still much to do.

After LtCol Chester Salazar briefed him, Fabian ordered that the gap that had been burned in the pier when Japanese mortars had ignited a fuel dump on D-Day morning be built over.

The seaplane ramp was badly battered by boats that had been running into it for upwards of 28 hours, and it had been gnawed at by thousands of bullets fired from the beach and *Niminoa*.

In response to worries and rumors about abnormally low tidal conditions, Commodore McGovern had fortunately ordered the fabrication of hundreds of pipe-metal structures that could be set at varying depths to support roller conveyers, over which supply crates could be pushed and upon which men could stand to work. Lou Fabian ordered these contraptions brought in and put to immediate use.

Gunfire from at least three directions initially prevented the supply handlers from standing to do their work. Rather, they crawled on their stomachs to push or tug heavy wooden crates farther and farther down the pier. The first crates with non-lethal contents to reach a forward area were set on the outer edges of the pier, and a clear space was left in the middle. Slowly, walls comprised of the crates were built up until a protected aisle took form. In time, supply handlers stood within the protected area and moved yet more crates along the extended roller conveyer running down the middle of the lengthening aisle.

The pierhead crews broke all the rules. Except for munitions, supply types were not segregated, so any given crate might contain food or dry mops or spare tripods or volleyball nets. The chaos was unbelievable. Hundreds of men milled about at the pierhead. Some unloaded boats. Others ran messages. Others stowed crates. Others unstowed crates. Some gave orders. Others ignored orders. Hundreds of men did hundreds of jobs with a minimum of rest and a minimum of organization. In time, the right kinds of equipment got to the beaches.

Shortly after sunset, Salazar and Fabian found that many junior Navy control officers had departed from the pierhead; they had gotten tired or hungry or fearful and had returned to their ships, leaving a serious command void. The waters off the pierhead were filled with boats and tractors that had to be directed. Lacking even one officer he could spare, Lou Fabian asked Coxswain Joseph Jiminez to try to restore order among the boats. Jimenez was very young and spoke very broken English, but he talked his way into de facto command of the boats, and he restored order.

By 2300, Fabian and Salazar agreed that the pier might collapse if more cargo were landed. Besides, the supply handlers were exhausted and needed a rest. When Salazar's sergeant-major found a small open area at the tip of the eastern branch of the pierhead, he called the two senior officers over and ordered them to get some sleep. Lou Fabian had just dozed off, when he was abruptly awakened by, of all people, Comdr John McGovern.

McGovern was incensed at finding the two senior officers asleep. Fabian attempted to explain that everyone was exhausted and the pier was in danger of falling into the lagoon. McGovern replied that, if the Marines were too far gone, Fabian should have requested bluejackets from the transports. Next, relying on his expertise as an engineer, McGovern insisted that the pier would be able to hold considerably more weight than it already was holding. He issued positive orders to get on with the unloading and then returned to *Pursuit*.

The tip of the pier caved in at 0300, taking a radio jeep with it. Nonessential personnel were evacuated, and a perversely pleased Lou Fabian messaged the commodore. Dozens of sleep-starved men went into the low water to boost sunken crates back onto the standing sections. Work continued through the night. The men refused to stop working.

Col Red Mike Edson, 2nd Marine Division's chief of staff, left *Maryland* at 1750, bound for Red-2 to succeed Dave Shoup as assault-force commander.

Colonel Edson officially took over when he arrived at Shoup's CP at 2030, and Shoup was glad of the change. Two weeks before, the regimental commander had been a lieutenant colonel commanding a staff section—an important staff section, but not a regiment, and certainly not seven rifle and nearly five support battalions in combat. For two days, he had been working out of a hole in the ground, beset by snipers, limping on a wrenched knee, and reduced to catching catnaps between urgent, frantic calls from this or that superior or subordinate. With Edson ashore, all Shoup had to worry about was his augmented regiment of seven rifle and nearly five support battalions, which he would direct from a hole in the ground, beset by snipers, limping on a wrenched knee and reduced to catching catnaps between urgent, frantic calls from this or that superior or subordinate.

Pfc Tom Deese drew the routine job of guarding a pile of gear on the pier at dark. After a few hours on the job, Deese noticed a large gasoline drum floating under the pier. Something was not right, but it took a minute before he realized the drum was moving against the current.

The sentry bellowed a challenge. No response.

Two rounds from Deese's Garand rifle prodded a Japanese bluejacket out from behind the floating drum, and Deese shot him dead.

The drum was half-filled with gasoline, and the dead man was armed with explosives.

The tide had turned, but there was still a long way to go.

Part IV
THE THIRD DAY

31

D + 2: The third day.

Division contacted LtCol Kenneth McLeod of the 3rd Battalion, 6th, at 0319, November 22, and ordered him to stand by off Beach Green at 0800. At 0359, Col Red Mike Edson, now working out of Col Dave Shoup's Red-2 CP, also ordered McLeod to stand by off Beach Green at 0800 to receive further orders.

At 0400, immediately after speaking with McLeod, Edson and Shoup contacted Col Elmer Hall of the 8th Marines to discuss the day's fighting. Then Edson sent Maj Tommy Tompkins to Beach Green to confer with Maj Willie Jones, whom Edson was unable to contact by radio.

Edson's order to Major Jones, relayed by Major Tompkins, was to pass his battalion through Ryan's and attack eastward along the south shore in order to gain firm physical contact with elements of the 1st and 2nd Battalions, 2nd, on Beach Black—precisely what Jones had already decided on his own to do.

Maj Larry Hays's 1st Battalion, 8th, was to assault westward along the northern beach to eliminate the beach boundary strongpoint. And Colonel Hall was to oversee the activities of the 2nd and 3rd Battalions, 8th, which were to attack eastward to break out of the Red-3 pocket.

The Bairiki positions held by LtCol Ray Murray's 2nd Battalion, 6th, were to provide a base for additional artillery supports. At 0300, the 2nd Battalion, 10th, was ordered into its boats. However, only E Battery and elements of the headquarters battery were in the water when an air alert stopped the operation and sent all the transports running for deeper water. The lone battery, with its supports, was ordered to immediately sail to Bairiki, and it arrived at 0630. F Battery and the remainder of Headquarters Battery would be landed by noon. D Battery, which was to have landed on Beach Green, could not get over the reef and also landed on Bairiki much later in the day. All of the 2nd Battalion's guns were tied by radio to the fire direction center of the 1st Battalion, 10th, on Red-2.

The commitment of the 2nd Battalion, 10th, to Bairiki had the effect of completely surrounding the Japanese on Betio, making it impossible for them to move large bodies of troops to better advantage without being observed and interdicted. The guns and Murray's battalion cut their line of retreat.

The third day looked promising. Colonel Edson had foreseen his greatest difficulties, and he had accounted for them in his orders. The third day was to be a day of consolidation and perhaps victory. Jones's battalion—and possibly McLeod's—was to be the instrument of that consolidation.

Short of winning on D+2, Edson apparently hoped to oversee the establishment of a unified eastward-facing line beyond the eastern extremity of his holdings on Red-3. This would enable his troops to conduct a mop-up operation from Red-1 to Black-1, and from Red-2 and Red-3 to Black-2. Several of the initial assault battalions might be relieved that day, possibly the entire 2nd Regiment.

The prevailing attitude among the commanders was voiced by Dave Shoup when Father Frank Kelly asked him how the division was faring. "I think we broke their backs," said the colonel to the priest, "but the bastards have a lot of ammunition left."

Early in the day, well before dawn, Edson's biggest headache was his lack of direct contact with Maj Willie Jones. Edson had much to say to the battalion commander, but he had to reply on inexact roundabout means to do so.

At 0505, Edson was forced to ask Division to relate the attack plan to Jones. This was, from the outset, a most unsatisfactory means for communicating because the message stood a good chance of being lost, either between Edson and *Maryland* or between *Maryland* and Jones. Lost messages had had a tremendous effect on the battle from the outset, but the 0505 message reached Jones intact. In the process, however, it was discovered that Jones was not in direct contact with his own regimental commander, Col Maurice Holmes.

Division contacted LtCol Kenneth McLeod to inform him—for the third time—that he was to have his 3rd Battalion, 6th, off Beach Green by 0800, at which time Dave Shoup would provide direction. However, Shoup was not in direct touch with McLeod.

A Company, 6th, mounted a limited reconnaissance at 0630 to look over the ground around the Singapore Gun. The complex was technically within the lines of the 3rd Battalion, 2nd, but there was a brief skirmish in which the newcomers killed several Japanese and captured five Korean laborers.

This was to be the last fruitful activity by the 1st Battalion, 6th, for over an hour. In the meantime, the niceties of command were observed in an abundance of radio messages.

At 0653, Division told Colonel Edson it had finally contacted Major Jones by radio. This was in apparent confirmation of Edson's 0505 message.

At 0720, Jones was contacted by 6th Regiment and told to postpone his assault pending specific orders from Col Dave Shoup. This had the effect of attaching Jones's battalion directly to Shoup's ever-burgeoning regiment.

At 0730, the 3rd Battalion, 6th—which had been on the water all night—was finally contacted by Division and ordered to land on Beach Green. This order apparently superseded all others, in which McLeod's battalion had been ordered to land, rendezvous, await orders, rendezvous, and finally land. McLeod would have seized the opportunity, but he was immediately told to await instructions as to the manner in which he was to land, and that left him pretty much where he had been all night, afloat in a sea of indecision.

Maj Tommy Tompkins contacted Colonels Edson and Shoup by radio at 0735 to say that he had just issued verbal orders to Major Jones. By then, however, Shoup had been in direct touch with Jones for some time, thus nullifying the latest of Tompkins's hazardous missions. Shoup directed Jones to be ready to push off at 0800. Jones would then be free to make his own tactical decisions for attacking the Japanese defenses between Ryan's and Kyle's battalions.

While two light and two medium tanks were being refueled, Jones's Marines closed on Ryan's lines and prepared to jump off. At length, the two light tanks moved to the front to support the leading files of C Company, 6th, with their 37mm guns.

Friendly ribbing marked the entry of C Company into the lines of I Company, 2nd. A short distance to the north, 2ndLt Jim Fawcett found no reason for amusement at the arrival of Jones's battalion; a few trigger-happy newcomers fired into Fawcett's left flank. The exhausted platoon leader brayed hoarse orders for them to secure, but the plea went unheeded. Finally, Fawcett stalked forward in the open, livid with rage, cranky from lack of sleep, and fed up with all the needless death he had seen in 48 hours on Betio. The former sergeant collared an unidentified captain and commenced to read him off. The recipient of Fawcett's tirade was so taken aback by the platoon leader's foaming rage that he neglected to ask Fawcett to identify himself. His anger spent, Jim Fawcett turned on his heel and rushed to see if any casualties had resulted from the indiscriminate fire. There was none.

H-Hour came and went, but the 1st Battalion, 6th, did not jump off; the tanks were not in position. Then, at 0805 the tanks clanked through the infantry files and the attack was on.

With a zone of action stretching only 100 yards from south to north, it was possible for C Company, 6th, to employ only one rifle platoon at a time. Third Platoon had the lead. As soon as it ran into opposition, the next platoon advanced to the front, and then the next, then 3rd Platoon again, and so forth.

The tanks flailed a path through the Japanese emplacements 50 yards ahead of the riflemen. They were far enough ahead to reduce danger to the riflemen but close enough to be supported by them. In addition to the tanks, C Company was supported by six flamethrower teams, deployed two to a platoon. The tactic they evolved called for the employment of two flamethrowers in the assault and four for mopping up bypassed emplacements.

Progress, while steady, was not without its hazards. There was a constant average of six pillboxes within every 100 square yards of jumbled terrain.

Midway through the initial thrust, one young Marine screamed at a particularly stubborn machine gun crew, "You bastards! I'm coming in!" He dropped his rifle, pulled a grenade from his pocket, and stalked forward to drop the explosive through the firing aperture of the emplacement. The pillbox was blown and the crazed Marine, by then flat on his stomach, began pounding the ground with his fist, laughing at a hysterical pitch.

Pfc Felix Kranc moved alone to attack three pillboxes that had caught his squad in a crossfire. He crawled up behind a standing coconut tree about 30 yards from the nearest pillbox and emptied a full eight-round clip into the firing embrasure. The Japanese machine gun kept firing, so Kranc called for a BAR and emptied a full magazine, without effect.

Kranc next got to his feet and loped back to his original position to collect three hand grenades. Then he turned back, passed the tree from which he had made his earlier effort, and advanced to within ten yards of the gun before lobbing all three grenades in quick succession. The position was blown and Kranc returned to his squad, where he spotted a wounded Marine between the two remaining pillboxes.

Private First Class Kranc grabbed a poncho, cajoled another Marine into joining him, and rushed into the open. As Kranc's squad fired to support him, he rolled the injured Marine onto the poncho and he and his companion pulled the wounded man to safety.

The two remaining pillboxes fell to Kranc's squad following a brief fight.

Within minutes of the fall of the pillbox strongpoint, PhM3 Milton Price was walking right behind Felix Kranc when he saw two Japanese with smoldering clothing leap from the trench and make a beeline for the company commander, Capt Joseph Golding, who was leading the way. One of the Japanese was felled as Marines nearby riddled him with bullets. The second man raised his fist at the company commander but fell under Kranc's rifle fire.

Jones's battalion gained visual contact with Marines on Black-2 at 1000. All C Company, 6th, had to do was link up and begin a passage of the lines.

In all, advance from Beach Green had been a relatively simple affair. Japanese casualties, virtually all killed, were estimated at from 50 to 250.

While Jones's 1st Battalion, 6th, was advancing toward Black-2, McLeod's 3rd Battalion, 6th, was getting its final set of orders for landing on Beach Green.

At 0810, just as Jones started moving, Colonel Edson sent

the following message to McLeod: "On landing, reinforce present lines ashore. Do not advance east. 1st Battalion, 8th Marines, is advancing west on north coast to reach you."

The message, while informative, did not actually specify that McLeod was to land. It only told him what to do once his battalion was ashore.

Finally, at 0850, the necessary order was issued: The 3rd Battalion, 6th, was to land on Green-North, reorganize on the beach, and prepare to attack at Division's order.

The battalion immediately started in but got hung up on the reef at low tide and did not get ashore until 1100.

First Lieutenant Ott Schulte, who was on the beach awaiting transportation to a hospital ship, was flabbergasted to see the battalion wade in standing up. Although slowed by deep potholes all along the way, the fresh Marines moved smartly in long lines, their rifles at high port. The only mishap occurred when the battalion's dentist stepped into a pothole and snapped his ankle.

McLeod's companies deployed behind the 3rd Battalion, 2nd; I Company, 6th, moved into the antitank ditch by the Singapore Gun to a point about midway across the island; L Company, 6th, tied in on the left and extended itself to the water at Red-1; and K Company, 6th, was the reserve. Thus came the relief of the battered, brilliant 3rd Battalion, 2nd.

32

In compliance with orders issued by Colonels Shoup and Edson the preceding evening, the rag-tag elements under Maj Wood Kyle began preparations for an eastward assault along Black-2. The object was to clear the opposition and link up with Crowe's battalions on Red-3.

Major Kyle, who had to oversee the defense of the entire trenchline, turned the command of the assault over to Capt Maxie Williams, who had a company-sized mixed bag to work with: one officer and 39 Marines from his own B Company; 26 Marines from A Company; 15 Marines from C Company; two machine gun platoons, and one officer and 30 riflemen from the 2nd Battalion, 2nd.

Williams's objective was a well-defended area along the beach. His troops were tired almost beyond ability to comprehend their orders, and at least a few were really ambulatory wounded. They had little ammunition.

As Williams made the rounds to brief the troop leaders, he stopped off at the eastern end of his sector to talk with 2ndLt Walt Yoder, whose machine gun platoon would support the initial phase of the assault. As the two officers lay down to confer, the foot of coral sand between them erupted under gunfire. The only possible source of the fire was a tree overlooking that end of the trench. Before either Williams or Yoder could react, a machine gun squad leader sawed off the top of the tree, using a precious chest of ammunition to do it. Out fell a dead Japanese sniper. Without pausing to see if the area was safe, Yoder's Guadalcanal-trained looters erupted over the end of the trench, stripped the souvenir-laden corpse, and presented Yoder with an enamel chrysanthemum-and-anchor *rigosentai* cap badge and a small strip of cloth bearing three gold bars.

Maxie Williams promptly and coolly got on with the

briefing. The attack was to be preceded by a naval bombardment and air support, which would be guided by a naval gunfire officer and a Navy air liaison officer who would be arriving at Yoder's position in a short time.

Within minutes of Williams's departure, a guide brought up the two liaison officers and informed Yoder that his platoon sergeant, GySgt Henry Gregerson, had been killed a little earlier by a sniper. Yoder took a few moments out to view Gregerson's body. The gunny was still carrying his map case and fieldglasses, and Yoder was again glad that he had ditched his. Since Gregerson's brother was in the battalion communications platoon, the lieutenant took the gunny's watch for him.

As soon as Yoder returned to his position, a medium tank arrived. The tank commander told Yoder that he was to support the attack until his limited supply of 75mm ammunition was exhausted.

Capt Williams's troops lined up, all set to go. B Company strung itself northward from the trench. On the left was 1stSgt Wilbur Burgess and 25 A Company riflemen. On the right were the remaining mixed elements, strung out to occupy the area between the trench and the water. Yoder's guns and the medium tank were in the center, and a second .30-caliber gun platoon was a bit to the north.

The attack began at Captain Williams's order. Progress on either side of the trench, which was relatively unsupported, was slower than in the center, where the tank and Yoder's guns helped clear the way. After the tank commander extracted a promise from the gunners to keep the Japanese from swarming over his vehicle, his tank lashed out at a line of pillboxes and bunkers about 50 yards beyond the gun platoon. In order to destroy the sand-covered emplacements, the tank's gunner first fired a dead-head armor-piercing round, then followed with a high explosive round aimed at precisely the same spot. As the tank fired, a swarm of *rigosentai* emerged and went after it. Surprised to see one attacker wielding a sword, Lieutenant Yoder ordered his gunners to cut loose. Three guns using a chest of ammunition apiece beat off the attackers, killing or maiming many.

The opposition appreciably stiffened as Captain Williams pressed on. It was discovered that the Japanese were occupying an elaborate and extensive network of trenches and that they possessed an inordinately large supply of automatic weapons.

Grenades were often useless against the bunkers and pillboxes and, much to everyone's surprise, large TNT charges were often insufficient for reducing the opposition. The only worthwhile weapon was the medium tank, but it ran out of ammunition too soon and clanked off to find more on Red-2.

Almost as soon as the medium departed, the Navy air liaison officer called in a fighter strike, which sprayed the occupied area with .50-caliber machine gun fire. The Navy F6F Hellcat fighters did little material damage, but since no Marines were inadvertently hit, they boosted morale a bit.

As soon as the Hellcats were clear, the naval gunfire team talked a destroyer into position south of the beach. The steady barrage of 5-inch rounds started "long" and was steadily pulled back to within 50 yards of the waiting Marines. Again, no Marine was injured by the friendly fire, and morale climbed accordingly.

As the engagement broadened, fresh troops from the north passed through Lieutenant Yoder's base of fire, and replacement stocks of ammunition began appearing. Among the new arrivals was a demolitions team, which toted in several large cases of TNT. The team leader talked Yoder into firing cover while he hit the still-active pillboxes in front of the gun platoon. Yoder instructed the crews of two guns to fire across the fronts and rears of the pillboxes while the engineers placed their charges on the blind sides facing the American gun emplacements.

The demolitions men moved out under heavy covering bursts and planted their explosives atop the nearest emplacement. Then they scuttled back to the trench, and everyone ducked as the charge went off. After shaking off a liberal covering of sand, all hands looked up to check the results of the blast. There was no perceptible damage.

On the next attempt, an entire case of TNT was primed and worked into position. As the engineers scuttled back again to the trench, one said that he was going to watch and invited the machine gunners to do the same. The gunners declined. The charge blew with a mighty roar. When Walt Yoder looked up, the curious engineer was being led away to the north, his face a sandblasted mess, his eyes destroyed. However, the top of the bunker had caved in.

The Marine assault teams under Captain Williams came to a halt after moving forward almost 200 yards against steadily increasing opposition. To the west, the 1st Battalion, 6th, was just coming into view, and the advance had to be stopped to allow Major Jones's Marines to pass through Major Kyle's.

Almost as soon as the trenches occupied by Maj Wood Kyle's troops were spotted by the crews of three tanks supporting Jones, the armor roared ahead. In the rush, the tankers passed all the way through a line of pillboxes, which immediately fired on the leading files of C Company, 6th. Without the armor, the riflemen felt they could not safely proceed.

Fortunately, a damaged tank just behind C Company, 6th, was still in radio contact with the others, and it called them back. As the tanks turned to rejoin Jones, Sgt Clifton Fomby advanced on his own initiative to guide them in against the pillboxes. As the first pillbox was being blasted, Fomby was shot in the stomach. He died a short time later.

Elements of C Company, 2nd, moved on the pillboxes from the east as C Company, 6th, attacked them from the west. Capt Jim Clanahan had long been planning to assault those pillboxes, and his platoons were ready to go.

As 2ndLt Bill Howell furiously crawled up to the nearest bunker, he peeked through the firing aperture and was amazed to see a face staring back at him. Howell's M2 carbine was virtually resting on the tip of the man's nose, so Howell pulled the trigger. Nothing happened. Howell forced his body to twist out of the line of fire and scooted behind a nearby palm tree. As soon as he felt he was out of immediate danger, he pulled open the bolt of his errant weapon. A small grain of coral was lodged on the firing pin.

Before Howell could return to the duel, one of his riflemen moved on the bunker with a primed hand grenade while others shouted instructions. Growing anxious under the mounting pressure, the Marine rose to toss his grenade, but a shot from within the bunker killed him. As the dead man's body rolled from atop the bunker, Howell's BAR-man lost his head and ran into the open, spraying long bursts at each of the bunkers in the complex. He regained his composure in a few moments and returned to his platoon in one piece.

By then, one of the light tanks supporting Jones's battalion appeared on the scene and fired 37mm armor-piercing, high-explosive, and canister rounds through each bunker in turn.

The bunkers were then scoured by waiting riflemen, who took no prisoners.

After the tanks had done all they could, the six flamethrower teams operating with C Company, 6th, moved in and really finished the job. Over 100 Japanese were killed in this engagement. Others who survived the onslaught were killed later while sniping at Kyle's Marines.

C Company, 6th, linked up with C Company, 2nd. It was 1100.

33

Crucial to Red Mike Edson's master plan of action for D + 2 was the assignment of Maj Larry Hays's 1st Battalion, 8th, to attack westward from the right flank of Red-2 to reduce the Japanese beach boundary strongpoint.

After a day of heavy fighting, Hays's troops already knew that progress would be slow and extremely costly without some sort of heavy support. So, through the second night, Division had made every effort to supply Hays with the types of weapons he would need.

At 1700 in the evening of D + 1, there arrived on Red-2 two waterlogged light tanks from C Company, 2nd Tank Battalion. Originally assigned to support the 3rd Battalion, 2nd, on Red-1, the six-tank platoon of which they were a part had been rerouted to Red-3 early on D-Day. In attempting a passage along the eastern side of the pier, four LCMs had been sunk, and four tanks had been lost. The two survivors had been withdrawn and, after spending most of D + 1 afloat, had been sent into Red-2. They worked with Hays's battalion until nightfall, when they were pulled back.

At the time the two C Company tanks were going into Red-2, the 18 light tanks of B Company, 2nd Tank Battalion, were bound for Beach Green. Only two landed there before the rest were sent to the reef off Red-2. Moving as best they could in the dark, without markers or other aids, the B Company LCMs had broken into small groups. Three, commanded by PlSgt Leonard Sines, finally arrived off Red-2 at about 0215, November 22.

Sines's tank, *Burp*, refused to budge when its LCM lowered its ramp at the reef; its starter had burned out. A tow was passed from one of the other tanks and, with Sines and the other tank commanders walking ahead on foot, the three vehicles worked in over the reef and through the waist-deep water. They arrived on the beach by 0300. The tanks were hurriedly parked on a bit of open ground while Sines rushed off to find someone to tell him what to do. While Sines was gone, a brief concentration of Japanese mortar fire knocked *Burp's* turret askew and put it out of commission.

The next group of light tanks arrived on the beach at 0730. These three, also from B Company, were hurriedly attached to the two C Company tanks that had landed the previous afternoon and ordered to support the 1st Battalion, 8th.

Three more B Company tanks that arrived off Red-2 at 0800 were all flooded out as they attempted to pass to the beach.

At about that time, the last two of Platoon Sergeant Sines's B Company tanks were sent to bolster the five tanks already operating with Hays's battalion.

Second Lieutenant Al Tidwell of A Company, 8th, knew it was going to be a rough day within minutes of waking.

Tidwell had spent the night in a shellhole about twenty feet from the front line. With him were his runner, a corpsman, and a staff noncom. During the night, Tidwell had been awakened by a loud noise and had asked the runner, who was on guard, what had happened. The Marine replied that he had looked up to see a Japanese officer standing over the hole looking down on the group. The intruder had fired his pistol into the hole and had taken off. Then the runner had shot him. The story was too farfetched for Tidwell, and he dozed off without further comment. As soon as it was light enough to see, Tidwell spotted a crumpled human form midway between his shellhole and the platoon line. It had not been there the night before. When Tidwell checked the body, he discovered a pistol clenched in one of the outstretched hands, a sword, and two hand grenades. Why the Japanese naval officer had not silently attacked with the grenades was to remain one of life's little mysteries.

Hays's battalion jumped off at 0700. B Company, such as it was, held the beach flank. A Company, such as it was, held the center, with Al Tidwell in command of its oversized infantry platoon. On the left, C Company, such as it was, was spread as far as it could be stretched, and its left flank was dangling. Interspersed through the line was a hodgepodge of attached units, including some engineers, a few pioneers, communicators, and some headquarters people from the 3rd Battalion, 2nd; scattered elements of D Company's mortar and machine gun platoons; and one civilian correspondent, Keith Wheeler, of the *Chicago Times*.

Using well-honed fire-and-move tactics, the infantry line immediately began taking ground. The Japanese defenses were fairly dense and mutually supporting. Flamethrower teams, tanks, and demolitions teams armed with TNT and bangalore torpedoes (long pipes filled with TNT) ranged alongside infantry teams firing heavy covering concentrations. Within minutes of jumping off, the entire battalion was engaged to the last man in an exceptionally hot, largely disorganized fight.

The preceding night, Maj John Schoettel had established his CP in a large shellhole beside a partially destroyed bunker. In the morning, shortly after the assault began, Sgt Chester Brown, one of Schoettel's communicators, grew curious and clawed the dirt away from the half-buried entrance. Then, with a carbine in his right hand and a flashlight in his left, Brown crawled in. His muffled voice was heard moments later by the men in the shellhole CP; he was yelling for ammunition. Cpl Lew Benton, another communicator, heaved two magazines through the entryway. Brown continued to fire; then there was silence. At length, Brown emerged to report, "We'll have to haul 'em out. I killed five in there. There were two dead already. That makes seven."

A short distance away, by the seawall, a flamegunner directed a burst of oily flame into a pillbox just overhead. After the fire inside died out, four dead Japanese were found sprawled about their machine gun.

A short while after going into action, one of the light tanks was blown up by what appeared to be a magnetic mine, a second tank was immobilized by Japanese mortar fire, and a third was lost when it toppled into a large shellhole. A fourth tank burned out its ignition and dropped out of the fight.

Although the light tanks lent moral support, they were virtually useless in this phase of the operation. The crews were willing enough to grapple with the Japanese, but their small 37mm guns were no match for Japanese defensive engineering. The only mobile weapons large enough to do the job were the 75mm guns aboard two halftracks from Weapons Company,

2nd Marines, which were called forward to replace the light tanks.

The halftracks moved up behind B Company, 8th, and fired liberal doses of 75mm armor-piercing and high-explosive rounds along the front. Each gun was moved to within about 60 feet of an offending line of pillboxes, then a dozen rounds were fired in quick succession as each gun slowly traversed a 60-degree arc. The guns were so close to the targets that the firing report and contact detonation were indistinguishable. One blast tossed a man 50 feet into the air. The body, with sword flapping at its side, pinwheeled upward, stopped at the top of its arc, then crashed earthward, head first.

A number of emplacements survived even this rough handling, so B Company officers had to direct riflemen against the survivors of the destroyed or damaged pillboxes. For reasons known only to themselves, the Japanese decided to scurry to and fro through the debris of the wrecked emplacements, thus exposing themselves to deadly fire. Had they stayed put, they might have been invaluable as snipers. Dust-covered, they were almost invisible, even at close range, unless they moved in the open.

First Lieutenant Charles McNeil of B Company was shot through the groin by a Japanese who did stay put; he clung to life for several days but died without ever regaining consciousness.

Another Marine troop leader ordered his B Company riflemen to pull back while he moved against another dust-obscured emplacement. He rose to his feet and poured the contents of a full clip through a hole in the gently sloping mound, but he was felled as he reached for the second clip. Cries of "Corpsman!" rose as soon as he went down. Correspondent Keith Wheeler lifted himself from his protective hole and sprinted to a low log building just as the wounded Marine was brought in. The man was on his stomach on a stretcher, gasping horribly. His shirt was pulled off to reveal blood flowing so thickly that it took precious moments to find the gaping wound. A rifleman egged the nimble corpsman on, exclaiming how brave his friend had been, begging the corpsman to keep the man alive. But the gasping ceased, and the corpsman closed one eye with his blood-covered thumb. It took a moment for the message to sink in. The crouching rifleman refused to believe that his buddy was dead, but he finally calmed down, removed his helmet, and stared silently at the death-shriveled body.

The halftracks withdrew to replenish their ammunition stocks, so riflemen worked in with grenades, hoping to put the time to use. First Lieutenant Gordon Leslie arrived to help, but his engineer team lacked explosives and flamethrower fuel, so it was sent to the beach to help collect the dead.

As soon as the halftracks returned, one took machine gun fire through its radiator and had to retire. The surviving vehicle led the way westward along the beach.

34

Between 0700 and 0720, battleships standing well off Betio—far enough to achieve the high firing angles they had arrogantly neglected to achieve on D-Day—fired 14- and 16-inch guns at targets ranging from the eastern end of Betio to within 500 yards of Crowe's lines on Red-3. Next, carrier aircraft pummeled the area for 30 minutes. Between 0830 and 0850, the battleships resumed firing. Then more air. Then, from 0930 to 0950, the battleships fired again. Then more air, and then from 1030 to 1050, more battleship gunnery. The goal was to destroy the Japanese reserve manpower pool and resources in the rear.

Early on D + 2, Maj Jim Crowe issued general orders calling for an all-out assault against the defensive complex on his left flank below the Burns-Philp wharf. The complex, consisting primarily of the large covered bombproof and two supporting pillboxes, had stymied F and K Companies for nearly 48 hours and had barred the way to the wharf and the entire eastern end of Betio. After spending nearly all of D + 1 preparing the way, the two badly understrength rifle companies and assorted mixed units under Maj Bill Chamberlin were ready to go.

The remnant of F Company drew the steel pillbox covering the wharf and the northeast corner of the bombproof. G Company was in support. A short distance to the south, K Company, supported by two 37mm antitank guns and its own 60mm mortars, was to hit the coconut-log pillbox guarding the south and southeast portions of the bombproof. Assault teams from the most successful unit would take on the bombproof itself. There were no plans for further advances by any of the units on Red-3; they would be issued when the bombproof fell. If the bombproof fell.

Preparations for the assault began at about 0930, when most

of the machine guns along the front, particularly those supporting F Company, were shifted to what was hoped would be better advantage. At the same time, Marines began cleaning their rifles and automatic weapons in relays; the crud of the two days of battle had fouled many weapons to the point of unreliability.

Also at 0930, the 60mm mortars supporting K Company were unleashed against the coconut-log emplacement and the area around it. No fire was directed against the covered bunker as that would have been a waste of precious ammunition. One round from a K Company mortar hit an uncharted ammunition dump, which blew with a loud bang. The dump, to the amazement of all, had been *in* the very emplacement that held up the advance for two full days. Machine gun fire from this quarter ceased to be a problem.

While the infantry's preparations continued, *Colorado*, the lone surviving medium tank of 1stLt Lou Largey's platoon, slowly advanced through the riflemen huddled along the beach to a position behind the easternmost extremity of F Company's seawall line. Largey directed his 75mm gun against the steel pillbox, and a quick succession of direct hits flattened the position, giving F Company free reign over the area.

At 1000, moments after *Colorado* destroyed the steel pillbox, the assault on the bombproof was cancelled. Rather, F Company was to assault eastward to outflank the defensive keypoint. Then the main event would commence.

The haggard remnants of F Company had only 30 yards to take, the same 30 yards they had conceded the day before to consolidate their position on the beach. A lot had happened to weaken and demoralize F Company in two days of battle, so it took Capt Martin Barrett several hours just to get his troops into position.

F Company struck at 1300 and immediately met with ferocious defensive fire from infantry positions along the beach and just across the seawall. Although small gains were achieved, it was decided that the assault on the bombproof would have to be made without the added benefit of flank control.

As the covered bunker was the main objective in his sector of Red-3, Maj Bill Chamberlin was more or less left with the task of organizing the proceedings. With F Company bogged down at the seawall and K Company engaged on the bomb-proof's western flank, it was impossible to draw upon any organic infantry formations for the assault. Chamberlin began scrounging.

One of the first men nabbed in the major's roundup was TSgt Norm Hatch, the only combat movie cameramen on Red-3 (and the only one on Betio through D-Day and D + 1). Using his rank and considerable bulk to bolster his native talents for organization, Hatch helped Major Chamberlin gather a mixed group of stray riflemen and specialists. Once organized, the group huddled below the seawall for a quick briefing. Chamberlin pointed to the crest of the bombproof and told the men, "When I yell 'Follow me!' you follow me up that bombproof."

Hunched up against the wall with Technical Sergeant Hatch, Chamberlin watched and waited for a few moments. The fire did not slacken, and the scene changed not one jot. The major shrugged and, without looking back, rose to his feet and yelled "Follow me!" Norm Hatch raced with him to the top.

At the crest of the mound, the major and the cameraman—who was carrying his movie camera—stared in amazement as a squad of Japanese broke into the open and spotted them silhouetted against the smoky skyline. Chamberlin instantly prepared to fire. Only then did he realize that he was unarmed.

Norm Hatch wordlessly looked on. The major looked at him, snapping him into action. Hatch placed his precious camera under his arm and began sifting through his film-filled bandoleers in search of his .45-caliber pistol, which had long since been twisted out of reach behind his back. He looked at Chamberlin in helpless dismay, and Chamberlin muttered one curt suggestion, "Let's get the hell out of here!"

They turned and barrelled off the mound, unhurt, furious.

Like Chamberlin and Hatch, 1stLt Sandy Bonnyman of F Company, 18th, put together a mixed group of engineers, pioneers, and stray riflemen to mount an assault on the bombproof. The group worked through the F Company seawall line and sought the protection of a six-foot-high wooden fence running at right angles to the seawall just off the bombproof's northwest corner.

The bombproof was the closest to a hill on Betio. Since it had proved impossible to breach either of the entryways, the only tactic left to Bonnyman was a direct uphill assault. The Japanese engineers who had designed the bomb-proof had left a number of large black ventilators protruding from the well-camouflaged roof. Those ventilators would be Sandy Bonnyman's key objectives. A bit of flaming fuel fired into them would certainly force the defenders into the open. The alternative was air too hot to breathe and thus asphyxia-tion.

So, supported by 37mm antitank guns, 60mm mortars, and an assortment of automatic infantry weapons, Bonnyman's group lined up single-file below the seawall and stepped off.

Each of Bonnyman's men individually vaulted the seawall to the higher ground behind the L-shaped fence. From there, following hand signals from observers who could clearly see the objective, the men worked along the fence to the foot of the slope, where they were stopped by heavy gunfire.

Cpl Harry Niehoff's demolitions team was intercepted by Major Chamberlin as it returned from a minor foray farther along the beach. Chamberlin asked Niehoff if there were any explosives available, and Niehoff replied that he still had several charges. "Where do you want them used, Sir?" Chamberlin motioned to the covered bombproof and explained that the Japanese were reinforcing from the southeast but that their avenue of approach was well camouflaged and had not yet been found.

Harry Niehoff hurled several charges over the bombproof and ducked behind the seawall as a flurry of fire sought him out. When the firing subsided, he led his engineers around to the L-shaped fence and prepared to move on the summit.

Pfc Johnny Borich, who was operating one of two flame-throwers on Red-3, was the pointman. He lightly doused the top of the bunker while Harry Niehoff tossed a big charge in hopes of subduing the defenses. Next, Borich moved forward to spray a concentrated burst of flame. As Niehoff prepared to throw another charge, Borich screamed, "Grenade!" Every-one hit the dirt.

The instant the dust settled, Corporal Niehoff threw another big charge. It blew, and every man behind the fence piled into the open and legged uphill to the summit.

All over Red-3, Marines curious about the commotion stopped what they were doing to look on as Sandy Bonnyman and a half-dozen Marines made it to the top. TSgt Norm Hatch captured the breakthrough with his movie camera.

The first key had been turned by Johnny Borich and Harry Niehoff. The combination of flame and TNT had killed the crew manning a machine gun at the top of the bunker and had set the palm-frond camouflage afire to cover the breakthrough.

The next key was turned by a pioneer named Earl Coleman. As Sandy Bonnyman sparked the team and issued a steady stream of orders, Pappy Coleman yelled for TNT and tossed fused charges as fast as he could light them. In moments, he had blown the cover off a camouflaged entryway on the southeast corner of the huge structure. As hundreds of helpless Marines looked on, a large knot of Japanese burst from the exposed entryway and formed to counterattack Bonnyman's team.

There were only a half-dozen men atop the bombproof at that moment. Pfc Johnny Borich was firing burning diesel into the ventilators, forcing the Japanese to evacuate. Pappy Coleman, Cpl Harry Niehoff, and Sgt Elmo Ferretti were furiously heaving blocks of TNT. Sandy Bonnyman faced the Japanese alone with his light M2 carbine.

Bonnyman leaped to the forward edge of the toehold beside Harry Niehoff, rammed home a full 15-round clip, and rapidly fired into the oncoming *rigosentai*. Some fell. Most kept coming. With the Japanese only yards away, Bonnyman rammed home another fresh clip and killed three, just as Marine reinforcements attacking up the backside of the bunker blunted and turned the Japanese drive.

But the help arrived too late for Sandy Bonnyman. He had been shot dead in the final moments of his one-man defense of the bombproof summit.

As soon as Harry Niehoff heard the killing shot thud into Sandy Bonnyman's body, he flattened himself against the ground. It was just in time, for one of Pappy Coleman's potent charges arched back over the knot of the defending attackers, bowling men from their feet. Sgt Elmo Ferretti was badly dazed and had to be led back down to the seawall.

Moments later, as Harry Niehoff was firing his carbine in the midst of another Japanese sally, he heard something drop next to his head. He saw a grenade from the corner of his eye. Without thinking, he leaped across the dead lieutenant's body and wedged himself between it and a dead Japanese machine gunner. But nothing happened. Long moments later, Niehoff ventured a peek and saw an unarmed American grenade, thoughtfully provided by the men at the foot of the bombproof.

Tension, smoke, and the stench of burning flesh finally got to Harry Niehoff. Since he was out of TNT and ammunition for his carbine, the engineer corporal ambled to the rear for a break. He had not suffered a scratch, although 13 of the first 21 men to reach the top of the bombproof were dead or wounded.

On losing their bid for the summit, the Japanese sought to abandon the position; they cascaded from the two entryways and legged off to the east. Most of them were cut down by F Company, 8th. Many defenders who turned south to escape F Company were felled by a pair of 37mm guns firing canister rounds as fast as the gunners could reload.

After leaving the bombproof, Cpl Harry Niehoff wandered down the beach to his platoon's CP and found a large cache of TNT. Rising above his exhaustion, he loaded an ammunition cart with explosives and, eliciting help from nearby Marines, hauled it to the beach by the bombproof. By the time Niehoff got there, however, dozens upon dozens of Marines were swarming over the area, rooting out survivors and snipers.

Corporal Niehoff decided to call it a day. He sat down to rest and, following a few nearsighted reveries, found a pile of glass at his feet. The glass was of a sort known to all Marines—the kind they make beer bottles with. Niehoff idly poked through the shattered debris and found the best reward he could ever have hoped for. He pulled one tantalizing, if warm, full and unopened bottle of Kirin beer from the wreckage of what had once been a goodly supply. As his tongue madly quivered, Harry Niehoff prepared to open his prize. But a voice from behind shattered his solitude. Commenting on the corporal's ideal luck, Maj Bill Chamberlin stared at the lone bottle of beer through eyes that had become a gateway to his soul. The major looked precisely as bad as the corporal felt. Succumbing to one of the hardest decisions of his life, Harry Niehoff silently handed the major the prize of a lifetime.

Following the annihilation of the bombproof defenders, the rifle companies got set to move. Maj Jim Crowe ordered his command to attack eastward along the northern shore until stopped by the onset of darkness or a Division order.

While F Company occupied a holding position, E and G Companies moved around the north side of the bombproof. To the south, K Company stood down to cover a demolitions team as it moved to seal the southeastern entryway of the bombproof. No one was about to enter the building, and no one wanted any more Japanese vacating it after dark, by which time it would be well behind Marine lines.

Next, K Company and *Colorado* attacked parallel to E Company along the southern side of the bombproof.

A team of riflemen who were left to guard the southern side of the bombproof whiled away the afternoon by chucking grenades into any openings they could find. In time, a bulldozer with a jury-rigged armor-plated cab arrived and commenced to seal the entire structure with sand; doubtless, any Japanese still cowering within were asphyxiated.

E, G, and K Companies had a field day. Everything fell before them. Trenches, buildings, and pillboxes were blown wherever encountered. Although a number of Marines were wounded, no one was killed. First Lieutenant Robert Rogers, leading E Company, had a close call when, on turning, he saw a Japanese officer bearing down on him, sword held high for a killing blow. The attacker was shot dead in his tracks by a nearby rifleman.

The last major objective of Crowe's advance was the massive concrete bunker housing the headquarters of Admiral Shibasaki's 3rd Special Konkyochitai. For nearly three days, gunners on the flat roof of the headquarters bunker had had an unobstructed view overlooking Marine dispositions. Their machine guns had taken the lives of many Marines.

While a line of machine guns was positioned to keep the Japanese from manning the bunker's numerous firing embrasures, a large group of combat engineers tactfully approached the bunker in short hops. The objective was the bunker's massive steel doors, which had been banged shut by seven fleeing *rigosentai* only minutes earlier.

The engineers set and ignited a powerful charge and ducked around the corner. The door was buckled and thrown open, and Pfc Johnny Borich stepped through the billowing dust and smoke to douse the bunker's innards with a stiff dose of flaming fuel. When Borich turned to let waiting riflemen pass, he was greeted by a tremendous cheer from scores of Marines who had watched his calm actions.

Marines streamed by. The advance was so swift and steady that *Colorado*, which was backing K Company, was never called to help.

Later estimates concluded that nearly 100 Japanese throughout the area committed suicide in the face of the successful Marine attacks. This, more than anything, accounted for the low casualties among the assault units; only three men were wounded after the leading files passed the Burns-Philp wharf.

In the end, Jim Crowe's two mixed battalion landing teams covered almost 400 yards straight out. Late in the afternoon, however, orders from Division pulled Crowe's forward elements back almost 150 yards to the airport turning circle. It was feared that Crowe's fields of fire might endanger the 1st Battalion, 6th, which was rapidly approaching the area south of the turning circle.

35

At 1050, just as the 1st Battalion, 6th's leading elements were about to join with the 2nd Regiment troops on Black-2, Maj Willie Jones was ordered to Red-2 to confer with Col Dave Shoup. He left the battalion in the care of his weapons company commander, Maj Francis Beamer, and struck out overland with his staff.

On arriving at Shoup's CP, Jones was informed that the 1st Battalion, 6th, was to begin passing through Kyle's troops at 1300. Shoup then gave the major a complete briefing on the situation all over Betio: The entire west end of the island was in Marine hands, except for the beach boundary strongpoint, now the beach boundary pocket; Crowe was beginning his advance to the east, and it was hoped that he would be in a position to support Jones's advance later in the day.

All available supporting arms, including armor and artillery, were assigned to assist Jones's battalion, as needed. It was hoped that Jones would be able to draw abreast of Crowe's battalions by nightfall and relieve them if all went well.

Earlier in the morning, in light of the decided change in the fortunes of his division, MGen Julian Smith decided to venture ashore, accompanied by BGen James Underhill, the senior 4th Marine Division observer, BGen Thomas Bourke, commander of the 10th Marines, and a security detail of ten officers and Marines drawn from the Division CP.

General Smith's party left *Maryland* and made directly for Beach Green, where it arrived at 1155. Smith inspected elements of Maj Mike Ryan's force and looked over some of the Japanese defenses the 3rd Battalion, 2nd, had reduced in 40 hours of combat. Smith then asked to be taken to the CP on Red-2 to confer with Colonels Edson and Shoup.

The best way for the general to get to Red-2 was aboard an

amtrac. One was readily secured and the party set off. On the way, the amtrac received fire from the beach boundary pocket. Its driver was wounded and the vehicle went out of control for a few moments. The general and his subordinates transferred to a second amtrac and reached the Red-2 CP at 1355.

The assumption of command ashore by General Smith was far more symbolic than substantive, for Red Mike Edson and Dave Shoup had already issued just about all the orders that could be issued for the final reduction of Japanese forces on Betio.

While General Smith was en route to Red-2, Edson had called a meeting of all available senior troop commanders: Col Dave Shoup of the 2nd Marines, Col Elmer Hall of the 8th, Maj Willie Jones of the 1st Battalion, 6th, LtCol Presley Rixey, of the 1st Battalion, 10th, and Maj Charles McCoy of the 2nd Tank Battalion. Edson's directives were verbal: Jones's battalion, with armor, was to finish passing through Kyle's lines and assault eastward at 1330. Its initial objective was the tank trap at the eastern end of the main runway. Crowe's battalions were to take all the ground north of the northeast taxiway or at least encircle and seal the area. Colonel Hall was to coordinate Crowe's efforts with Jones's. The entire 2nd Regiment, with the 1st Battalion, 8th, attached, was to encircle and reduce the beach boundary pocket and mop up throughout the western half of Betio. Rixey's 75mm pack howitzer battalion was to provide on-call fire for Jones. Edson concluded by pledging to provide naval gunfire and air support in advance of the various assaults up to 1330, after which he would put a stop to general bombardments to avoid hitting Marines on the move.

While Major Jones was involved at the CP conference, Maj Francis Beamer, his weapons company commander, set to work reorganizing the battalion and getting it set for the afternoon's fighting. The first thing Beamer did was order C Company into reserve. A Company was to be in the vanguard, with B Company in support. The entire battalion was tired, hungry and thirsty after the 800-yard fighting advance from Beach Green. The extreme heat, combined with tension and exhausting work, had already resulted in several cases of heat prostration, and the hottest part of the day was yet to come.

True to his promise, Red Mike Edson dispatched all

available armor to bolster the one medium and two light tanks still supporting the 1st Battalion, 6th. During the passage of Kyle's lines, however, the armored reinforcement amounted to one light tank, which had been sent south immediately upon landing on Red-2 at noon. More would follow.

A Company began the passage of lines at 1230. Advancing in combat formation with the tanks in support, the lead platoon broke into unoccupied terrain at precisely 1300. The immediate objective was a complex of rifle pits and machine gun emplacements interspersed among a tight knot of concrete pillboxes. Some of the pillboxes had steel cupolas mounted on their roofs, each equipped with a machine gun commanding a 360-degree field of fire. They looked quite formidable to riflemen and tankers alike.

Due to an extremely limited supply of 75mm ammunition, *Cecilia* was held in reserve as the three light tanks moved forward. But the 37mm guns were too puny to contend with the ferroconcrete emplacements. Riflemen were called forward to try their hand, but they battled mightily for over an hour to gain nothing. *Cecilia* was called forward at 1400. Her big gun was too valuable to withhold any longer.

The lone medium clanked to the front amidst shouts from the riflemen. It stopped for a moment when it reached the front and swung its big gun to bear on the nearest pillbox. Then *Cecilia* fired. And again. And again, until the pillbox was reduced to rubble.

Several yards behind the lead assault platoon, manning a radio link, 1stLt Baine Kerr, A Company's exec, rose to follow the advancing squads. When Kerr's radioman drew fire down on both of them, Kerr, who had been shot on Guadalcanal, sprinted like a madman across thirty yards of open ground to the next depression. As he dived to gain speed, he landed smack on top of a ripe, dead Japanese.

Kerr was alone. The trench was very shallow, and the slightest attempt at movement brought a hail of overhead fire. There was no way out, forward or back. The battlewise Texas lawyer whimsically removed his helmet, placed it on a stick, and waved it for the Japanese gunners to see. The ruse worked. The helmet was shot full of holes.

In quiet desperation, Baine Kerr decided to get moving. He thought he should advance rather than retreat, to throw the Japanese gunners off. However, just as he was flexing for a start, a terrific commotion on the right heralded the arrival of a trusty squad of Marine riflemen, who made short shrift of Kerr's oppressors.

At 1430, after 90 minutes of grueling battle, A Company, 6th, broke through the battered defenses and began gaining ground.

The battalion's first water replenishment arrived at 1500, and all hands rotated to the rear to draw shares of the tepid liquid. The last of the light tanks from Red-2 arrived at the same time, three in all, bringing Jones's immediate supports to a total of six lights and one medium. Two of the lights would be lost in the afternoon fighting. One burned out its ignition; the other plunged into an unseen shellhole.

At 1530, Jones was ordered to dispatch one company to relieve the 2nd Battalion, 8th, at the airport turning circle. He sent C Company at 1600. At the same time, Jones replaced A Company in the vanguard with B Company, which continued the advance against steadily increasing opposition. The anti-tank ditch at the end of the main runway was practically within reach, but Jones's troops were nearing exhaustion and could not gather the strength to complete the drive.

At 1625, while directing his company's attack, B Company's commander, Capt George Krueger, was shot in the head. He was evacuated in critical condition and replaced by his executive officer, 1stLt Norman Thomas.

The attack was stalled by 1830. Since it was nearly nightfall and the final objectives were beyond reach, Major Jones ordered the battalion to dig in on line. A Company drew abreast of B and placed its right flank on the beach. An outpost screen was stretched out 50 yards ahead of the main line. Ahead of A and B Companies was a large expanse of open ground, including the airport turning circle, which had to be covered at long range by many machine guns. C Company, which was holding the turning circle, was in visual contact until dusk, after which even radio contact was lost.

Only ten minutes after occupying the main battalion line, all officers were informed that a major counterattack was expected. This news was identical to rumors passed around on the two preceding evenings, but the situation had changed: The Japanese were losing.

Thirty wounded Marines were evacuated aboard two amtracs after nightfall. Then Jones's battalion settled in to wait.

During the afternoon advance, which covered only a few hundred yards, the 1st Battalion, 6th, had killed 200 Japanese, a total of 450 for the day. In the coming hours of darkness, and without gaining any new ground, the battalion would nearly double the score.

36

The tedious task of tidying up began that third afternoon. Men were still dying on Betio, but for many of the veterans of the badly mauled battalions of the 2nd Marine Regiment and its service and support units, there came a moment when the pressure seemed to physically lift, a moment when pure instinct for survival finally gave way to some careful planning. In most cases, respite took the form of seeking some water, some food, some rest, some companionship.

For 2ndLt John Cannon, it meant noticing the cloudy stench that hung over Betio. Before that afternoon, Cannon had been too busy staying alive to notice the foul blanket of putrid air. It meant sitting down on a dirt-covered log, or what appeared to be a dirt-covered log, only to find that it was the leg of a dead adversary who was otherwise buried beneath a pile of wood splinters, gritty sand, and palm fronds. Somewhere within the young platoon leader, a soundless voice questioned that hitherto unrealized insensitivity to matters concerning the demise of so many mortals so alike or so different from himself. And, in the end, he got up and moved to another spot, too dog-tired to give the matter any more of his energy. Later, on the beach, Cannon turned to the lagoon and looked upon uncountable bodies, Americans all, gently lolling against the sloping shelf as the surf carried them a few feet back, a few feet forward, a few feet back. . . . And he saw one live Asian man, probably a Korean, the first he had been able to see in nearly 57 hours on Betio. The man was miserable and obviously fearful. Stripped to a G-string in a diligent body search, he flitted his black eyes back and forth among the tall, unshaven, haggard Americans, no doubt wondering which one would offer the *coup de grace*. The young Americans stared back, eyes cold and hot at the same time—passionate over the remembered dead, dispassionate over this captive's fate.

First Lieutenant Ott Schulte, who had been evacuated from Red-1 shortly after noon, awoke aboard one of the transports from his first sleep in three days. The former platoon leader's wounded arm was swathed in bandages and splints and securely wired to the bunk overhead. A compassionate sailor asked Schulte if he wanted to eat. The answer was a firm "Yes!" and the young man returned with a huge bowl of stew. Ott Schulte gulped the food down and readily agreed to seconds. It was the first he had eaten since the "last meal" of steak and eggs 60 hours earlier.

Maj John Schoettel, commander of the 3rd Battalion, 2nd, finally reached Red-1 and resumed command of far fewer than the 1,000 men he had sent to the beach on D-Day.

Cpl Jerry Kubinski and the survivors of his E Company, 2nd, squad had a hell-raising afternoon, sampling from a cache of *sake* they found as they rummaged through a blasted pillbox.

On the beach behind the regimental—now divisional—CP, Father Frank Kelly and his clerk laid 1stLt William Deane Hawkins and scores of his fellow Marines to rest.

While many members of the nearby 3rd Battalion, 2nd, were easing the pressure on frazzled nerves, the 1st Battalion, 8th, was still plodding into the beach boundary pocket, killing and being killed.

A Company in the center and C Company inland made relatively steady progress during the afternoon, and they even managed to reduce one of the keystones of the defensive complex. But B Company, on the beach, ran into the bitterest opposition of the day, which forced the two companies on the left to slow their advances. Still, the Japanese remaining on the western portion of the island were confined to the area directly in front of Hays's battalion. A counterattack mounted by those desperate Japanese in the late afternoon was easily beaten off.

The quietest advance on D+2 probably took place in the eastern half of the airfield triangle.

For the first two days of battle, a small force built from elements of I and L Companies, 8th, had been manning a southward-facing line extending from the northeastern taxiway to a point about midway along the triangle's center, about 125 yards short of the positions held by the 1st Battalion, 2nd, on the first night. The force was commanded by 1stLt Ashby Fristoe, the L Company exec.

Fristoe and his subordinates had done the best they could to organize their lines, but the area they occupied was exposed on two flanks to heavy fire from beyond the coral-topped runways. Movement was out of the question on D-Day, and the situation was little improved by the second night. However, more men trickled in throughout D+1, and a bit more ground was seized.

Things livened up considerably on D+2. First, Fristoe's company commander, Capt Osborne LeBlanc, arrived from the north after spending the first two days coordinating the movements of the entire 3rd Battalion, 8th. Second, word got around that a major offensive action was under way to the south and that the 2nd Battalion, 8th, was attempting to sweep by to the north. If those thrusts succeeded, the Marines in the triangle would have to wrest more ground in their sector and draw abreast of the units on either flank.

Captain LeBlanc's command could actually see the 1st Battalion, 6th, by 1300, and that was the signal to begin moving.

Both the 1st Battalion, 6th, and the units to the north were up to their collective ears in Japanese, but, as LeBlanc's group wheeled eastward and moved out, it encountered almost zero opposition. The triangle was virtually undefended.

By late afternoon, the Marines in the triangle had advanced to the junction of the northeast taxiway and the main runway and had established a wedge-shaped position pointing to the east. The turning circle was dead ahead. Jones's advance carried well to the east of LeBlanc's position, but there was ample cover in the triangle and none out on the flat surface of the turning circle, so LeBlanc's force stayed where it was.

C Company, 6th, passed behind LeBlanc's front near dusk and established its line to the north. K Company, 8th, was withdrawn from Crowe's front and was charged with establishing a secondary line of defense. And the 2nd Battalion, 8th, was virtually relieved of all duties.

Physical exhaustion was depleting the pierhead crew.

Supply handlers started collapsing shortly after dawn, and from then on there were always a few men out cold. A number of the young Navy officers asked to be relieved as the pace became too much for them; a few just picked up and left. While LCdr Lou Fabian was helping to move a jeep that had become disabled when the pierhead had collapsed during the night, he slipped through a weak section in the decking and badly scratched a leg from ankle to groin. He was so exhausted and the shock of the accident was so overwhelming that the squadron beachmaster lapsed into unconsciousness for at least 20 minutes. When Fabian came to, he got up and went back to work. Lou Fabian was 40 years old, nearly twenty years older than most of the quitters.

Col Dave Shoup's CP messaged The Flag at 1505: "Land available personnel of Combat Team 2 on Beach Green and labor details." Most of the men on Betio would soon be working rather than fighting. At 1530, Shoup's CP broadcasted a second message to *Maryland*: "B [Company], [2nd] Medical [Battalion,] land on Bairiki, establish a field hospital as soon as possible. Medical officers and corpsmen A and C [Companies], Medical, land on Beach Red-2 as soon as possible. Bring morphine, plasma, dressing and stretchers." It was time to start taking better care of the wounded and screening the lightly wounded out of active fighting organizations, as infection of untreated wounds and scrapes was an emerging threat. A message at 1550 asked Division to "Land guns, ammunition and personnel of 2nd Defense Battalion as soon as possible at pier." Betio was to be turned into a fortress—an *impregnable* fortress.

MGen Julian Smith contacted BGen Dutch Hermle, who was running the Division CP aboard *Maryland*, at 1606: "Situation not favorable for rapid clean-up of Betio. Heavy casualties among officers make leadership problems difficult. Still strong organized resistance . . . [and] many emplacements intact eastern end of island. . . . In addition, many Japanese strongpoints to westward of our front lines within our positions have not been reduced. Progress slow and extremely costly. Complete occupation will take at least five days more. Naval and air bombardment a great help, but does not take out emplacements."

In fact, GySgt Jared Hooper's Scout-and-Sniper Platoon had returned from a mortar spotting mission two hours earlier and, after spending an hour scrounging explosives, had gone to work on the many isolated buildings that still provided safe havens for snipers near Smith's CP.

Col Elmer Hall of the 8th Marines landed with his command group in the early afternoon, and Col Maurice Holmes landed with elements of the 6th Marines command group in the late afternoon to establish his own CP ashore. Shortly after landing, Holmes was called to a regimental commanders' conference at General Smith's CP to discuss operations for November 23.

As the plan evolved, elements of the 6th Marines were to revert to Colonel Holmes's direct control at 2100 hours, November 22. LtCol Kenneth McLeod's 3rd Battalion, 6th, had already been directed to move in behind Jones's 1st Battalion, and LtCol Ray Murray's 2nd Battalion was to move from Bairiki to Beach Green in the morning. The 3rd Battalion was to pass through the 1st after sunrise, with all available tanks in support. Murray's battalion would move eastward upon landing to support McLeod. If possible, McLeod was to drive all the way to the eastern tip of the island. The attack would probably begin on a two-company front, then steadily contract as the island tapered off to the east.

Before leaving General Smith's CP, Colonel Holmes made all the necessary arrangements for air and naval support.

Elements of the 2nd Military Police Company undertook two important operations that afternoon.

In the first, 1stLt Douglas Key, who had received antimine training, was assigned with two MP sergeants to clear the mined beaches. The sergeants received a quick course, following which the three men crawled up and down the beaches, very gently prodding the sand with long bayonets.

All the other MPs on Betio collected and incarcerated prisoners.

The job did not go well at all, until a fast-talking Korean convinced the MP to let him help. The man was so servile that the MPs dubbed him "Tojo the Earbanger," a salty term for bootlick, and put him to work. The first thing Tojo did was point out the hiding place of four *rigosentai*, who refused to come out. A light dose of TNT brought three Japanese peacefully to the surface. The fourth man came up shooting and was killed.

Tojo led his mentors to a second pillbox, where a total of 22 docile fellow Koreans were taken alive.

In the end, Tojo the Earbanger brought in 81 men, nearly all Korean laborers who were clearly happy to be out of the war.

The only naval action attending the seizure of Betio began at noon, when picket destroyer *Gansevoort* picked up, then lost, a submarine contact on her sonar. Destroyer *Meade* made and lost a similar contact at 1245.

Nothing more happened until 1530, when contact was again made and lost. Destroyer *Frazier*, which was sent to help *Meade* and *Gansevoort*, was aggressively patrolling in its sector at 1627, when she made contact and immediately dropped a pattern of depth charges. To the amazement of all, a submarine conning tower broke the surface.

As soon as the sub's periscope was visible, *Meade* and *Frazier* both poured 5-inch, 20mm, and 40mm fire into it. The shooting was a bit cramped because the sub came up directly between the two American warships.

When the hull appeared, *Frazier* rammed it at full speed. The submarine immediately sank, losing great bubbles of air as she went. Three Japanese naval ratings were fished from the water, and they identified the intruder as *RC-35*, an old short-range ocean-going vessel.

Frazier suffered some damage to her bows, but she only had to slow a bit to keep the water out.

37

Victory was in the air. There was no doubting it. Optimism was enormous for most. The medical team aboard transport *Doyen* had not the slightest inkling that the battle was to be a Marine victory. They only knew that the Marines had suffered hideous casualties and that the suffering seemed endless.

LCdr James Oliver's five-man surgical team had been planning for the welfare of the casualties for many months. The doctors had had some practice at Kiska, in the Aleutians, where most of the casualties had resulted from booby traps and mistaken identity. *Doyen's* junior medical officer was Dr. Albert Kelly, who had been aboard since her commissioning in 1942. Kelly was a perfectionist, and he insisted that the ship's authorized supply of medical gear be tripled. Extra operating tables had been installed, and a surgical team from the 2nd Medical Battalion had been attached to Dr. Oliver's staff. An enormous supply of sodium pentathol had been laid in, along with ample supplies of every available sulfa compound. The latest in bandages and plaster casts was in abundance. Everything to cover every eventuality had been thought of and stowed away.

Doyen began taking the wounded aboard within an hour of H-Hour. Hardly a moment went by without another boat or tractor coming alongside with at least one damaged Marine. The less serious casualties were sent on to ships farther out, while the more serious cases were carefully hoisted aboard and doled out to the surgical teams.

The doctors worked so many miracles so often that the miraculous seemed to become commonplace. Lt Von McAtee, the ship's dentist, became an expert anesthetist on the run, while the surgeons sawed and sewed, probed and prodded, padded and patched every sort of wound. Decisions had to be made in an instant: who is the most serious case; who can be adequately handled by a corpsman; should we cut; should he be placed in an upper bunk or lower bunk, where he can be more carefully watched? No matter how close to death a Marine seemed, *Doyen's* doctors gave him the very best care possible.

The doctors were brutalized by their ordeal. Dr. Oliver was dead on his feet, and Dr. Kelly stopped smiling as soon as he started work; his smile did not return until many weeks later. Dr. Robert Watkins often howled "London Bridge is Falling Down" at the top of his lungs in order to drown everything out while he made an unending series of life-or-death decisions.

Capt John McClaughry, *Doyen's* master, did not hold back an inch when it came to providing supplies, manpower, or space for the wounded.

The doctors ate on their feet and slept in the passageways in 15- to 30-minute snatches. Black coffee was a constant source of new energy. Each morning, a cardboard case of 2-oz. brandy bottles was set out, and Dr. Oliver told the men to take as much as they needed to keep going; he was not overly astonished to learn that no one took advantage of the offer.

Every time General Quarters sent the rest of *Doyen's* crew to battle stations, every medical man thought about how nice it would be to drop everything and run. The fear of a Japanese air raid was deep-rooted, but the urge to run was transient. Not one man hesitated to carry out his duties, despite repeated alarms.

The most amazing things happened. Dr. Oliver found one case before him that looked ridiculously easy. A Marine was lying bellydown on a litter and a small piece of shrapnel was sticking out of the back side of one knee. Preparing to bandage the tiny wound, the doctor pulled the steel from the boy's leg, releasing a sudden surge of blood that spattered the overhead. The shrapnel had been lodged in the popliteal artery. There was no time to lose; moments of indecision would have left the Marine near death.

Supplies began running short on the third day. Dr. Oliver grudgingly assented to the use of ether in place of the sodium pentathol, although a bomb hit would have blown *Doyen* off the surface of the planet. When sheet wadding for padding casts ran out, one of the doctors came to the rescue by recalling where an extra issue of blankets for the Kiska operation had been stowed; these were cut up and used in place of more acceptable materials. The same doctor also improvised scores of wooden and metal splints and other retentive apparatus. Plaster bandages ran out, so powdered plaster and regular bandages were broken out. Transfusion units containing anticoagulants were in constant use by corpsmen, who occasionally availed themselves of the opportunity to match and transfuse blood directly from volunteer donors to patients, if donors were available.

Keeping men conscious was another of the rougher tasks. An inordinate number of men had been equipped with morphine syrettes, so Marines arriving from the beaches were usually overdosed with the narcotic, which appeared to have been administered at every opportunity. The morphine depressed breathing, and many men, otherwise well off, might have asphyxiated.

The doctors became inured to ragged stumps where strong, youthful arms and legs had been, to eyes that had been shattered by concussion, to an unending variety of holes in human flesh, to grisly burns, to oozing hamburger-like chests and backs and abdomens, to exposed intestines, to the beseeching eyes of damaged teenagers.

Late in the third day, Dr. Oliver was informed that *Doyen* had taken aboard 400 casualties. He was flabbergasted, for the number was unprecedented. And it rose toward 500. By the time *Doyen* set sail for Pearl Harbor, she had 550 wounded men below decks. This put her, an ordinary fleet transport with good but rudimentary medical facilities, in the class of a large hospital ship. (*Doyen* would surpass her Tarawa record by treating 600 shipboard patients at Iwo Jima.)

For the moment, however, neither Jim Oliver nor any member of his staff had time to keep a tally.

38

Since the earliest days of the Guadalcanal fighting in mid 1942, Marines had known that the Japanese reacted to miscarried plans in an irrational and suicidal manner. The name the Marines gave to the manifestations of this tendency was *banzai*. Roughly translated, *banzai* means "ten thousand years." However, it is not the name for a suicide attack; it is a victory cry.

Used properly, a massed assault by a nearly-beaten force might buy enough time for a different decision to be reached, or it might destroy the ability of the nearly-victorious enemy to carry its effort to a successful conclusion. More often, as would be dramatically shown in the expanding Pacific War, a massed assault by Japanese confined to a corner of an indefensible island was a sign of desperation, of defeat, of a desire to take ten of the enemy for every Japanese killed, of a hope to cripple the enemy on the spot while defenders of bastions farther along the route of conquest prepared a better defense.

With eight Marine rifle battalions facing them and one rifle and one artillery battalion blocking their only route of retreat, the *rigosentai* compressed into the eastern tail of Betio had no hope for ever attaining a victory. They might only hurt 2nd Marine Division more grievously than it had already been hurt.

The Marines of A and B Companies, 6th, anticipated a last-ditch assault. An alert was issued at 1840, only ten minutes after they were ordered to halt in place for the night.

Approximately 50 *rigosentai* began to infiltrate the outpost line screening Jones's battalion at precisely 1930 on the evening of Monday, November 23. The infiltrators were able to open a small gap between A and B Companies within a short time.

Marine response was immediate and ruthless.

Withholding automatic-weapons fire to avoid giving away key positions, the Marines on the main line fired small-arms concentrations into the gradually enlarging pocket. At the same time, the flank platoons of both companies attempted to re-fuse the line, giving way slightly to form an inward salient at the line's center, around the Japanese pocket.

Within fifteen minutes of the initial action, at 1945, Capt Lyle Specht, the weapons company exec, moved forward with the battalion reserve of 81mm mortar crewmen to mop up. The gunners unsheathed bayonets and went to work against the almost-invisible infiltrators, hand to hand. They, and several headquarters warriors who joined them, literally pried the Japanese from hiding places across the infiltrated area.

While Captain Specht's force worked in among the infiltrators, Maj Willie Jones took precautionary measures against any other Japanese who might have been awaiting an initial breakthrough. First, since he had no reserves left, Jones asked Maj Wood Kyle to rush riflemen forward as quickly as possible. Kyle's nearest troops were 300 yards behind Jones's line, but he sprang to action and soon had a small mixed unit on the move; this unit was eventually placed 100 yards behind Jones's main line.

In the meantime, Jones placed a hurried call to his B Company commander, 1stLt Norman Thomas, who said, "We need reinforcements. Another attack like that and the line may break."

Jones: "I can't now. You've got to hold."

Thomas: "Aye, aye, Sir. We'll hold the line."

Jones turned to the men in his CP and said, "If they don't hold, we may lose the entire battalion. . . . C Company must stay where it is, in case the Japs break through." Then, to Thomas, "Water and ammunition are coming up on *China Gal*. At 2000, we're going to open with naval gunfire. Let us know how the shells are landing. They'll be pretty close, you know. Good luck!"

Two types of artillery support were available. The entire 1st Battalion, 10th, was standing by, and there were several destroyers ringing the tiny island. The destroyers' guns were under the control of Lt(jg) Charles Corben and his specially trained four-man shore fire control party. Aside from Corben, the party was comprised of Marines from Jones's battalion, most of whom were Guadalcanal veterans.

As soon as the shooting began, Corben's two wiremen sprang to action, laying telephone wire to the battalion CP; lines were already in to the rifle companies. Second Lieutenant Norman Milner, a forward observer from A Battery, 10th, who was operating from a hole near the CP, consented to spot for the ships' fire. In addition to Milner, Marine troop leaders with access to telephones were patched into the fire control net.

The first salvo was fired at 2000, exactly 30 minutes after the fight began. Lt(jg) Charles Corben was in direct radio contact with seaborne gunnery officers. Switching to 1stLt Norman Thomas, Corben said, "Salvo! Here it comes."

Loud explosions sounded a few moments later.

Corben: "How was that? . . . Okay, that's good." Turning to Major Jones, he reported, "They fell 50 yards in front of our lines. They want more in the same spot." It had been Jones's original intention to fire into possible staging areas 75 yards beyond his own front. Apparently Lieutenant Thomas was content with screening his line with a curtain of fire. Returning to the phone, Corben said to Thomas, "Can do. If you want them that close, we'll deliver." Corben turned to his radioman and said, "More on the same target. Tell them the shooting's great."

The naval gunfire continued for 30 minutes, until 2030.

Captain Specht's small reaction force continued to claw away at the infiltrators until about 2130, two hours after initial contact. The gap itself had been closed at 2030, but, although A and B Companies had straightened their lines at the center, many Japanese remained roving about behind the Marine lines.

Farther to the rear, Major Kyle's original reinforcement had been bolstered by 40 Marines from the 2nd Battalion, 2nd. And the entire 3rd Battalion, 6th, was being readied to relieve Kyle's small force and establish a strong secondary line.

The fact that the initial action had ended in success meant very little to anyone in Jones's battalion. A mere 50 Japanese had been involved, and it was presumed that over 500 remained in front of Jones's lines. The naval gunfire had served to keep others away, but it did not kill many of them.

A and B Companies were afforded a 90-minute respite.

• • •

A strong second contact was made at precisely 2300 hours, when another 50 Japanese attempted to create a diversion near the beach, in front of A Company. These men fired weapons and hurled grenades at the Marine line, but they did not attack. While this ruckus was in full flower, a hitherto unperceived force moved on B Company.

The Marines came right back with 60mm mortar fire, followed by automatic-weapons fire which cut deeply into the oncoming files of *rigosentai*. Hand grenades shattered the leading ranks as soon as they came into range. The Japanese recoiled, then withdrew. The attack was put down as a "strong probe."

During the "probe," B Company came very close to losing its second commander that day. Right in the midst of the melee, as Lieutenant Thomas attempted to control the fire of his machine guns, he found an intruder in his foxhole. Thomas had had his carbine shot out of his hands a moment earlier and was just pulling his .45-caliber pistol from its holster when he was attacked. He grabbed his assailant's wrists, threw the man off balance, and clouted him in the head with the pistol. When the man fell, Thomas aimed and pulled the trigger. But the pistol was empty, useless. As the man began stirring once again, the Marine officer felled him with another blow. Then Thomas rammed a fresh magazine into the butt opening of the automatic pistol and fired a round through the dazed man's temple.

The 3rd Battalion, 6th, completed its 600-yard advance as the second attack was ending. I Company relieved 2nd Marines units on the secondary line 100 yards behind A and B Companies. At the same time, *China Gal* arrived near Jones's CP with a cargo of ammunition, hand grenades and water. Carrying parties were immediately organized to move the goods to the lines.

Maj Willie Jones requested fire support again, and Lt(jg) Charles Corben's shore fire control party contacted a destroyer and had her fire for effect. The shells harmlessly caromed across the island. A correction was called in, and, once on target, the destroyer commenced to pump 5-inch shells 500 yards east of the Marine front in the hope of disrupting Japanese communications and movements. One round landed in an ammunition dump, and a searing burst of light flashed over the island and the sea. Shells in the dump continued to cook off for hours.

While the destroyer was firing long, Marine forward observer 2ndLt Norman Milner directed his 12-gun 75mm pack howitzer battalion to fire into the intervening ground, between the Marine line and the naval gunfire target line. Hours passed before anything more was heard from the Japanese.

Things began heating up again at about 0300, when Japanese machine guns opened from a small collection of wrecked trucks about 50 yards in front of the Marine lines. As the Japanese guns were a bit too close for pinpoint accuracy by the artillery or less accurate naval gunfire, Jones's Marines had to get them.

The .30-caliber water-cooled machine guns on Jones's line accounted for several of the Japanese gun crews, but they could not accomplish the entire job alone, so a small group of Marines crawled out of their foxholes and snaked forward to the trucks. Using hand grenades and fast-moving infiltration tactics, the Marines destroyed three more guns and withdrew. The Japanese fire ceased, because all the guns had been destroyed or because the survivors knew when enough was enough. Whatever the case, the front was quiet. But not for long.

The Japanese hit hard at 0400. An estimated 300 *rigosentai* barreled into B Company's line and A Company's left front, while a smaller group ran diversions along the beach.

This was the main event.

Second Lieutenant Milner, the artillery forward observer, placed a call for immediate fire support. The 1st Battalion, 10th, cut loose its 12 75mm pack howitzers, firing down to ranges only 75 yards from Jones's embattled line. They caught many Japanese in the open. Calls from the front became so frenzied that senior artillery officers dispensed with the usual procedures to exhort the gunners to fire as fast as they could reload. In the end, a respectable two rounds per gun per minute would be expended.

Marines were fighting back along the front with the proverbial "everything they had." Screaming, yelling, shooting, grenade-throwing Japanese were battering themselves on the Marine line. Many positions were in danger of being overrun.

At about 0430, after 30 minutes of quick-paced fighting, Pfc Jack Stambaugh, a B Company rifleman, was firing into the oncoming Japanese when his M1 rifle suddenly jammed. Stambaugh's buddies were a short distance away, yelling for help. Stambaugh tossed his useless weapon aside and ran toward his buddies' foxhole. He was accosted by a bayonet-wielding Japanese before he could get there, but he cut the man down with his own bayonet and moved on. Working rapidly, the Marine carved the lives from three more *rigosentai* he encountered in the open. As he drew his blade from the last, however, a Japanese officer ran his sabre through Stambaugh's back. Another Marine shot the officer and dropped to Stambaugh's side to help, but Pfc Jack Stambaugh was already dead.

Lt(jg) Charles Corben's shore fire control party was in the midst of directing fire from destroyer *Sigsby*, when a call to secure came in; a few rounds had fallen into Marine positions, wounding several friendly troops. Corben checked the range and directed *Sigsby* to a safer impact area. The destroyer, which had been supporting the battalion all night, fired several salvoes, then informed Corben that her 5-inch magazines were empty. A radio patch was hurriedly established, and Corben began laying in destroyer *Schroeder's* guns. Within minutes of the switch, *Schroeder* was firing as fast as her guncrews could reload.

First Lieutenant Norman Thomas got a quick message through to Major Jones at 0440: "We are killing them as fast as they come at us, but we can't hold much longer. We need reinforcements."

Jones's reply: "You've got to hold!"

The attackers got so close that Cpl Willie Miles, a B Company 60mm mortar gunner, found his most pressing targets only 40 yards away from his tube, a shot that would have been difficult for even the best gunners in daylight. But it was really black out then, and time was racing by. Firing by dead reckoning, Miles put every round to work and did not fire a single "short." At one point, he spotted several Japanese moving a machine gun into position. Miles aimed in on the moving targets by dead reckoning and nailed them cold, a miraculous shot.

The attack broke up about 0500. Jones's battalion had done more than stand, it had broken the back of the remainder of 3rd Special Konkyochitai, an act that would hasten the fall of Betio.

A bit over an hour after the shooting stopped, when it was light enough to see, an actual body count would reveal over 200 *rigosentai* had died behind, on, or within 75 yards of Jones's line, and another 125 dead were counted over 75 yards out, pummeled by Marine artillery and naval gunfire. The 1st Battalion, 6th, had lost one officer and 44 men killed and five officers and 123 men wounded. Destroyers *Sigsby* and *Schroeder* had been fired dry. And the 1st Battalion, 10th, had expended between 1,300 and 1,600 75mm rounds, many of which had been rushed directly from the pierhead while the guns were firing.

Banzai had been a dismal flop.

Part V
THE LAST DAY

39

Tuesday, November 23, 1943. D+3.

While preparations for the final assault down the long axis of Betio were nearing completion, the 1st Battalion, 8th, began its final sweep through the beach boundary pocket. To the west, elements of the 3rd Battalion, 2nd, were also set to assault the pocket in the hope of joining in the final victory.

Maj Larry Hays's three small rifle companies drove in from the east in a semicircle with support from a pair of halftracks and flamethrower and demolitions teams from C Company, 18th.

Gains were rapid, but the real breakthrough began when a rifle platoon and the two halftracks crossed the lagoon to the reef to bring enfilade fire to bear against the remaining bunkers and pillboxes.

In the meantime, 1stLt Gordon Leslie of A Company, 18th, reported to his company headquarters on Red-2 to pick up some explosives. He was met there by an assault squad, which he bolstered with eight volunteers from the engineer company's headquarters. The ad hoc team rushed to join with the 1st Battalion, 8th, and had startling success; it demolished nearly three dozen emplacements during the morning.

By 1000 hours, the elimination of a number of Japanese emplacements, mainly on the southern flank, enabled Hays's battalion to forge a solid link with Schoettel's, which swung a line through the area of airfield construction south of the pocket and rested its left flank on the beach west of the Japanese defenses.

Elements of the 1st Battalion, 2nd, were sent to bolster Hays's and Schoettel's battalions, which were both severely understrength. Schoettel's Marines were also charged with mopping up Red-1, Green, and Black-1.

The Japanese in the beach boundary pocket were beaten.

There was no doubt about that. But they were worthy fighters, and they continued to stand against repeated infantry assaults, bombings, and shellings. Their position—what was left of it—was a going concern. Excellent fields of fire, the result of meticulous planning, remained to all emplacements. But the number of defenders was steadily declining.

Shortly before 1300, the ragged remnants of 2ndLt John Cannon's 3rd Platoon, I Company, 2nd, moved steadily northward through the airfield construction area. Dead ahead was a large covered bunker, clearly filled with spirited *rigosentai*.

Cannon could not see the entrance to the bunker, so he left his Marines and crawled forward to a better vantage point. Many more Marines than Cannon had seen in three days on Betio were moving to surround the bombproof, which they ringed within minutes, despite heavy fire from within.

A small group of Marines—Gordon Leslie's engineers—moved through the lines to plant bangalore torpedoes, hand grenades, and potent satchel charges. There was a massive blast, but, by the time the dust settled, the bombproof's defenders had resumed firing. The light inshore breeze carried Japanese voices to the Marine line.

A flamethrower team moved up next and quickly doused burning fuel through a number of firing embrasures. But the Japanese continued to fire, and the voices from within continued their haunting singsong litany.

A 75mm howitzer was wheeled into position only 100 feet from the massive steel doors, and its crew pleaded for an opportunity to fire head-on. Permission was refused because there were too many Marines too close to the impact area.

Following a brief lull, the flamethrower teams moved in again; this time, they made for the ventilators. Burning fuel pouring down the airshafts ignited the bunker's spare ammunition. There was a loud, brief *WHOMPF*, followed by smoke and flame pouring out through all the building's openings. Bullets cooked off for hours. The voices from within the bunker were not heard again.

Continued sweeps through the pocket reduced all the remaining opposition.

40

Col Maurice Holmes radioed LtCol Kenneth McLeod just after sunrise and ordered the 3rd Battalion, 6th, to pass through Jones's battalion and form a line completely across Betio. Assaults were to be launched to the eastern tip of the island, some 2,000 yards distant, as soon as air and naval supports finished prepping the objective at 0800.

Carrier aircraft bombed and strafed the Japanese-held areas between 0700 and 0730, assisted by Navy air liaison teams on the ground. As soon as the aircraft departed, the entire 1st Battalion, 10th, hit the Japanese-occupied tail of the island for 15 minutes, following which all available warships conducted a final 15-minute bombardment.

McLeod's battalion passed through Jones's between 0700 and 0800. L Company, on the right, by the southern beach, was strung out to a point about midway across the tapering island to join with I Company, which was advancing eastward on the left (north) flank. K Company was in reserve. Accompanying the battalion were two medium tanks, *Colorado* and *Cecilia*, and seven light tanks from C Company, 2nd Tank Battalion.

McLeod's first phase line was the antitank ditch running tangential to the eastern edge of the turning circle, about 150 yards from the line of departure. The battalion commander expected to stop there to rest and regroup his troops; it was assumed that they would face a heavy fight to get that far.

The first 150 yards fell without opposition in a matter of minutes. The battalion briskly plowed on and rapidly claimed another 200 yards. At that point, I Company, in the north, ran head-on into a bombproof complex.

When Lieutenant Colonel McLeon realized that L Company had good cover all the way along its axis of advance, he ordered I Company to surround the defensive complex on its front and stand to while the remainder of the attack force ground forward.

K and L Companies, with most of the tanks and headquarters troops, ducked past the strongpoint and surged eastward. The island had narrowed to a mere 200 yards, so L Company strung itself across the entire front, and K remained in reserve.

I Company's adversaries were holed up in three enormous mutually supporting bunkers with numerous satellites. The I Company officers were confident, for they had been left with *Colorado* and several flamethrower teams. The flamegunners moved forward under heavy covering fire and spurted burning fuel into ventilators and firing apertures. Large explosive charges were set. Two of the three bunkers were quickly reduced to rubble, and all the smaller outlying emplacements fell almost as a matter of course.

The garrison of the third bombproof, the center of resistance, was probably reinforced by *rigosentai* fleeing the destruction of the other bunkers and pillboxes. The riflemen fired, and the flamegunners moved in. Just as the flamethrowers began firing, the bunker's massive steel doors were thrown open, and all of the defenders surged through the narrow exit channel into the open.

First Lieutenant Lou Largey had just brought *Colorado* into position at the head of the exit channel in the hope of blowing the doors open with his 75mm turret gun. The 75 cut loose at pointblank range. Largey later estimated that he spread the viscera of at least 50 Japanese over a wide arc with that one round. The few survivors were shot to death as they milled about in confusion and despair.

The Japanese facing L Company were not up for a fight. Most were found in hiding. There were no lines as such, just a number of emplacements and large guns facing out to sea. There was no room for cross-island defenses. The advance was swift and, most important, cheap. L Company called for naval gunfire support at 1250. The Japanese survivors were crammed into a few score square yards of the island. Warships and the entire 2nd Battalion, 10th, were on hand to prevent a mass exit in the direction of Bairiki.

L Company moved as soon as the supporting arms ceased fire. The last part of the advance took only 15 minutes.

At the cost of nine dead and 25 wounded, the 3rd Battalion, 6th, had advanced 2,000 yards down the long axis of Betio's tail and had killed 475 and captured 14 Japanese along the way.

At 1305, a Marine radioman on the eastern tip of Betio broadcast the three words his 20,000 fellow Marines had been waiting precisely 76 hours and ten minutes to hear:

BETIO HAS FALLEN.

APPENDIX A

A Word About Organization

At the time of the invasion of Tarawa, 2nd Marine Division numbered about 20,000 men. Most were Marines, but the division also included several hundred Navy doctors and corpsmen (medics) and a battalion of Seabees (Navy construction engineers).

The main strength of the division lay in its three infantry regiments, the 2nd, 6th, and 8th Marines. Each regiment was composed of three 1,000-man rifle battalions, a heavy weapons company, and a headquarters-and-service company, plus various detachments and special service units. In all, the average regiment—and each one was slightly different from the others—comprised about 3,500 officers and men.

Each infantry regiment's three rifle battalions (a total of nine in the division) consisted of three rifle companies, one weapons company, and one headquarters-and-service company. The rifle and weapons companies were identified by alphabetical designators as follows: *1st Battalion*, A, B, C, D (the last is the weapons company); *2nd Battalion*, E, F, G, H; *3rd Battalion*, I, K, L, M. (There was no J Company.)

Each rifle company consisted of three rifle platoons and one weapons platoon. The rifle platoons numbered about 40 men, divided into three 12-man squads and a platoon headquarters. The company weapons platoon manned .30-caliber light machine guns and three 60mm mortars. The battalion weapons company consisted of three .30-caliber medium machine-gun platoons of six guns each and an 81mm mortar platoon of six guns. The battalion headquarters-and-service company incorporated battalion staff officers and enlisted clerks and specialists plus a communications platoon, a medical section (all Navy personnel), and several attached liaison teams, such as air, artillery, or naval gunfire observers.

The division's fourth regiment was the artillery regiment. At the time of Tarawa, the 10th Marines had three 12-gun 75mm pack howitzer battalions ("light" artillery, in the vernacular of the day), which supported each of the three infantry regiments. A 105mm medium howitzer battalion, and a 155mm heavy gun battalion completed the tactical arm of the regiment. The whole was commanded by the regimental headquarters and supported by a large service battery. The firing batteries, three to a battalion, were designated A through P, skipping J. The 155mm battalion was not at Tarawa, and the 3rd and 4th Battalions, 10th Marines, were not committed. Technically, each 75mm battery was assigned to support one of the rifle battalions, and at least two junior lieutenants lived with the rifle battalions to which their guns were assigned; these lieutenants and a team of communicators were called "forward observer" teams, an adequate enough description of their combat role.

The fifth regiment of 2nd Marine Division was the 18th Marines, consisting of a battalion each of combat engineers (1st Battalion), pioneers (2nd Battalion), and Seabees (3rd Battalion). Each of the three companies of each battalion (A through I) was to support a different infantry regiment, one platoon per infantry battalion. (Thus, 1st Platoon, A Company, 18th Marines, might support the 1st Battalion, 2nd Marines; 2nd Platoon, A Company, 18th, which might support the 2nd Battalion, 2nd; and so on, up to the 3rd Platoon, C Company, 18th, which might support the 3rd Battalion, 8th.)

The combat engineer platoons each contained 60 Marines. They were trained to build and destroy fortifications and roads with equal skill. The pioneers, also grouped in 60-man platoons, were to be used as shore party (stevedores), but they were also trained to enter combat as needed. The Seabees, who were not employed at Tarawa, served in much the same manner as the Marine engineers, but their specialty was building such things as airfields and roads, and defending what they built.

In addition to the special units incorporated into the 18th Marines, a number of special battalions and companies served as divisional organic units. One was a tank battalion of three companies of three 6-tank platoons—one platoon per rifle battalion, one company per regiment. The same applied to the special weapons (antitank) battalion (not employed at Tarawa), the medical battalion, the amphibian tractor battalion, and several special companies attached to what amounted to a divisional headquarters battalion (military police, communicators, etc.). All of the special organic units were under the direct authority of the division commander. Although they were intended to take care of the needs of the infantry units to which they might be attached, they were, in fact, used in various configurations as the action required. For example, all of the amphibian tractors were initially attached to Combat Team 2—the reinforced 2nd Marines—and not parcelled out a platoon at a time to each of the nine rifle battalions.

The overriding characteristic of the organization was its flexibility. Whatever troops, weapons, and equipment it had on hand could be used however the needs of the moment dictated.

APPENDIX B

Medal of Honor Recipients

ALEXANDER BONNYMAN, JR.
First Lieutenant, USMCR
C Company, 18th Marines
November 20–22, 1943
Killed in Action

WILLIAM JAMES BORDELON
Staff Sergeant, USMC
A Company, 18th Marines
November 20, 1943
Killed in Action

WILLIAM DEANE HAWKINS
First Lieutenant, USMC
2nd Marines
November 20–21, 1943
Died of Wounds

DAVID MONROE SHOUP
Colonel, USMC
Commanding Officer, 2nd Marines
November 20–22, 1943

INDEX

WAR BOOKS FROM JOVE

0-515-08918-4	BATAAN: THE MARCH OF DEATH Stanley L. Falk	$3.50
0-515-08674-6	BLOODY WINTER John M. Waters	$3.95
0-515-07294-X	THE DEVIL'S VIRTUOSOS David Downing	$2.95
0-515-07297-4	HITLER'S WEREWOLVES Charles Whiting	$2.95
0-515-07427-6	U-BOAT OFFSHORE Edwin P. Hoyt	$2.95
0-515-09030-1	A DISTANT CHALLENGE Edited by Infantry Magazine	$3.50
0-515-08054-3	INFANTRY IN VIETNAM Albert N. Garland, U.S.A. (ret.)	$3.95
0-515-08365-8	HITLER MUST DIE! Herbert Molloy Mason, Jr.	$3.95
0-515-08810-2	LITTLE SHIP, BIG WAR: THE SAGA OF DE343 Commander Edward P. Stafford, U.S.N. (ret.)	$3.95
0-515-08513-8	PANZER ARMY AFRICA James Lucas	$3.50
0-515-08682-7	THE END OF THE IMPERIAL JAPANESE NAVY Masanori Ito	$3.50
0-515-07733-X	THE INCREDIBLE 305th Wilbur Morrison	$2.95
0-515-08066-7	THE KAMIKAZES Edwin P. Hoyt	$3.50
0-515-07618-X	KASSERINE PASS Martin Blumenson	$3.50
0-515-08732-7	PORK CHOP HILL S.L.A. Marshall	$3.50
0-515-08940-0	THE LOS BANOS RAID Lt. Gen. E. M. Flanagan, Jr.	$3.50
0-515-08913-3	FOUR STARS OF HELL Laurence Critchell	$3.95
0-515-09066-2	DROP ZONE SICILY William B. Breuer	$3.50
0-515-08896-X	BLUE SKIES AND BLOOD Edwin P. Hoyt	$3.50
0-515-09005-0	PAK SIX G. I. Basel	$3.50
0-515-09230-4	THE BATTLE OF LEYTE GULF Edwin P. Hoyt	$3.95
0-515-09159-6	ACE: A MARINE NIGHT FIGHTER PILOT IN WWII Colonel R. Bruce Porter with Eric Hammel	$3.95
0-515-09074-3	RINGED IN STEEL Michael D. Mahler	$3.50
0-515-09367-X	DEVIL BOATS: THE PT WAR AGAINST JAPAN William Breuer	$3.50
0-515-09511-7	WE LED THE WAY: DARBY'S RANGERS William O. Darby and William H. Baumer	$3.50
0-515-09485-4	76 HOURS: THE INVASION OF TARAWA Eric Hammel and John E. Lane	$3.95
0-515-08236-8	WAKE ISLAND Duane Schultz (On Sale April '88)	$3.50

MARINE SNIPER

CHARLES HENDERSON

Sergeant Carlos Hathcock is an unparalleled Marine marksman. Able to lie in one position for days, control his breathing and heartbeat, and hit his target with a single bullet. He stalked the Vietcong behind enemy lines and came out with 93 confirmed kills. An unbelievable record... an incredible hunter...a true story.

A MAIN SELECTION OF THE MILITARY BOOK CLUB

___ 0-425-10355-2   MARINE SNIPER $3.95